The Medical Offset Effect and Public Health Policy

THE MEDICAL OFFSET EFFECT AND PUBLIC HEALTH POLICY

Mental Health Industry in Transition

John L. Fiedler
and
Jonathan B. Wight

PRAEGER

New York
Westport, Connecticut
London

Library of Congress Cataloging-in-Publication Data

Fiedler, John L.
   The medical offset effect and public health policy: mental health
industry in transition / John L. Fiedler and Jonathan B. Wight.
      p.   cm.
   Bibliography: p.
   Includes index.
   ISBN 0-275-92859-4 (alk. paper)
   1. Mental health services—Economic aspects—United States.
   2. Mental health policy—United States.   I. Wight, Jonathan B.
   II. Title.
   RA790.F44   1989
   362.2'0973—dc19   88-28927

Library of Congress Catalog Card Number: 88-28927
ISBN: 0-275-92859-4

First published in 1989

Praeger Publishers, One Madison Avenue, New York, NY 10010
A division of Greenwood Press, Inc.

Printed in the United States of America

The paper used in this book complies with the Permanent
Paper Standard issued by the National Information Standards
Organization (Z39.48-1984).

10 9 8 7 6 5 4 3 2 1

CONTENTS

EXHIBITS

FOREWORD

This book began as part of a National Institute of Mental Health (NIMH) study entitled "Mental Health Impact on Medical Care Cost and Utilization Under Medicare and Medicaid—A Study Design," which was completed in June 1986 (Contract No. 278-83-0013). Valuable comments were obtained on that initial draft from Paul Widem at NIMH. We thank Glenn Silverberg for his interest and discerning eye. He recognized the potential of that initial report and encouraged pursuing its transformation into the present work. Additional helpful reviews of the Georgia and Michigan empirical chapters were obtained in 1987 and 1988 from Matthew Hendryx (SUNY–Fredonia) and Kristine Jones (SUNY–New York), respectively.

Robert Schmidt at the University of Richmond provided able support in generating table output from SPSS-X, among other things, and the University of Richmond generously provided summer research funding in 1987, as well as secretarial, telephone, computer, and mailing resources. Ronald Eggleston at the Michigan Department of Social Services and Burt Skelley of the Georgia Department of Medical Assistance supplied us with valuable insights. The various editors who have worked on this project—George Zimmar, Susan Baker, and Jessica Ryan—deserve special mention for their patience, attention to detail, and unflagging commitment which substantially improved our early drafts. The authors would like to gratefully acknowledge and thank each of these institutions and individuals for their generous contributions to this work, absolving them, of course, of any shortcomings that may still remain.

On a personal level, I (Jack Fiedler) would like to express my gratitude for the love, understanding, and crucial support my family—Eryka, Desraeli, and especially my wife, Renee—has provided me throughout this project. I (Jonathan Wight) would like to recognize my parents and siblings—JoJo, Billy, Pickett, Web, and Jody—for their abundant love and support.

The Medical Offset Effect
and Public Health Policy

INTRODUCTION

The great question is, not so much what money you have in your pocket, as what you will buy with it.
— John Ruskin (nineteenth-century social reformer)

WHAT WE DON'T KNOW

Mental illness is a widespread and costly disease; it reduces productivity, increases absenteeism, shortens longevity, and produces untold human suffering. It is estimated that the provision of mental health services alone in 1980 accounted for an expenditure of between $23 and $30 billion in the United States. Adding the indirect costs of mental illness might bring the total annual burden to society to $54 billion or higher (Klerman, 1985: 588; Frank and Kamlet, 1985: 165; Research Triangle Institute, 1984: 4).

While there is agreement about the importance and seriousness of mental illness, there is no corresponding consensus about what to do about it. This, for the most part, is the result of two closely interrelated factors: first, the still inconclusive analyses of the effectiveness of psychotherapy; and second, the relative paucity of policy-related (specifically economic) analyses of mental illness and mental health treatment. Discussion and understanding of the mental health industry remain what they have long been: limited and piecemeal. As a result, policy-making about mental illness—in the public and private sector alike—continues to be based far too often on opinion, presumption, and hunch.

Meanwhile, economic forces march along to a different drummer. The staggering expenditures have induced a new cost consciousness resulting in "cost containments" that are now transforming the mental health industry, with few safeguards for quality and access considerations. John Ruskin's words, which are quoted above, are worth repeating here: "The great question is, not so much what money you have in your pocket, as what you will buy with it."

In that regard, two vital questions about how we spend our health care dollars remain to be answered. Can the timely purchase and provision of mental health treatment services reduce a person's overall physical health treatment costs? And, if so, what types of mental health insurance policies and other public financing incentives would promote such gains in efficiency? We hope, in the course of this book, to establish a means by which researchers will be able to help answer these controversial questions about what is called the medical offset effect.

THE MEDICAL OFFSET EFFECT

We have noted that the treatment of mental illness alone is a staggering cost burden on society. But this is just the tip of the iceberg; for persons who suffer from mental illness consume an inappropriately large amount of general health services. This link between mental and physical illness, and their treatments, brings us to the heart of this book, the medical offset effect.

Providers of mental health services, such as psychologists, psychiatrists, clinical social workers, and others, have long asserted that the timely treatment of mental illness generates a corresponding reduction in the use of physical health care. If this is so, then the cost of mental health treatment is offset partially, if not entirely, by savings in the physical health sector. Hypothetically, a dollar spent on psychological evaluation and treatment could generate savings of two and three dollars for private insurance companies, Medicaid, and others involved in health care insurance and financing.

Although this alleged phenomenon, the medical offset effect, has been studied for two decades, there is nothing approaching a consensus about even whether or not such an effect exists. Until now, we believe that researchers in this area have labored under great difficulties, among which are different definitions and different measures of the concept, unique study populations, different experimental designs, and different statistical procedures. More fundamentally, research efforts have largely focused on identifying factors associated with the offset, rather than seeking to explain a consistent theory behind it. As a consequence, the results are difficult to compare and nearly impossible to reproduce: researchers are "talking past" one another.

So we are left with opinions and presumptions to guide policy about any potential offset. But to rely on opinion and presumption in a field as poorly understood by the public, as historically neglected and shrouded in mystique, and as subject to arbitrary and sometimes discriminatory policies as in the mental health industry, is to risk being very far from where an informed profession and polity should be. In short, there is an urgent need for those in the industry, whether practitioners, researchers, or policymakers, to begin a dialogue starting from square one.

There is a growing awareness that a larger framework for understanding, measuring, and estimating mental illness and treatment paradigms is essential if we are to develop rational public and private policies regarding the mentally ill. It is in light of these considerations that we offer this book as an attempt to compile a comprehensive stocktaking of what is known about the hypothesized offset effect, and the forces which are presently affecting and will continue to affect it in the foreseeable future. Beyond this, we would like to synthesize the underlying theory behind the offset and provide a framework which will be useful for understanding and coordinating research methodologies employed in the future.

The book is therefore geared not only to active researchers in the field but also to mental health treatment providers, insurance companies, and government agencies that are directly affected by an offset. We hope the book will also serve as a useful reference to the general student on the evolution of the mental health industry, as well as a valuable compilation and review of the literature.

WHAT YOU DON'T KNOW CAN HURT YOU

We cannot dally to reach some answers about the issues raised here; nor can we hope that these unresolved issues will somehow sort themselves out to our satisfaction. The mental health industry is being buffeted by powerful forces on an increasingly frequent basis; for example, the 1981 repeal of the Community Mental Health Act of 1963; the introduction of Medicare's prospective payment system—diagnostic-related groups (DRGs)—and the general supplanting of the cost-based reimbursement mechanism with one based on price; the rapid growth of prepaid-capitated care plans and of for-profit medicine; the aggressive and cost-conscious purchasing of health insurance along with a more effective use of utilization review; the growing physician glut; the slowing rate of growth of states mandating the offering of mental health insurance coverage; the rolling back of private insurance plan coverage. Together these forces are revolutionizing the American health care system.

Relatively little inquiry, analysis, or understanding of the implications for either the mentally ill or their providers was sought before most of these measures were undertaken. As far as the mental health industry input was concerned—with the conspicuous exception of psychiatric DRGs (shortly to be discussed)—these changes for the most part were fait accompli. Together these changes constitute a fundamental restructuring of the financial side of the mental health industry. It is hardly surprising, therefore, that they are having major and not always intended impacts on the patients and the providers of mental health services.

These forces transforming the health industry create powerful incentives to underserve the lower-income segment of clientele and to avoid altogether the indigent population. With increasingly less room for cost shifting, uncompensated care becomes an onerous burden, one which is unequally distributed and is having an inequitable impact on some hospitals' abilities to survive in this newly price-competitive world.

As dialectical processes, "the structural transformation of American medicine" (Starr, 1982) and the "industrialization of American psychiatry" (Bittker, 1985) are certain to continue. As they do, cost containment will continue its ascension to the assailable but unquestionably paramount position, further eclipsing the quality imperative and consumer sovereignty concerns.

Since people with mental disorders receive most of their care from the general medical care sector and account for a disproportionate amount of the total services of that sector, the question as to whether or not there is an offset effect is, and will be for some time, of major policy interest. Preoccupied with trimming budgets, eliminating "unnecessary" services, altering Medicaid incentive structures, and improving the performance of Health Maintenance Organizations (HMOs), public and private policymakers alike will increasingly turn to medical offset research findings for an understanding of present and future relationships between general medical care and mental health care services.

In his path-breaking *The Phenomenon of Man*, Jesuit philosopher Tielhard de Chardin wisely admonishes his readers, "So please do not expect a final explanation of things here." This caveat should serve to remind us, in this endeavor, not to expect to find easy answers or to provide the last word on the subject. Rather, we hope this work will contribute something to the ever-unfolding knowledge of man, his illnesses of the mind, and their effective treatments.

Before concluding this chapter with a brief overview of the book, we would like to acknowledge our deep debt and sense of gratitude to past and present researchers who have lugged the wagon of knowledge up the incline to its present point. That this present work owes much to many pioneers who charted many difficult courses in this field should be obvious to those familiar with the wealth of literature which we draw upon. And we do not doubt that this book is a first step, which with hindsight will appear obvious and primitive.

AN OVERVIEW OF THE BOOK

Chapter 2 traces the revolutionary transformation of the mental health industry in the post–World War II era, and provides a context for understanding the growth of public interest in the industry, specifically in the medical offset effect. Chapter 3 winnows through the offset literature in a stylized review, extracting and examining the major issues, problems, and findings of medical offset research.

To facilitate the conceptual integration of these studies and to synthesize their diverse findings, a behavioral model for explaining the medical offset effect is constructed in chapter 4. Estimation of a behavioral model offers the most precise and conclusive method for ascertaining the existence of the offset, as well as simultaneously providing an understanding of the underlying causal relationships. An understanding of these causal relationships is essential if policymakers are to gain insight into how to design policies to most effectively alter behavior of the mentally ill and their families, of psychotherapists, or of public and private insurance companies, to maximize any potential medical offset effect.

Empirical estimates of the offset effect are made in chapter 5, using a multivariate regression model and longitudinal (1980–82) Medicaid data from Georgia. In chapter 6 additional policy issues are analyzed and the Georgia results are compared to offset results for a similar Medicaid population in Michigan. The final chapter discusses the policy implications of our findings against the backdrop of the larger picture of mental health care, the mental health care industry, and general public health care policy as it evolves through the 1990s.

STUDY DOMAIN

Hospital and nursing home mental health care was estimated to account for 85 percent of total mental health treatment outlays in 1980. As documented in the next chapter, however, by far the largest and most rapidly growing component of mental health care is outpatient (as opposed to inpatient) care. This observation, coupled with our untested hypothesis that recipients of inpatient care are far more likely to be chronically ill—and, to the extent that they remain inpatients for long periods, are less likely to generate an offset—prompted us to concentrate on outpatient treatment. Although we occasionally discuss inpatient care—notably in the narrative account of the evolution of the industry since World War II contained in the next chapter—the primary focus (especially in the review of literature and the empirical sections) is outpatient care.

Frequently the mentally ill are defined to include alcohol and drug abusers. In the interest of precision we take a more narrow focus in our empirical section to ensure a more homogeneous study group. Technically, the types of mental illness examined in our empirical estimation include clinical module diagnostic codes 290, 293-302, and 305-316, of the International Classification of Disease (version 9). As in any empirical analysis, the unique characteristics of the data base demarcate the extent to which the results may be generalized. These considerations and a more complete discussion of the empirical analysis are covered in chapters 5 and 6.

GROWTH AND CHANGE IN THE MENTAL HEALTH INDUSTRY

> They start the fog machine again and it's snowing down cold and white all over me like skim milk, so thick I might even be able to hide in it if they didn't have a hold on me. I can't see six inches in front of me through the fog and the only thing I can hear over the wail I'm making is the Big Nurse....
>
> —Ken Kesey, *One Flew Over the Cuckoo's Nest* (1961)

The frightening and stereotypical portrayal of the treatment of mental illness in Ken Kesey's novel is a stark reminder of the attitudes about mental illness and treatment methods that were prevalent until the middle of this century. But this portrayal scarcely reflects the mainstream of attitudes or treatment methods that prevail today. The mental health system has been transformed from one in which the overwhelming majority of patients were involuntarily incarcerated in public institutions to one which is both more voluntaristic and more pluralistic, in terms not only of its clientele but also of its treatment regimens, settings, and providers.

Before examining (in chapter 3) the impact that this transformation has had on possibilities for a "medical offset," we must first review this transformation of the mental health industry, and seek clues as to how it will evolve in the near future. We end the chapter with a sobering reflection that, even with the rapid growth of mental health access and treatment we have witnessed, the vast majority of those in mental distress remain undiagnosed and untreated by the mental health care sector.

INCREASING UTILIZATION AND THE PLURALIZATION OF THE MENTAL HEALTH INDUSTRY

Throughout the post–World War II era, and especially since the mid-1950s, mental health service utilization has grown dramatically. In 1955, only about

1 percent of the U.S. population visited a mental health professional; by 1980 approximately 10 percent of the population sought professional help for a mental health problem (Klerman, 1985: 587).

There is no single, definitive source for information on the prevalence of mental illness or mental health service utilization. The studies most widely recognized as providing reliable estimates are: (1) Regier et al. (1978), which is based on 1975 data pooled from a variety of epidemiologic and health service research organizations, and includes institutional care; (2) the National Ambulatory Medical Care (NAMC) survey of 1973 and 1975 (Schurman et al., 1985), which is information obtained from a national probability sample of private, office-based physicians; (3) the 1977 National Medical Care Expenditures Survey (NMCES), which used a national probability sample of the U.S. population and included non-physician providers; and (4) the Epidemiological Catchment Area (ECA) study based on three survey interviews, conducted between 1980 and 1982, of probability samples of 3,000 to 3,500 noninstitutionalized persons aged 18 and over, in New Haven, St. Louis, and Baltimore (Myers et al., 1984; Shapiro et al., 1984).

Despite the biases inherent in these different data sources, a relatively consistent picture emerges from the four studies. Where estimates or measures vary widely, an attempt has been made throughout this chapter to indicate that there are discrepancies and to present the ranges of the most variable estimates.

These trends, reflecting the reduced stigma associated with having a mental health problem or seeking care for an emotional disturbance, manifest the public's changing attitude toward mental health. Public attitudes toward mental illness and utilization of mental health services have undergone a quiet revolution in the past thirty years. In 1957 a national survey, with a probability sample representative of all Americans at least twenty-one years of age and living in private households, found that 15 percent of the population had used some type of mental health service at least once (VandenBos, 1980: 11). In a 1976 replication of the survey it was learned that 26 percent of the population had used mental health services at some time in their life, and an additional 34 percent reported that they would utilize mental health services if they ever confronted particular types of problems (Douvan et al., 1976).

More positive attitudes toward mental health services have not, of course, evolved in a vacuum. Changing attitudes and changing utilization behavior have been concomitant and mutually reinforcing. Attitude changes have been in part the result of increased service use, which has meant greater visibility and concern for mental illness, and given greater visibility and legitimacy to its treatment.

Given the growth of the United States population since World War II, the significant increase in the proportion of the U.S. population utilizing mental health services translates into a rapid growth rate in the number of mental health services provided. The absolute number of individuals entering the mental health service marketplace grew from 24,688,200 in 1955 to 56,444,700 in 1980; constituting a cumulative annual growth rate in excess of 4.5 percent.

Not only has the rate of utilization changed markedly, but the pattern of utilization has changed as well. The rapid growth in the number of individuals served and in the pattern of utilization has been transactionally related to four major structural changes within the mental health industry. These changes together have resulted in what, for lack of a better term, we shall refer to as the *pluralization* of the mental health industry. The four major changes, each evidencing a distinct force acting to pluralize the industry, are:

- the development of new philosophical attitudes and treatment therapies,
- the creation of new treatment settings and organizational structures,
- the broadening of the population seeking treatment,
- the broadening of the number and types of treatment providers.

First, the development of new philosophical attitudes, new drug therapies, and new psychosocial treatment therapies in the 1950s undermined the standard approach to treating the mentally ill, long stereotyped by the large, public mental institution (Weissman and Klerman, 1978; Klerman, 1985).

These new developments in psychotherapeutic techniques accommodated an assortment of new treatment settings and organizational structures, notably the development of outpatient care. While the proportion of the population hospitalized for mental illness has not changed appreciably (vacillating between 0.8 and 0.9 percent of the total population), the proportion of total mental health services provided on an inpatient basis has dropped persistently and precipitously. In 1955 more than three-quarters of all mental health care episodes were inpatient encounters. By 1975 the relative shares of outpatient and inpatient care were reversed: outpatient visits then accounted for more than three-quarters of all services (McGuire, 1981: 18). This dramatic shift in the mix of treatment sites is accompanied by another significant change, the pluralization of inpatient care. Most inpatient services are no longer provided in public institutions, but are primarily in the psychiatric units of private for-profit, private nonprofit, or general hospitals.

The third major structural change in the mental health industry is in part a consequence of the development of new psychotherapeutics along with the development of new (less imposing) treatment settings. Because these treatments are less resource-intensive and less disruptive of individuals' lifestyles, they have enabled and encouraged the treatment of more individuals, more individuals with less severe disorders, and more individuals who voluntarily seek care.

Finally, in addition to the rapid expansion in the number of ambulatory (outpatient) services already noted, there is the very telling change in the nature of these ambulatory services, and in particular the growth in reliance on other-than-psychiatric providers. The most complete recent data for mental health service utilization by source of care comes from the 1979 National Survey of Psychotherapeutic Drug Use IRSB/NIMH Collaborative Study. This data (shown in exhibit 2.1) documents the growing plurality of outpatient mental health care providers, such that social workers, counselors, and psychologists provided over twice the services of psychiatrists in this 1979 sample. Exceeding this group was the number of those enrolled in self-help groups, as well as those who sought help from clergy or pastoral counselors.

Having identified the major structural transformations in the mental health industry, we will, in the next section, investigate the reasons behind these transformations.

CAUSAL FACTORS IN THE GROWTH AND TRANSFORMATION OF THE MENTAL HEALTH INDUSTRY

What accounts for the tremendous growth in the number of mental health service encounters in recent years? In part it is attributable to a growing population. But, as already noted, since the proportion of the American population entering the mental health marketplace has also been growing, that is only a partial explanation. Other possible explanatory factors include additional determinants of demand—especially (1) an increasing prevalence of mental illness in American society; (2) an enhanced predisposition toward mental health service usage; (3) greater access to mental health services resulting from the expansion of private insurance coverage; and (4) changing supply parameters in the mental health industry, including the greater availability of providers, as indicated by higher mental health specialists-to-population ratio(s), and the growth of a government-sponsored community mental health center network. The discussion now turns to a brief investigation of each of these factors.

Prevalence

As Murphy et al. (1984) have pointed out, relatively commonly occurring phrases in the psychiatric literature such as "the neurotic personality of our time" (Horney, 1937), "the age of anxiety" (Weissman and Klerman, 1978), and "the decade of depression" (Schwab et al., 1979) suggest that the prevalence of mental illness in our society is rising. This appears to be the general public's perception as well. Notwithstanding, the general consensus among mental health epidemiologists is that the incidence of mental illness has not changed appreciably in North America in recent decades (Murphy 1980; Murphy et al., 1984; Myers et al., 1984).

While there is no doubt that discussion of mental illness is a much more common topic of public discourse today, this is attributable to changes in attitudes, the development of new treatment protocols, and debate about the changing role of government within the industry, rather than to the changing incidence of mental disorders.

Exhibit 2.1

Prevalence of Receiving Treatment, Advice or Help
from Various Psychosocial Therapy Providers
Among the Noninstitutionalized Adult Population

Type of Therapist or Help	Percent Using		
	Men	Women	All Persons
Psychiatrists	1.4	2.6	2.1
Other mental health professionals:			
Psychologist	1.1	0.8	1.0
Social worker or counselor	2.3	4.3	3.4
Other individual or group therapy	0.5	0.9	0.7
(Any mental health professional)	(3.8)	(7.0)	(5.6)
Clergy or pastoral counselor	4.0	5.9	5.0
Personal growth or self-help group	4.5	6.9	5.8
(Any of the above)	(10.3)	(17.2)	(14.1)
Number of individuals	1334	1827	3161

Source: 1979 National Survey of Psychotherapeutic Drugs Use
IRSB/NIMH Collaborative Study

There is a growing body of psychiatric epidemiological literature concerned with estimating the incidence of mental illness in the U.S. population. The Graduate Medical Education National Advisory Committee (GMENAC) panel on psychiatry estimates that 18 percent of Americans have a mental disorder (Pardes and Pincus, 1983). The NIMH-sponsored Epidemiological Catchment Area (ECA) Program has estimated that a very similar rate, 18.5 percent, was found in the population of its four study site communities (Myers et al., 1984).

The most frequently cited rate, however, is 15 percent. An analysis of psychiatric epidemiological literature of the past twenty-five years (Regier et al., 1978: 638) estimated that roughly thirty-two million Americans (15 percent of the total population) have a mental disorder over the course of a year and that, at any moment in time, 10 percent of a population is mentally ill. The general consistency of data from a variety of studies, including what have been labeled "the four landmark epidemiological surveys conducted since World War II" (in addition to the three authoritative sources already mentioned) suggests the relative stability of this 15 percent range.[1]

Since the higher rate of mental health service utilization is not attributable to any significant secular change in the incidence of mental disorders, its explanation must be based on other causal factors.

Enhanced Predisposition Toward Mental Health Service Use

As already noted, the general public's attitudes toward both mental illness and mental health service utilization have been substantially revised in the last thirty years. Probably this has been primarily due to accelerated and continuing changes in the socioeconomic fabric of our society. Increased urbanization, a quickened pace of life, the displacement of the extended family by the nuclear family and the single-parent family, the reduced number and effectiveness of social networks, and the increased labor force participation of women have complicated efforts of family and friends to care for the mentally ill (Hansen, 1981: 86). As a result, people have more readily turned to mental health specialists. This increased predisposition to seek the assistance of professionals has been further enhanced by the public's increasing recognition of the complexity of mental health problems and treatment.

In addition to the development of new treatment methods, which have given patients more options regarding both the type and setting of the treatment, another—and perhaps the most significant—factor increasing the demand for mental health services has been the generally held belief that psychotherapy is effective. While a number of other important influences have encouraged the use of mental health services, individuals would not seek mental health care were it not for their conviction—or at least their hope—that it would help them.

Due to numerous methodological shortcomings, however, the numerous studies intended to assess the effectiveness of psychotherapy which have been conducted in the past three decades, while helping to distill the major issues, have often resulted in claims that have been equivocal, overstated, or simply wrong.[2]

Chapter 3 will focus on the subset of this literature pertaining to the "medical offset" or "cost offset." This effect is one outcome indicator of psychotherapy. Briefly, it refers to the hypothesized notion that providing appropriate mental health treatment interventions, by offsetting (reducing) the use of other, general health services, can be not only effective, but cost-effective.

Individuals' enhanced predisposition toward use of mental health services due to their belief in its effectiveness has established psychotherapy as an accepted, integral part of medical care (Kogan et al., 1975). The discussion turns now to other factors which have encouraged and/or facilitated this development.

Increasing Access to Mental Health Services: Insurance[3]

The growth of mental health insurance coverage—both private and public, in the form of Medicare and Medicaid—has been a major contributing factor in the secular increase in access to and utilization of mental health care in the last forty years. Notwithstanding, the role of insurance has been ambiguous: periodically there have been controversial reversals in the nature and extent of private insurance coverage.

Insurance coverage for medical care first became widely available during the 1930s. During World War II coverage grew very rapidly; and by 1945 thirty-two million Americans were enrolled in plans which covered, almost exclusively, inpatient care (McGuire, 1981: 6). Initially inpatient psychiatric care was included in these plans with the same coverage as that provided for other ailments. In the early 1950s, by the time insurance coverage had expanded to include outpatient medical services (offered primarily in major medical policies of group plans), treatment for mental illness was again part of the general expansion of the "all-illnesses" coverage. Fairly quickly, however, commercial insurance carriers revamped their policies pertaining to outpatient care, particularly for mental health patients (McGuire, 1981: 6–8).

The companies became concerned over the appropriateness and equity of paying out significant portions of total benefit payments to a very few individuals who were not disabled and were continuing to earn or to carry on their usual functions. (Reed, Myers, and Scheidemandel, 1972: 61, cited in McGuire, 1981: 7)

That is, the insurance companies felt that the primary beneficiaries of such coverage were a few individuals who were not "that" sick; at least not in any readily apparent, demonstrable way. Accordingly, insurance companies subsequently reduced their coverage of outpatient services for treatment of mental illness relative to that for other ailments: maximum benefits per year or per lifetime were adopted, and relatively high coinsurance rates introduced.

What was construed as inappropriate or inequitable during the early 1950s, however, may have been largely a reflection of the predominant mode of psychotherapy at the time. Those who entered the system generally were treated with individual psychoanalysis provided by a psychiatrist. With the introduction of new techniques, such as drug and group therapy, and the substitution of less expensive providers for psychiatrists, this pattern of utilization changed dramatically.

Despite these innovations, there has been no major restructuring of the insurance coverage of mental health services, at least not until the advent of state-mandated coverage in the late 1970s. Thus the private insurance industry has maintained a relative inequality of physical and mental health services insurance coverage, with little empirical evidence on which to base such a policy.[4]

Nevertheless, as the general level of insurance coverage of Americans expanded, so did the proportion of the population which had some insurance coverage for mental health services. The impact of Medicare and Medicaid in particular has been of major significance (Taube and Rupp, 1986; Taube et al., 1986).

The differential pattern of coverage for general vis-à-vis mental health services has been a major focus of the spate of demand studies which finally began in earnest in 1985. Unfortunately, the starting point of some demand analysts seems to be the presumption that the relative disparities are the result of fully informed, rational actors (such as insurance carriers) operating in a free market. For instance, based on this presumption, Thomas G. McGuire (in the pioneering econometric work which stands as one of the most comprehensive economic analyses of the demand for psychotherapeutic care) largely dismisses out of hand the existence of a medical offset effect. He adopts something of an agnostic stance:

Health insurance carriers are in a position to capture many of the offset effects of psychotherapy. Eagerness would not aptly describe the attitude of most carriers toward psychotherapy. In spite of numerous experiments in progress, most insurers severely restrict such (ambulatory mental health service) coverage. This negative attitude, built on the experience of those whose business it is to know the extra costs of additional coverage, is evidence against the proposition that insurance for ambulatory psychiatric treatment affords substantial savings in other services. (McGuire, 1981: 76)

The differential pattern of general vis-à-vis mental health insurance coverage has been a major issue in the mental health services demand literature, although the discussion has been recast into a slightly different form. Generally, the issue has been split into two topics. One addresses the severity issue as it historically evolved: is it true that the individuals who use mental health services are generally not those who are in greatest need of them? Or, a slight variation thereon (which is more directly testable by econometric methods): is there a systematic relationship between the demand for mental health services and the severity of mental illness?

The second issue strives to determine if users of mental health services are more sensitive to changes in the net price (the after-insurance or "out-of-pocket" price) of mental health services than users of general health services are to changes in the net price of general health services. Most commonly, this topic of price sensitivity is discussed using the economic concept of elasticity, and the issue becomes one centered around the relative sizes of the elasticities.[5]

"Price elasticity of demand" measures the degree to which consumers are responsive to higher or lower prices in the market. The more responsive the consumer demand is to price changes, the more "elastic" the demand is said to be. Such goods are often found to be either luxury items, such as expensive meals at fancy restaurants, or not very important items in the consumer's budget, for example, chewing gum. If the price rises, consumers will cut back on their demand. In contrast, if consumer demand is not very responsive, demand is said to be "inelastic"; an example of this would be for a necessary item such as food.

So, what are the implications of the controversy over the relative elasticities of mental versus general health services? If the demand for mental health care is more elastic than that for general health services, consumers will be less willing to bear increases in their "out-of-pocket" costs (due, for example, to a reduction in insurance coverage, or an increase in insurance copayment requirements) for mental versus general health services. For equal increases in "out-of-pocket" costs, mental health service use will fall proportionately more than general health service use, because consumers perceive mental health services as less essential.

Historically, as we have seen, insurance carriers have generally presumed that the price elasticity of demand for mental health services is greater than that of general health services: hence their differential insurance coverage. The empirical evidence, however, is mixed. Those who have found the demand for general health care more inelastic than that of mental health service include McGuire (1981), Frank (1985), Taube et al. (1986), and Horgan (1986). The Rand Health Insurance Study (HIS), on the other hand, found them to be about the same (Wells et al., 1982), while Watts, Scheffler, and Jewell (1986) come somewhere in between.

In judging the issue, it is not enough to simply count up the number of studies in each "camp." These studies are based on different populations, estimating the demand for different types of providers (some restrict the analysis to only mental health specialists; others make no restrictions), employing different (often second-best) measures of net price, and their findings have different policy implications. Furthermore, the policy-relevant issue should not be limited to simply ascertaining whether or not elasticity differentials exist; for if they are found to exist, their absolute magnitudes are important as well.

The analysis of these demand studies can be rather technical, and is included for the interested reader in an appendix to this chapter. It is clear that much more work on the demand for mental health services remains to be done. In light of the major structural changes occurring in the health care industry, results to date must be viewed as tentative. The completion of the second National Medical Care Expenditures Survey by the National Center for Health Services Research will provide a rich database for using the increasingly sophisticated analytical tools being applied to the study of mental health services demand, and will serve as the basis for our best, most precise, and definitive estimates to date.

As already noted, a common perception is that many who seek mental health treatment are not seriously disturbed. Let us now look at this second issue in the mental versus general health insurance relative disparities debate. The presumption that those who seek mental health care are not very ill, or not the most severely ill, continues to be marshaled as "evidence" of the need for, and justification of, cutbacks in the insurance coverage of mental health services, especially relative to that of general health services (see, for example, Simon, 1976). The argument goes something like this: insurance benefits are already so high that those who are not really mentally ill, or at least not very ill, are being encouraged to obtain care. If benefits are slashed, it won't deter those who really need care.

The genesis of this misperception may be the various analyses which have been based on physician/provider claims, much as that of insurance carriers. Such studies may be misleading:[6] analysts have found that physicians frequently assign minimally severe diagnoses to their patients in the interest of protecting the "confidentiality" of their clients (Hustead and Sharfstein, 1978; Towery et al., 1980). Both of these studies, which are based on the Federal Employees Plan (FEP), suggest that this practice results in distorting insurance reimbursement payment-by-diagnosis patterns. It is very likely that this practice of "protecting" the patient has created the inaccurate impression that insurance companies pay out disproportionate amounts of money for individuals afflicted with relatively minor mental illnesses.

The empirical evidence generally suggests just the opposite. Wallen et al.'s 1986 analysis of a natural experiment—the introduction of a copayment for the heavily insured United Mine Workers of America—found that men who were more severely ill, but who sought less care relative to women, were the most affected by the change. With the introduction of the copayment, they reduced their already (relatively) too-low levels of mental health treatment.

Turning the relationship around, the Rand HIS study found similar results: "Both the probability of any mental health care and the intensity of treatment provided by mental health specialist increases significantly with increases in psychological stress" (Ware et al., 1984: 1090). In a more focused analysis comparing HMOs to fee-for-service plans in Seattle, Rand investigators found mental health status to be a powerful and important predictor of the probability of use of any provider, the probability of use of a mental health specialty provider, and the intensity of any use (Wells et al., 1986).

Further corroboration of a systematic relationship between the severity of mental illness and the demand for mental health specialty services comes from McGuire's 1981 study (McGuire, 1981: 114–19) and Horgan (1986).

The lack of congruence between the low level of insurance coverage for mental health services and the public's long-term growing demand for and use of mental health services, coupled with arguments concerning (1) the need to enhance access to and utilization of such services and (2) the existence of a medical offset effect, have together, since 1971, prodded more than two-thirds of the states to intervene in the mental health insurance marketplace (McGuire and Montgomery, 1982). Twenty-nine states have required private health insurers to provide specified minimum coverage for mental health services (Frisman et al., 1985). Thirty-six states have mandated that carriers are either required to insure the treatment of alcohol and substance abuse or that they must offer it as an option (Sullivan et al., 1987: 25).

The nature and extent of insurance coverage for mental health treatment have had an important influence in shaping the demand for mental health services. That the impact of private insurance has been poorly understood is largely due to widely varying characteristics of insurance policies, making direct comparisons impossible, and is a reflection of the rudimentary state of our knowledge of mental health service demand.

In the public sector, on the other hand, the impact and role of insurance have not been so elusive or ambiguous. Mental health benefits have been provided by Medicare and Medicaid since 1966, and for various lengths of time by an assortment of other public agencies, including the Civilian Health and Medical Program of the Uniformed Services, the Civilian and Medical Program of the Veterans' Administration, the Indian Health Services, and other federal, state, city, or county payers or providers (Horgan, 1985: 569). By 1977 public insurance reimbursements accounted for 30 percent of total ambulatory mental health expenditures (in both the specialty and general medical sectors); nearly twice the share covered by private health insurance carriers collectively.

There is little doubt that Medicaid has enhanced the access and utilization of mental health care for the poor: people covered by Medicaid have a higher probability of using ambulatory mental health services than either persons who have private insurance or who are uninsured (Horgan, 1985: 567; Horgan, 1986; Taube and Rupp, 1986).[7]

In sum, it is evident that the growth of private insurance, and various actions of all levels of government—directly by the provision of insurance, and indirectly by the more recent introduction of mental-health-specific insurance regulations—have increased the level of mental health services covered by insurance, and thereby increased access to and utilization of mental health services over the past few—especially the last two—decades.

Greater Availability of Providers

The increased availability of mental health specialty providers has increased access to care. This growth has had important quantitative as well as qualitative dimensions. In 1955 mental health services were provided almost exclusively by psychiatrists, then numbering about ten thousand. Since then, while the number of practicing psychiatrists has more than doubled, other mental health professionals have grown even more dramatically both in their numbers and in their number of patient contacts (both in absolute terms, and relative to psychiatrists). Today there are more than 125,000 fully trained professional mental health service providers (VandenBos, 1980:10). Psychologists, psychiatric social workers, psychiatric nurses, and mental health counselors are estimated to number more than one hundred thousand, and to account for 65 to 75 percent of all mental health services (Klerman, 1985: 587–88). Once the mainstays of the industry, psychiatrists are now the minority mental health provider type.

Passage of state "freedom of choice" laws (starting in the 1970s) increased the demand for, and perhaps the supply of, psychologists. Such laws require equal treatment of psychologists and psychiatrists for insurance reimbursement if the psychologist is licensed to provide specific covered services. States with such laws comprise 80 percent of the U.S. population (Kelvorick, 1981).

To the extent that it is discussed in the literature, it is generally (simplistically) noted that this development created the possibility of receiving treatment from mental health practitioners other than psychiatrists. Almost predictably, this mindset has led to two sharply conflicting assessments of what has come to be regarded as the substitution of other mental health providers' services for those of psychiatrists. One view maintains that the substitution has not significantly altered the quality of services; less costly, more available, and adequately skilled providers, it is explained, have expanded in number relative to psychiatrists in order to meet the increased demand for care. The second view asserts that the increased demand has been met by these alternative providers only at the sacrifice of the quality of services provided (McGuire, 1981: 29).

The issue, however, is far more complex. In part, the growth in other-than-psychiatrist mental health providers has been a reflection of those new psychotherapeutic techniques which have created a need for new types of services. Many of these techniques (for example, a psychiatric social worker's counseling and monitoring the daily activities of a patient in a community-based treatment center) were non-existent before the 1950s. To the extent that new mental health specialties have taken over these activities, they have not displaced psychiatrists. These services would be most accurately described as complementary to the still-needed and very different activities of the psychiatrist. Other activities, however—such as a psychologist or a psychiatric nurse practitioner providing counseling—may actually serve as substitutes for the psychiatrist's services.

Whether or not the growth in the numbers and types of mental health specialists has resulted in a net reduction in the quality of mental health services is therefore not an easy question to answer. Its resolution requires a detailed, disaggregated analysis which first identifies the types of things each provider does, and then compares the process and/or outcome of those things they do in common. Given the division of labor among these different provider types, those activities which they all perform are not likely to constitute an equal proportion—or a very large proportion—of the total activities of any single provider category. Accurate comparison, therefore, if possible, requires development of techniques to compare different types of activities with different types of skill and time requirements; a difficult task of dubious value.

Although there has been a great deal of research on the importance of provider and client variables to the outcome of therapy, the relevance of these variables to this issue is unknown. The research that has been done has been based overwhelmingly on the work of psychiatrists and, to a lesser extent, psychologists. Bergin and Lambert have carefully reviewed this literature and concluded: "We believe the hypothesis is supportable that the largest proportion of variation in therapy outcome is accounted for by preexisting client factors, such as motivation for change, and the like. Therapist personal factors account for the second largest proportion of change, with technique variables coming in a distant third. . . . It appears that these personal factors are crucial ingredients even in the more technical therapies" (Bergin and Lambert, 1978: 180).

Although the discipline-specific nature of this literature (its either psychiatrist- or psychologist-specific character) suggests that it is unlikely to be true without qualification, it also seems to suggest the possibility that the substitution of the less-qualified and less expensive mental health specialists need not result in markedly different therapeutic outcomes. To determine this unequivocally, however, requires additional research along the lines suggested above. All that may be stated unequivocally is that the growth in the number and type of mental health providers has increased the access to and the variety of mental health services.

Finally, there is at least one bit of recent evidence that suggests that the presumed quality-cost trade-off embodied in the two extreme views about the growth of other-than-psychiatrist providers may no longer be accurate. Care provided by psychiatric social workers in the Civilian Health and Medical Program of the Uniformed Services (CHAMPUS) has slowly increased in cost and is now at par with, or even more expensive than, that provided by psychiatrists and psychologists (Sullivan et al., 1987: 25).

Government-Sponsorship of Community Mental Health Centers

The proliferation in the numbers and types of mental health providers has been complemented by an analagous proliferation in the numbers and types of mental health treatment sites, which together have greatly enhanced access to mental health services. Most important in terms of its impact on access and utilization of care has been the federal government's initiation and sponsorship of community mental health centers.

In 1963, Congress passed Public Law 88-164, the Mental Retardation Facilities and Community Mental Health Centers Construction Act. The act authorized the National Institute of Mental Health to develop local community mental health centers (CMHCs), and provided seed monies in the form of long-term construction and short-term services development grants. Within two years 125 federally funded CMHCs were in operation, and their numbers continued to grow. By 1970 there were 196 CMHCs, and by 1980 they numbered 691 (Manderscheid et al., 1986: 536).

CMHCs are not the only type of facilities offering mental health services which have increased in number in recent decades. During the 1970s, the years of the most rapid growth in the industry, the total number of facilities offering mental health services rose by 43 percent, from 3,005 to 4,302. While the number of state and county mental hospitals fell, psychiatric outpatient clinics—led by CMHCs—increased dramatically. In January 1970, CMHCs constituted 7 percent of all specialty mental health facilities. By January 1980, they accounted for nearly one-fifth (19 percent) of all such facilities (Manderscheid et al., 1986: 536–37).

Not surprisingly, this change in the relative mix of facility-types has been paralleled by a change in the patterns of care. Although annual inpatient admissions have increased—accommodated in large part by the growth of nonfederal general hospitals providing psychiatric services—the total number of inpatient days has fallen by more than half, declining from 168.9 million to 77.1 million from 1969 to 1981. Correspondingly, the annual number of outpatient visits more than doubled over this period, from 1.1 million to nearly 2.5 million.

More closely mirroring the change in the mix of facility-types, the share of services provided by the most rapidly growing component of outpatient care-providing facilities—community mental health centers—has increased dramatically. By 1980, CMHCs were treating 1.2 million persons—nearly half of all persons receiving ambulatory mental health care—and were providing more than three million visits annually (Manderscheid et al., 1986: 536–37).

The factors which accounted for the rapid growth and change in the mental health industry (discussed in the preceding pages) continue to be affected by dramatic upheavals in the financing of health care, specifically the financing of mental health treatment. In the next section we review some of these important changes.

THE IMPACT OF RECENT CHANGES IN THE STRUCTURE OF FINANCING

Block Grants and the CMHCs

The Omnibus Budget Reconciliation Act of 1981 (OBRA) marked the advent of block grant funding for mental health services. This legislation aggregated all funds for alcohol, drug abuse, and mental health categorical grants into a single block grant. In addition, it replaced the federal government with individual state governments as the authority responsible for the planning, administration, allocation, and monitoring of these monies. The act slashed the level of federal funds allocated to these programs in 1982 to 75 percent of their 1981 level, and allowed the transferring of up to 7 percent of the allocations from any one of the four health-related blocks to another block in any year.

In the mental health area, the impact of OBRA was most dramatically felt by the community mental health centers. The number of "essential services" that centers were required to offer was reduced from twelve to five (outpatient services, emergency services, partial hospitalization, screening of patients at risk of state hospitalization, and consultation and education), and inpatient care activities were made ineligible for federal funding. Finally, vague guidelines charged that states must use at least some of the monies to provide care to the chronically mentally ill, children, the elderly, and other "underserved" populations (Okin, 1984: 1118).

The introduction of these changes has resulted in fairly predictable impacts on the centers. Very few states have used block grant monies to develop new centers. The progress which had been recorded in terms of the increased access to and utilization of mental health services resulting from growing numbers of CMHCs was largely halted in its tracks. The original goal—having at least one CMHC in each of the seven hundred identified catchment areas in the country—probably will not improve upon the roughly 50 percent coverage which presently exists.

Another access-related issue is that there has been an increased reliance on fees for service. But, as Robert Okin has noted,

even before the recent federal cutbacks, the contribution of federal funds to the budget of the average center had decreased from 34 percent in 1973 to 22 percent in 1980, while the state contribution increased from 27 percent to approximately 34 percent. It could be argued that the 1981 transfer of administrative authority to the states recognized the shift that had gradually occurred in the primary source of government support over the years. (Okin, 1984: 1120)

There has also been a change in the kinds of services provided by CMHCs. In part this stems from the prohibition of the use of federal funds for inpatient services; in part it stems from increasing economic constraints. Evidence suggests that OBRA was initiated in an era during which several long-term trends were reversed. Starting in 1982, the staff mix changed (becoming less psychiatrist-intensive). More dramatically, the average number of staff per center fell, which—coupled with the increasing number of part-time staff—resulted in increasing caseloads (Estes and Wood, 1984; Okin, 1984; Thompson and Bass, 1984).

The future of the community mental health centers is probably not in serious jeopardy; they have demonstrated over time that they are remarkably resilient institutions. But the future of the centers in terms of how they will be funded and how they will provide services (and to whom) is in question. With uncertainty about the organizational entity that now provides the bulk of care comes uncertainty about the future of the industry as a whole: an uncertainty which is highlighted by the tenuous and changing nature of financing—public and private alike. Medicare's prospective payment system constitutes another case in point.

Medicare's Prospective Payment System

On October 1, 1983, a prospective payment system to pay hospitals for the stays of Medicare beneficiaries was introduced. Under the system, 468 diagnosis-related groups (DRGs) were implemented to serve as the basis for determining the basic level of reimbursement (several additional weighting factors further adjust the level of payment). There are nine DRGs for psychiatric conditions. To date these DRGs have not been universally applied. At present (mid-1987), exemptions have been granted to psychiatric hospitals as well as to distinct-part psychiatric units of general hospitals that apply for an exemption and meet certain staffing, record-keeping, and treatment requirements.

Reimbursement Levels and Costs

Mental health researchers have demonstrated that the psychiatric DRGs are particularly poor reimbursement tools: they are poor predictors of length of stay and general resource use. Taube, Lee, and Forthofer (1984) reported that the psychiatric DRGs explain less than 3 percent of the variation in psychiatric length of stay. (In contrast, most medical DRGs explain 30 to 50 percent of such variation.) Taube and his colleagues then devised alternative DRGs, incorporating several additional variables, including psychiatric history and type of hospital. Their constructs significantly improve the predictive capability of the "model," but still can explain only about 20 percent of the variation in length of stay.

In a similar study, Janet Mitchell and colleagues (1987) analyzed the performance of two alternative patient classification systems: disease staging, developed by SysteMetrics, and their own clinically related groups. Although both of the alternative systems performed better than DRGs, both were still poor predictors of resource use, suggesting the need for additional work.

Implications for Inpatient Mental Health Treatment

At least two simulations of the universal implementation of the mental disorder DRGs suggest that they would have unintended and potentially disastrous consequences. In two companion articles, McGuire and his associates (1987) and Freiman, Mitchell, and Rosenbach (1987) analyze the impact of alternative psychiatric prospective payment systems on different types of hospitals. Freiman et al. found that Medicare DRG-based reimbursements for substance abuse and psychiatric admissions (considered together) would be greater for general hospitals with exempt, distinct-unit psychiatric units than those to hospitals without exempt units (because of their different severity of case mixes).

They also found, however, that the differences in the costs of the two types of facilities were greater than the payment differences that would occur if DRGs were implemented across both facility types. The obvious implication is that if the scheme were made universal, hospitals with distinct psychiatric units—as presently organized and managed—would not be economically viable in the long run. In addition, like the Taube et al. (1984) piece, this analysis suggests the need to incorporate some weight for different hospital characteristics into the psychiatric DRG formula.

In the companion article, McGuire et al. (1987) found that implementation of a uniform national prospective payment for substance abuse and psychiatric-diagnosed admissions would systematically underpay general hospitals with specialized facilities, while overpaying those without specialized units. The potentially disastrous implications of enactment of such a scheme are again self-evident.

For most psychiatric facilities, however, Medicare constitutes a relatively minor payer. Hence one might be tempted to discount the impact of Medicare's DRG system on the mental health inpatient care system.

However, the Health Care Financing Administration's policy toward prospective payment for ADM (alcohol, drug abuse and mental health) conditions may be viewed as a precedent by other payers. It is therefore critical to study—for payers other than Medicare and in settings including the full range of facilities that treat ADM disorders—the potential redistributive impact of prospective payment. (McGuire et al., 1987: 616)

Unintended Incentives and the DRG System

The implementation of DRGs has created a set of new incentives, many having direct or indirect effects on the treatment of the mentally ill. The Medicare system's prospective payment scheme has significantly reduced lengths of hospital stay, and created financial troubles for many hospitals. One response has been for hospitals to change their mix of services to capture a larger proportion of more lucrative patient-types.

Relative to psychiatric specialty hospitals, an increasing share of inpatient care is being provided in general hospitals, both those with and those without psychiatric units. The empty beds left by Medicare's prospective payment system have encouraged acute care hospitals to convert beds formerly allocated to medical and surgical patients into beds dedicated to psychiatric patients. Simultaneously, the number of private psychiatric hospitals has been growing rapidly, as has the share of them owned or operated by investor-owned hospital chains. In 1984 the number of psychiatric beds owned and operated by multihospital, for-profit companies increased by nearly 15 percent (Sullivan et al., 1987: 25).

Unintended Disincentives, DRGs, and Medical Indigents

Hospitals' DRG-related financial woes have been exacerbated by a constellation of other factors: the supplanting of the cost-based reimbursement mechanism with one based on price; employers' increasingly aggressive and prudent purchasing of health insurance; and the more effective use of utilization review. Together these forces are revolutionizing the American health system.

It is noteworthy that the forces shaping the transformation of the health care system create incentives to underserve their clientele, and to altogether avoid serving indigents. With less room for cost-shifting, uncompensated care becomes an onerous burden, one which is inequitably distributed, and one which has an inequitable impact on hospitals in this newly price-competitive world.

The indigent mentally ill, therefore, run the same heightened risk which has befallen the medically indigent in general: they are increasingly likely to receive no care, or they are at increased risk of being "dumped" at state mental hospitals. Studies commissioned by the National Association of Private Psychiatric Hospitals and the American Psychiatric Association both suggest that this situation will be exacerbated if DRGs are universally applied to the psychiatric units of general hospitals; costly patients, in particular, will be shifted to public institutions.

Prepayment Systems and Treatment: The Uncertain Future

The rapid growth of systems of prepaid care, specifically HMOs (enrollments which have been growing at annual rates in excess of 20 percent in the last few years), will bring with them reviews, reassessments, and changes in the treatment of mental disorders. Some lament the transformation of the fee-for-service system, citing evidence of HMOs inadequately treating and caring for the severely or chronically mentally ill (Cheifitz and Salloway, 1984; Levin et al., 1984; Diamond et al., 1985). Others, reviewing the findings of a recent national HMO survey, fear that present shortcomings portend the shape of things to come.

> HMOs may place psychiatrists and their patients at a disadvantage because they generally restrict coverage of mental illness, use mental health practitioners other than psychiatrists, and lack provision for treating chronic and indigent mentally ill patients. (Flinn et al., 1987: 255)

These failings are troubling. But are they unique to HMOs and prepaid systems of care in general? Most of these considerations, as we have seen, already exist in more traditional care settings, regardless of their basis of financing. While differences in degrees are important, there are reasons for greater optimism.

HMOs offer a unique opportunity to capture the cost savings that a medical offset effect—to the extent that it exists—can be expected to generate. This suggests that the opportunity for better-managed care, with greater continuity, offered by HMO arrangements, can mean that HMOs will better care for the mentally ill. This possibility looks even more attractive when one recalls the ongoing erosion of private insurance coverage of psychiatric services (Sharfstein et al., 1984). Concern must turn to structuring incentives to build on that opportunity. Here is where additional research on demand and the medical offset effect has an important role to play in public policy development.

RECOGNITION AND TREATMENT OF MENTAL DISORDERS IN THE PRIMARY CARE SECTOR

The scope and level of insurance coverage are both important determinants of the demand for mental health services. Insurance also influences the appropriateness of those services which are demanded. The relatively limited (or non-existent) insurance coverage of mental health treatment provides individuals with an economic incentive to have their emotional disorders treated by non-mental health specialists (Broskowski, 1981). This effect of differential insurance coverage reinforces several other factors which together act to heighten the proportion of the population with mental disorders who do not seek care in the mental health specialty sector. For a number of reasons, this, for many, is cause for alarm.

In the past few years it has come to be recognized that the majority of persons with mental disorders are not seen by mental health specialists, but by primary care physicians (Regier et al., 1978: 685; Houpt et al., 1979 and 1980; Kessler et al., 1985; Schurman et al., 1985).

While considerable evidence exists that there is a positive correlation between utilization of medical services and the presence of psychiatric problems (Broskowski, 1981: 17), a national survey of office-based physicians conducted by the National Center for Health Statistics found that the *primary* presenting ailment for 4.4 percent of all office visits is a diagnosed mental disorder (Delozier, 1975). In part (though there are no quantitative estimates) this is thought to be an artifact of the incentives of differential insurance coverage. In part, it reflects the attenuated, but still extant, stigma associated with emotional problems and the use of mental health services. Some individuals with emotional problems probably perceive less risk of being labeled and stigmatized if they obtain care in a primary health care setting rather than a specialized mental health care setting (Hankin and Oktay, 1979). This may also explain why—even when all outpatient visits to relatively expensive mental health specialists (up to fifty-two visits per year) are free—only one-half of the users of outpatient mental health services used mental health care providers exclusively (Wells et al., 1987a).

In addition to the 4.4 percent whose primary presenting ailment is a diagnosed mental disorder, a much larger fraction of the primary care population suffers from mental illness. As we noted earlier, the prevalence of psychiatric and mental disorders in such populations has been variously estimated to range between 7 and 25 percent, although the number generally cited is 15 percent (Locke et al., 1966; Locke and Gardner, 1969; Regier et al., 1978; Bittker, 1985: 150; Horgan, 1985; Shapiro et al., 1984: 975; Schurman et al., 1985; Orleans et al., 1985: 52). The wide range of the estimates is due to a variety of factors, including actual variability in the patient populations studied and physician characteristics, such as personality and attitude toward mental illness, which act to encourage or discourage persons with mental disorders from frequenting them (Marks et al., 1975).

Regier et al. (1978: 688) have estimated that of the nearly 32 million persons in the United States (roughly 15 percent of the total population) with a mental disorder, only 21 percent are treated within the specialty mental health sector. Most of this 21 percent, they maintain, are referred by primary care physicians. A far greater proportion, 60.1 percent, on the other hand, are receiving services (identified and/or being treated) from the primary care or outpatient medical services. Of those receiving their care in the general medical care sector, it has been estimated that between 70 percent (Regier et al., 1978: 688) and 87 percent (Schurman et al., 1985: 90) are treated by office-based primary care providers.

Moreover, Regier et al. have estimated that 90 percent of those treated in a primary care setting are treated exclusively therein. Overlapping care characterizes the utilization experiences of only a small fraction of individuals turning to the primary care sector. It should be noted, however, that there is recent evidence that the more severely mentally ill are more likely to be treated in the mental health specialty sector (Shapiro et al., 1984; Ware et al., 1984; Horgan, 1985; Schurman et al., 1985).

Given that these two sectors of the medical care system operate independently, and that there are several factors (such as lessened stigma and better insurance coverage) favoring entry into the non-mental health specialty or general health services sector, the question of the sectors' relative effectiveness and efficiency arises—inadequately addressed, hence, for policy purposes, unanswered. It begs a fundamental question: what happens to the mentally ill in primary health care settings?

Studies have consistently found that primary care physicians' recognition of mental disorders is poor (Kessler et al., 1985; Orleans et al., 1985; Brody, 1980; Marks et al., 1979; Thompson et al., 1983). Primary care physicians commonly underreport mental disorders among their patients (Hoeper et al, 1980a; Strumbo et al., 1982). This has been found to be the case even when patients self-report distress (Hoeper et al., 1980a; Brody 1980; Marks et al., 1979; Thompson et al., 1983). In a six-month longitudinal study, Kessler and associates (1985) found that 35 percent of a primary care population had at least one Research Diagnostic Criteria (RDC) disorder, and that nearly two-thirds of these (23 percent of the entire primary care population) had significant changes in their mental disorder diagnostic status. "Diagnosis of these transient and episodic cases by the primary care providers was under 10 percent, demonstrating the need for careful evaluation of the psychiatric status of primary care patients" (Kessler et al., 1985: 583). The implication of these findings is self-evident: unrecognized, the vast majority of mental disorders suffered by Americans go untreated.

In an earlier study, Shepherd and associates (1966) found that two-thirds of those with an identified mental disorder and who visited a general practitioner were identified and/or treated by the physician: another 5 percent were referred to specialty mental health care, leaving nearly one-third of such individuals (28 percent) receiving no treatment at all (they were only identified). At present it is thought that at least 3 percent of the total U.S. population has a mental disorder but does not receive treatment. (In other words, 80 percent of those with a mental disorder do receive some type of mental health treatment.) If Shepherd et al.'s estimate is accurate, it suggests that this rate is twice as large, leaving an additional 3 percent, or a total of 6 percent, of the U.S. population with an untreated mental disorder.

Contrary to Regier, Goldberg, and Taube's findings, both Hankin and Oktay (1979) and Shepherd and associates (1966) found that the majority of general practice patients with a recognized mental disorder are not referred for psychiatric treatment. The proportion referred, they maintain, is only 0.7 percent to 6.0 percent. Why are these referral rates so low?

In their comprehensive review of the literature on *Mental Disorder and Primary Medical Care* (1979), Hankin and Oktay note a variety of factors which have been found to influence referral from general and/or primary health care providers to mental health specialists: (1) the patient's fear of emotional illness (Raft, 1973; Moskowitz, 1968); (2) the physician's anger at a patient (Raft, 1973); (3) the physician's fear of patient reaction to the suggestion of a psychiatric referral (Follette and Cummings, 1967; Crede, 1968); (4) the existence of a negative attitude of the primary care provider toward psychiatry (Raft, 1973; Kessel, 1963); (5) the physician's anxiety about his own feelings toward the patient (Group for the Advancement of Psychiatry, 1964); (6) uncertainty about the appropriateness of the referral (Hilkevitch, 1965); (7) pessimism about success of outcome (Hilkevitch, 1965); and (8) treatment capacity of the mental health specialty providers (Follette and Cummings, 1967).

Most of the population with mental disorders, we have seen, is found in the primary health care sector, from which only a small fraction of them are referred to the mental health specialty sector. What types of factors influence whether or not they are treated in the primary care sector, and what treatment do they receive there? Again turning to Hankin and Oktay's review, they uncovered four factors in the literature which have been found to be related to the rate of physician treatment of the mentally ill: (1) the rate of identification of psychiatric patients (Shepherd et al., 1966; Kessler et al., 1985); (2) the general practitioner's personality (Pond, 1969; Marks et al., 1979); (3) physician specialty (Carey and Kogan, 1971); and (4) the psychiatric training of the physician (Hyams et al., 1971).

More recently, in a national survey of 350 family practice physicians, Orleans and associates (1985) found that about two-thirds of the respondents reported that they themselves had too little time to effectively treat emotional and psychiatric disorders (which they estimated nearly a quarter of their patients suffered from to the extent that they warranted evaluation and treatment). Still, many of the practitioners did attempt to treat the mentally disabled, relying—they reported—overwhelmingly on only the "therapy" of "advice and reassurance." Furthermore, the responding physicians reported referring only about 6 percent of "affected patients" although, it should be pointed out, they noted that many patients resisted referrals, suggesting the presence of a vicious circle.

What happens to those who are treated? Studies suggest that the quality of the care provided is a cause for concern: (1) psychotropic drugs are overprescribed; (2) systematic counseling and psychotherapy are rarely offered within the primary care setting; and (3) again, referral to mental health specialty providers is relatively uncommon. As Tracy Orleans and associates (1985) have pointed out, however, most of these findings come from studies with a variety of methodological shortcomings, most commonly reliance on small, regional samples of physicians.

In summarizing their literature review of primary care treatment of mental disorder, Hankin and Oktay carefully conclude that

there is some evidence that general practitioner therapy does not meet expectations of psychiatrists. . . . More work is needed to determine under what conditions particular psychotherapeutic interventions by general practitioners are appropriate. (Hankin and Oktay, 1979: 42)

While the piecemeal picture we have of the treatment of the mentally ill in health care settings is largely based on flawed studies of questionable validity, the consistency of the findings suggests that the general impression they provide is an accurate one, and one that is unsettling. A significant proportion of Americans who suffer a mental disorder in the course of a year go undiagnosed, never enter the mental health specialty sector, and, to the extent that they receive care, are treated exclusively in the primary care sector by physicians who are generally hesitant or incapable (for a variety of reasons) to provide effective treatment.

SUMMARY

The rapid growth in both the supply of and demand for mental health services in the United States in the last three decades has occurred for a complex set of reasons. A variety of scientific advances, socioeconomic, institutional, and even legal changes have had the effect of propelling the development of the mental health services industry in a variety of directions.

The current system, far from being an integrated set of services, rationally planned and designed to address efficiently and effectively the particular mental health problems of our society, is instead a patchwork of incremental additions to a system not designed and ill-equipped to deal with many of the demands made on it today. This is most dramatically evidenced by the fact that most Americans with a mental disorder remain generally unrecognized, undiagnosed, and untreated, and do not even enter the mental health care sector.

While the structure of the system has changed markedly since World War II, further major structural changes are already under way and still others are in the offing. Given, (1) that the direct and indirect costs of mental illness in our society have been, and remain, relatively high, (2) that most of the mentally ill are still not cared for in the mental health specialty sector, and (3) that the demand for mental health services continues to rise, it is clear that the evaluation of the effectiveness and efficiency of the sector will be of growing importance in the near future. Such evaluation will be the grist for policymaking mills as the twin calls for "accountability" and "cost-effectiveness" enter the mental health industry as they are certain to do in any arena (such as mental health) where consumers are so woefully ignorant, where the government has already had such an important role, and where growth has been so rapid. One of the most important issues in this evaluation effort is the focus of this study, the medical offset effect.

APPENDIX 2.1: EMPIRICAL EVIDENCE OF THE DEMAND FOR MENTAL HEALTH TREATMENT

This appendix presents a more technical discussion of the important research findings on the demand for mental health care. As indicated in the text, the bulk of these studies revolve around estimates of the price elasticity of demand for these services.

Price elasticity of demand is technically defined as the percentage change in quantity demanded divided by the percentage change in price. Because the quantity demanded for a good or service is usually inversely related to the price, the price elasticity of demand is a negative number. If the absolute value of this elasticity is a small number, less than 1.0, demand is said to be "inelastic" or "unresponsive" to changes in price. Thus as price rises, the quantity demanded falls, but by a lesser proportion than the price increase. Such inelastic-demand goods are generally characterized as "necessities."

Conversely, an "elastic" demand is one for which the absolute value of the elasticity is a large number, greater than 1.0. In this case, as price rises, consumers cut back their purchases of the service by an even greater percentage. Such elastic-demand goods are generally characterized as "luxuries."

We turn now to estimates of elasticity of demand for mental health services.

Noting that his seminal study "cannot tell how much insurance coverage increases the likelihood someone seeks treatment in the first place" (McGuire, 1981: 129), McGuire describes his findings as "illustrating that insurance does encourage utilization of psychotherapy [and that] the stimulus is at least as strong as the stimulus for physicians' services generally" (McGuire, 1981: 60). While he is unable to quantify the elasticity coefficients, McGuire suggests that the elasticity of mental health services is greater than that of general health services. Again, however, as pointed out in the text, absolute sizes of the coefficients—which, again, McGuire is unable to estimate—are also of interest. We do not know, for instance, if the demand for mental health services is elastic or inelastic.

In analysis based on a national probability sample (the 1980 National Medical Care Utilization and Expenditures Survey, NMCUES), Taube et al. (1986) estimate the price elasticity of demand to be between (-0.539) and (-0.98); inelastic, but larger (in absolute terms) than that of ambulatory non-mental health visits.

Using the 1977 National Medical Care Expenditures Survey (NMCES) data (based on another national probability sample), and limiting the analysis to mental health specialists, Horgan (1986) estimated that the level of cost-sharing affects the decision to use some—at least one—mental health specialty service less than it affects the level of use of services. While she found that both measures were greater in absolute value than estimates for ambulatory medical services based on the same database, both mental health elasticities were inelastic: (-0.27) for probability of use and (-0.54) for level of use. Hence, Horgan has found (as have Taube et al., 1986) that while the price elasticity of demand for mental health services is less than that of general health services, both are relatively insensitive to price changes.

What do these elasticity measures mean in terms of the level of use of services and its responsiveness to price changes? Based on Horgan's estimated elasticity coefficients, other things being equal, a 10 percent increase in the net price of mental health services results in a 2.7 percent reduction in the probability that an individual will have at least one mental health treatment visit, and will generate a 5.4 percent decrease in the number of treatment visits. Alternatively viewed, if insurance coverage is made more generous (e.g., a reduction of the coinsurance rate) such that there is a 10 percent reduction in the net price of a mental health visit, there will be a 2.7 percent increase in the probability that an individual will enter the mental health services market, and there will be a 5.4 percent increase in the number of treatment visits.

The only study in which the price elasticity of demand for mental health services has been estimated to be elastic is Richard Frank's 1985 analysis. This is also the only study in which the unit of analysis was not the individual. Based on aggregate, state-level data, Richard Frank (1985) estimated the price elasticity of demand to range from (-1.0) to (-2.0): a 10 percent reduction in the net price generates a 10 to 20 percent increase in mental health service utilization. Clearly the size differentials of these estimates have great policy relevance.

On the other hand, evidence suggesting that the physical versus mental health services insurance disparities are arbitrary and unfounded or unjustified comes from the Rand Health Insurance Study (HIS).[8] Rand analysts found that the price elasticity of demand for ambulatory mental health services was "roughly the same" as that for ambulatory medical care (Wells et al., 1984: 1087).[9] They found that the impact of cost-sharing was primarily on the probability of some use, as opposed to the level of use among users (Wells et al., 1982). That is, limiting analysis to those with at least one mental health treatment visit, Rand found that although the elasticity of demand varied considerably across the HIS's different plans' levels of copayments and deductibles, it was consistently price-inelastic (i.e., less than 1.0, in absolute value), and comparable to that of non-mental health ambulatory care demand. If a medical offset effect exists, relatively high coinsurance rates will likely preclude its being optimized. High coinsurance deters people from entering mental health treatment; if there were a medical offset effect, insurance coverage structure should be to encourage entry into treatment.

An intermediately positioned finding is that of Watts et al. (1986). Looking at a heavily insured population (Blue Cross/Blue Shield's Federal Employee Health Benefits Program), they found low and insignificant price elasticities of demand for both probability of use and level of use. These findings, however, may merely reflect the fact that when net prices are very low and do not vary a great deal—as in a heavily insured population such as this—changes in net prices are not likely to alter behavior a great deal. This is not surprising: basic economic theory and common sense tell us that the price elasticity of demand is a function not only of the individual's perception of the degree of "need" for the good or service in question but also of the price level relative to the individual's income. Other things being equal, the smaller the proportion of income a given purchase requires, the less sensitive the individual is likely to be to a percent change in its price. A 10 percent increase in the price of milk is likely to have a much smaller impact on the quantity of milk demanded than a 10 percent increase in the price of automobiles on the quantity of cars demanded.

NOTES

1. The four "landmark studies" are of Stirling County, Nova Scotia (Hughes et al., 1963; Leighton et al., 1963); the Baltimore morbidity study (Pasamanick et al., 1956; Commission on Chronic Illness, 1957); the midtown Manhattan study (Srole, 1962; 1975); and the New Haven, Connecticut study (Tischler et al., 1975; Weissman et al., 1978; Weissman and Myers, 1978). The appellation of "landmark" was affixed by a research team of the Epidemiological Catchment Area Program (ECA) (Regier et al., 1984: 934).

2. To avoid losing sight of the forest for the trees, the interested reader is urged to first consult the substantial body of literature reviews before tackling the primary literature. Particularly useful are Parloff et al., 1978; Hankin and Oktay, 1979; Jones and Vischi, 1979; VandenBos and Pino, 1980; Office of Technology Assessment, 1980; Smith et al., 1980; Schlesinger et al., 1980; Mumford et al., 1982; Devine and Cook, 1983; and Mumford et al., 1984.

3. More comprehensive historical accounts of insurance coverage of mental health services are found in Reed et al., 1972; Reed, 1975; Sharfstein, 1978; McGuire, 1981; McGuire and Weisbrod, 1981b; and Sharfstein et al., 1984.

4. These relative disparities have major implications for offset researchers. By affecting the magnitude and pattern of the demand for mental health services—generally reducing it from what it would be were it on a par with general health service insurance levels—differential coverage conditions the very existence of the offset. For instance, we might not observe the medical offset effect if the threshold level of mental health treatment visits required to generate it were on average greater than the number of visits generally made because relatively low insurance coverage has dampened utilization.

5. A more precise discussion of the concept of elasticity is given in Appendix 2.1.

6. An insured patient's medical records may be reviewed by the insurer, or, in the case when insurance is paid at least in part by the patient's employer, by the employer. These are the two most likely parties from whom the provider may want to keep his clients' records confidential (McGuire, 1981: 91).

7. The level of benefits under Medicaid varies by state, sometimes dramatically. The insurance variable in all three studies is a very simple, aggregative measure. It merely indicates whether the individual was insured, regardless of the extent of coverage.

8. See Newhouse (1974), Morris (1979), Wells et al. (1982), and Wells et al. (1984) for details of the design of the HIS, and its principal findings regarding mental health services demand and utilization.

9. Ellis and McGuire (1984) have argued that the Rand finding is probably an artifact of the peculiar structure of incentives in the HIS health insurance plans. This discussion is also detailed in Frank and McGuire (1986).

A STYLIZED REVIEW OF THE MEDICAL OFFSET LITERATURE

The Fifth, who chanced to touch the ear,
Said: "E'en the blindest man
Can tell what this resembles most;
Deny the fact who can,
This marvel of an elephant
Is very like a fan!"
So, oft in theologic wars
The disputants, I ween,
Rail on in utter ignorance
Of what each other mean,
And prate about an elephant
Not one of them has seen!
                    —John Godfey Saxe from "The Blind Men and the Elephant"

INTRODUCTION AND OVERVIEW

While the medical offset effect has been intensively studied for more than two decades, researchers continue to talk past one another, much like the comic arguments of the six blind men in Saxe's poem, each of whom describes by feel a different part of the same "elephant." The men dispute, "loud and long," over whether an elephant is like a wall, a spear, a snake, a tree, a fan, or a rope. So, too, without seeing the "big" picture of the offset, bits and pieces of what we know seem often to be in conflict and like the blind men we are " ... partly in the right/And all [are] in the wrong!" Thus, despite the persistent claims by mental health care providers that the timely treatment of mental illness generates subsequent reductions in non-mental health care expenses, skepticism about the very existence of an offset continues today.

The growing importance of medical offset studies for public and private policymaking means that a careful review of these existing studies is in order. Our review of the medical offset literature in this chapter is not intended to be totally comprehensive of the vast literature which has accumulated in the past twenty years. Several very good analytical reviews already exist (see especially the offset conference report edited by Jones, 1980). Rather, our review centers on seven methodological issues which have proved to be important limitations in the offset literature. We hope this approach will be most useful in taking stock of what in the past have been stumbling blocks which have kept researchers from synthesizing and building on previous works.

Before detailing these issues, we must first define more precisely what we mean by an "offset effect," since much of the ambiguity surrounding offset research findings stems from the different definitions and measurements of the concepts. Most researchers (including the present authors) have adopted a general and broad definition: an offset occurs if physical health utilization falls as a result of mental health intervention. This definition is independent of the level of mental health care utilization; that is, an offset exists so long as any reduction in physical health utilization occurs, regardless of whether it took two or twenty visits to a mental health provider to achieve this reduction. Whether the reduction in physical health charges only partially or more than completely offsets the cost of providing the mental health services—that is, whether mental health treatment is cost-effective—is obviously an additional crucial issue for public and private policy-making.

Others define an offset in a more narrow sense: an offset occurs only if the fall in physical health care utilization more than completely exceeds the increase in mental health care utilization. Investigators using this stricter definition focus on the total (physical plus mental) health care utilization following a mental health intervention rather than simply analyzing the impact on physical health charges.

In operationalizing these definitions of an offset, researchers have followed varying tactics, some looking at "utilization" in terms of the number of office visits, others in terms of dollar expenditures. Beyond these elemental differences in definitions and means, the ambivalence surrounding offset research findings stems from a variety of factors: principally, researchers seeking to address different issues, using different experimental designs and different statistical techniques.

These divergences are explained, in part, by the fact that the rich conglomeration of social scientists who together comprise the offset research "community" come from widely varying disciplines with widely varying trainings and predispositions on how to analyze the issue. This has contributed to researchers frequently "talking past" one another, and failing to build on what others have already done.

We have culled from the literature seven common methodological differences or difficulties around which to analyze these offset findings:

1. The definition of psychotherapy
2. The dearth of behavioral models

3. Unique study settings: Fee-for-service versus prepaid settings
4. Study design and selection biases
5. Controlling for the "peaking" phenomenon
6. The time dimension and functional form
7. Multiple regression techniques and issues

AN EXAMINATION OF THE MOST COMMON METHODOLOGICAL ISSUES OF OFFSET ANALYSIS

Defining Psychotherapy: The Need for Greater Specificity

The development of a plethora of psychotherapeutic methods is a reflection of the multifarious character and multifactorial etiology of mental illness. While the multiplication of treatment techniques has been the product of efforts to design more effective care, it has greatly complicated efforts to evaluate psychotherapy.

First, there has been a slow but constant expansion in what has generally been considered to be within the domain of psychotherapy. For example, many of the activities previously classified under the rubric of "health education" have come to wear the label of "psychosocial therapy" or "psychoeducational therapy." The advent in the 1970s of interest in health promotion in the general physical health sciences spawned a parallel development in the mental health field. The term "psychotherapy" is now generally understood to subsume techniques to enhance self-awareness and self-actualization (President's Commission on Mental Health, 1978, vol. IV). The result has been a blurring of the definition of psychotherapy, causing considerable confusion about what psychotherapy is and what it does. This confusion has undermined the reputability of psychotherapy for a substantial portion of the general public. As three of the most esteemed and prolific offset investigators have lamented,

while psychotherapy has been widely practiced under various names for millennia, it has the reputation in some quarters for being a vague treatment for vague complaints with no way of determining the necessity of treatment or assessing results. In fact, psychotherapy has been subjected to more controlled experiment and study than have most medical therapies, aside from drugs. (Mumford et al., 1981: 258)

Studies assessing the effectiveness of psychotherapy must, therefore, start by explicitly and unequivocally defining what it is that they are analyzing. Researchers should not analyze "psychotherapy" in general, but instead should more narrowly focus their analysis on specific psychotherapeutic techniques and modalities.

In addition, to avoid the further pitfall of comparing apples and oranges, the characteristics of the patient, the characteristics of the provider, and the treatment setting should be similarly disaggregated.

This is particularly essential in exercises which entail evaluating "psychotherapy," as well as those requiring aggregating and/or discussing different studies of psychotherapy, as in the case of analytical reviews of the literature. Too often, however, this has not been done, despite the fact that recent comparative psychotherapy research (see, for example, Karon and VandenBos, 1972; Sloane et al., 1975; Rush et al., 1977; Ellsworth et al., 1979) has demonstrated the need for and the importance of greater specificity (VandenBos and Pino, 1980).

Some of the implications of the growth in the field of psychotherapy and the need to clearly demarcate the content, domain, and relevance of any particular study are well illustrated by W. Lee Hansen in a discussion paper wherein he appropriately acknowledges this issue, even though his definition of psychotherapy is by no means concise or unambivalent:

For purposes of this paper, I take a broad view of what constitutes the mental health services sector and mental health manpower. The narrower view is reflected in the description of "The De Facto U.S. Mental Health Services System," developed by Regier, Goldberg and Taube, which is more fully described elsewhere. This system focuses on that part of the population suffering from mental disorders which is estimated to be about 15 percent of the U.S. population. A broader view encompasses, in addition, those people who experience "the more ubiquitous problem of living and emotional symptoms that may affect up to 85 percent of the population." Since these kinds of problems and symptoms often require treatment and hence affect the demand for mental health services, it is important to recognize this relationship. Moreover, this broader definition encompasses a larger more diversified group of providers of mental health services. While this makes the task of defining the field more difficult, it permits the exploration of certain issues that would otherwise be foreclosed. (Hansen, 1981: 85–86)

A second factor complicating the evaluation of psychotherapy is related to the first. With the quantitative and qualitative extension of psychotherapeutic modalities to a more diverse population it has become increasingly difficult to find a valid, reliable, and universally applicable outcome measure. As VandenBos and Pino (1980) recount, there has been a growth in the specificity of outcome and control group criteria in psychotherapy research. Because of its direct economic and other policy implications, one of the most useful outcome measures has been the pre- versus post-treatment changes in physical health service utilization—that is, the medical offset effect.

With few exceptions, general studies investigating whether or not mental health interventions are effective conclude that they are. Several reviews utilizing a quantitative aggregation technique known as "meta-analysis" have concluded the same. In the most comprehensive review of the literature, Smith et al. (1980), based on their meta-analysis of 475 studies of psychotherapy, assert that those receiving some psychotherapy are better off than 80 percent of those not receiving any mental health specialty care.

In reviews specifically investigating the offset effect, the findings similarly and preponderantly find psychotherapy to be effective. In fact, with very few exceptions, nearly all of the more than 100 diverse investigations of offset found that the effect existed.

In the three most important reviews of offset literature to date, Jones and Vischi (1979) found physical care utilization reductions in twelve of thirteen studies analyzed, with a median reduction of 20 percent; Devine and Cook's 1983 meta-analytic review of forty-nine studies of the relationship between brief psychoeducational interventions and the length of postsurgical hospitalization found that in most cases (about 70 percent of the studies) there was a reduction in the length of stay, with a mean reduction of about one and one-quarter days; and Mumford et al.'s 1984 meta-analysis of 58 studies assessing the experiences of 118 different groups of individuals found physical care utilization increased in only eleven of the groups (9.3 percent).

Focusing specifically on the offset literature, one of the major reasons that this overwhelming preponderance of evidence is not universally regarded as conclusive is that much of this research has analyzed psychoeducational treatment. Although the evidence of an offset in these studies is compelling, it tends to be discounted at least in part because of the non-traditional character of the patients. Rather than analyzing emotionally disturbed or mentally ill persons, the study population of most of these studies is not necessarily emotionally disturbed or mentally ill. Their eligibility for membership in the study group results instead from, in some studies, their having just been diagnosed as having a chronic condition, or, in other studies, having just experienced surgery. Their "mental health intervention" consists of one or more of what Devine and Cook (1983: 271) have labeled the three domains of psychoeducational care: information, skills training, and psychosocial support. This type of psychotherapy may be regarded as largely prophylactic: it smoothes what might otherwise (and in some cases might still) be a psychologically stressful transition, which, if unsuccessful, might encourage the onset of some form of mental illness.

This discussion is not intended to disparage such efforts, or to question their value. Rather, it is intended to elucidate a major source of misunderstanding which concomitantly underscores an important methodological consideration: the need to disaggregate psychotherapy and to analyze individual psychotherapeutic techniques.

The Need to Develop a Behavioral Model Approach

Studies based on matched comparison groups constitute the bulk of the (especially recent) literature on offset. The seminal work in this area is the study of Follette and Cummings at Kaiser Permanente twenty years ago. Follette and Cummings developed a comparison group matched on a variety of variables—including level of psychological distress, age, sex, and prior medical care utilization.

The goal of most subsequent studies for many years was a modest one: replication. Most of these studies not only failed to explore what other new or different variables influenced medical care utilization and/or the effectiveness of psychotherapy (and, therefore, should be controlled for), but failed even to match their study and control groups on several variables which had already been demonstrated to affect the offset.

The literature, thus, became characterized less by careful behavioral model building and incremental model elaboration, which is generally how scientific knowledge advances, and more by piecemeal—at times seemingly haphazard—explorations of what other variables might be statistically significant. The failure to include variables already shown to have an important influencing role may be analytically convenient, but the results of such analyses are generally imprecise and must be regarded (at best) as tentative. The empirical results reflect not only the influence of the particular variables under study, but usually also the effect of excluded, but correlated, variables. This problem undermines the precision and, more devastatingly, the internal validity of quasi-experimental evaluation. It is impossible to ferret out from such work what it is that has been learned. If multiple regression is the technique employed, this failure to include relevant variables results in what in statistical parlance is known as a "specification" error. For a discussion of this topic and its implications for multiple regression results, see p. 57 below.

In essence, research of the offset effect has become stuck on a kind of research treadmill. Not having taken advantage of what we think it is we do know about people's utilization of mental and physical health services, we are unable to discount a host of competing hypothetical explanations of the meaning of the latest, statistically significant finding.

Ten years ago, when the study of general health services utilization passed through a similar juncture, Hershey, Luft, and Giannaris wrote:

Many studies of health services utilization have been made in the past few years. . . . Occasionally, a specific model has been outlined and tested, but frequently little consideration has been given to exactly what behavior is being measured by the data. . . . A basic hypothesis of this paper is that using only a few independent variables can lead to an incorrect interpretation of the data in comparison with using an expanded set of variables. . . . Unfortunately, many investigators continue to be insensitive to the problems of omitting crucial variables. (Hershey et al., 1975: 838–39)

This is at once an accurate portrayal of, and pertinent advice for, many medical-offset-effect researchers. In the interest of maintaining our focus on past research efforts, we postpone presentation of our behavioral model of the medical offset effect until the next chapter.

The problems of defining psychotherapy and developing a behavioral model explaining and/or hypothesizing why an offset effect might be realized are per-

haps the two most common methodological shortcomings of the offset literature. There are others, however, some of which are closely related.

Unique Study Settings: Fee-for-Service versus Prepaid Settings

While much of the literature on the offset has found that there is indeed such
a phenomenon, these findings may be an artifact of the unique incentive structure of prepaid health plans, the setting of the overwhelming majority of offset
studies to date. There have been relatively few comparisons of the patterns of
mental health service utilization in fee-for-service settings as opposed to prepaid practice plans such as health maintenance organizations (HMOs), independent provider associations (IPAs), preferred provider organizations
(PPOs), and the like. Of those which have been conducted, even fewer have
analyzed the data disaggregated by source, or even presented the data to allow
interested readers to perform their own analysis. Moreover, the few studies
which have developed utilization patterns based on financing mechanisms
have had mixed results. Kogan et al. (1975), for example, found no differences
between the medical care use patterns of a prepaid practice's population and
a fee-for-service group. They did not, however, account in any way for the different characteristics of the two populations.

Studies by Paula Diehr and her colleagues (1984), on the other hand, dealing with the populations of an HMO, an IPA, and a fee-for-service population,
have been far more sophisticated in their analytical approach and have found
significant differences in utilization patterns. After transforming the population distribution of the variables of interest to take into account their non-nor-
mal distribution, and thereby increasing the reliability of their comparisons,
Diehr et al. also adjusted for sex and age. They found that while relatively
more of the people enrolled in the prepaid plans had mental health visits, the
number of mental health visits per person with at least one visit was substantially greater for the fee-for-service population. That the role of the providers'
incentive structures in the alternative-care settings was a powerful explanatory factor was corroborated by recognition that the IPA even used the same
community physicians as the fee-for-service enrollees. The researchers concluded, "The incentive system in this type of plan (fee-for-service) and the reliance upon psychiatrists seem to be associated with higher utilization once a
patient is in treatment" (Diehr et al., 1984: 11).

These findings suggest two things. First, that the common practice of aggregating across organizational structure (cf. Borus et al., 1985) is inappropriate.
Doing so results in an aggregation bias, which conceals important differences
and distorts the findings. Future investigations of the offset effect, therefore,
should avoid this possible source of bias, or should at least explicitly recognize
it and attempt to ascertain its magnitude.

Second, if the offset effect is defined as changes in total utilization (i.e., mental plus physical medical care utilization), the finding of an offset may be entirely attributable to differences in the mental health case management/treatment protocols of the alternative organizational structures, differences which seem to be attributable to their different incentive structures.

How might the impact of the incentive structure of prepaid practices manifest itself? There are several possibilities. First, the staff of a prepaid practice generally receive a salary which does not vary (in the short run) with the number of patients they treat. In addition, "Since physicians are at risk for all service costs, every reasonable and ethically sound effort is made to avoid long-term treatment and hospitalization" (Bittker, 1985: 151).

Furthermore, the integration of physical and mental health services in one organizational entity, in combination with the use of central patient records, creates the possibility of administrative oversight and control of especially inappropriate or "unnecessary" utilization.

Second (and consistent with the first), the treatment goals of prepaid practices are usually much more attuned to those of what is known in the psychiatric profession as "brief therapy." In short, "brief therapy" as opposed to more traditional forms of psychotherapy is more oriented toward "return to function" as opposed to "personality reconstruction."

Third, prepaid practices often extensively substitute less expensive professional personnel for psychiatrists or psychologists. These "substitute personnel," such as psychiatric nurse practitioners or psychiatric social workers, generally have less training in mental-health-related diagnosis and treatment.

Fourth, those mental health specialists who are hired by the prepaid practice are in fixed supply; therefore, so are the number of mental health service units the organization may provide. Depending on the level of demand, it may be necessary to ration that limited supply of providers and services by, for example, developing a waiting list (i.e., longer appointment time delays) or employing more and/or larger group therapy sessions. Like brief therapy, group therapy may be the preferred mode of some therapists independent of other considerations, but it might also be primarily motivated by financial considerations (McGuire, 1981: 58–59; Bittker, 1985).

These are the possibilities, but what has thus far been empirically ascertained? Thomas Bittker, drawing on his own research (Bittker and Idzorek, 1978; Bittker and George, 1980) has, in fact, found many of them to be borne out.

Prepaid psychiatry assumes a fundamentally different form than its fee-for-service counterpart. Heavy emphasis is placed on outpatient crisis intervention, time-limited and group psychotherapy, and collaboration with other mental health professionals. (Bittker, 1985: 151)

It is likely, therefore, that the processes of both diagnosis and treatment in prepaid practice plans are different from those in the fee-for-service sector.

Also, it is possible that the different incentive structure giving rise to different processes of diagnosis and treatment also gives rise to different outcomes: ones that are not necessarily as optimistic or positive with regard to the mental health treatment outcome as compared to those more generally discussed in the offset literature.

In light of these findings it may seem questionable to extrapolate the HMO-based offset research findings to the fee-for-service sector (which contains the majority of the American population). However, for purposes of planning the future of psychiatry, those studies in the prepaid arena are highly relevant. At the end of 1986, there were 626 HMOs in the U.S., with almost twenty-six million members. Moreover, HMO membership has grown at an annual average rate of more than 20 percent since 1982 (Ellwood, 1986). In addition, the Health Care Financing Administration (HCFA) has announced that it intends to move all of Medicare's hospital and physician reimbursement toward capitation by 1993 (Wagner, 1986).

Thus, the organizational structure and financial mechanisms for paying for care are additional variables that offset researchers must analyze in attempting to understand the offset effect.

Study Design and Selection Bias

The preferred method for establishing whether or not an offset exists would be to conduct an experiment, a randomized clinical trial. The ideal experimental design would entail first identifying a large number of individuals who have a mental disorder and are willing to receive mental health treatment.

Next, these individuals would be randomly assigned to one of two groups. One of the groups, the experimental group, would receive mental health treatment for their mental disorder; the second would not.

Properly executed, and with an adequate number of subjects, this selection and assignment procedure would ensure that the only significant (nonrandom) differences between the two groups would be group two's mental health treatment. Hence, the impact of the mental health intervention on medical care utilization could be isolated from confounding influences, and could be accurately measured. While there has been at least one effort to conduct this type of randomized, clinical trial (Follette and Cummings, 1967), none has, as yet, been successfully carried out.

The ethical considerations of withholding treatment from a randomly selected group of mentally ill individuals has encouraged most researchers to utilize an alternative (the second-best) research design; the quasi-experimental, matched comparison group, which we discussed earlier.

In all of the quasi-experimental studies utilizing matched comparison groups, the study and control groups vary—as they would in a "purely" experimental design—in that some of their members did and some did not receive mental health treatment. But an additional source of variation is found in the matched comparison-group-based studies, which is not found in those employing a pure experimental design. The source of this additional variation is an artifact of the different selection/assignment process they employ. In the pure experimental design, the process is one of random assignment: individuals are randomly selected to receive treatment. In the quasi-experimental design, on the other hand, those receiving treatment have themselves decided to receive it, and have successfully sought it out; whereas individuals in the control group (for a variety of reasons) have opted not to receive treatment. This suggests a number of possibilities: that those who receive treatment may have a more favorable view of mental health care, that they may be in greater need of mental health care, that they may have greater access to mental health care, and/or that they may be more predisposed to help-seeking behavior.

This difference in the selection process introduces a self-selection bias. As Jones and Vischi point out, "No one has yet determined the extent to which this may bias the results" (1979: 7). They offer, however, few insights as to what those biases might be—in terms of both sign and magnitude—or how they might be investigated. This is an important issue, worthy of investigation.

In their meta-analytic literature review, Devine and Cook (1983) suggest that the self-selection bias is relatively unimportant. They report that the method of subject assignment (self-selection or random) was not systematically related to the size of estimates of the offset effect.

On the other hand, in Mumford et al.'s meta-analytic review of literature (1984: 52), it is reported that although the offset effect appears under conditions of both random assignment and self-selection for treatment, it is smaller when only those studies using a random assignment process are analyzed.

Due to the level of aggregation in these studies and to their being subject to the three major criticisms already noted (lack of explanation as to why the offset should/might occur, the absence of a behavioral model, and too broad and non-specific a definition of the psychotherapeutic type, setting, and provider), these inconsistent findings are neither surprising nor to be regarded as the "last word" on the topic. Future research efforts need to incorporate investigations of the role of each of these influences in order to identify the size and magnitude of the self-selection bias.

Several years ago, Jones and Vischi (1979) suggested a creative technique by which to eschew both the self-selection bias as well as the ethical and legal consideration of withholding treatment through the use of waiting lists. A mental health care setting, they explained, with (especially) a large waiting list could serve as a site in which to develop either a randomized clinical trial or a matched comparison group of individuals as willing to obtain psychotherapy as the study group.

Since then, this approach has been incorporated into some study designs. Kessler and his colleagues (1982), for example, employed it in their longitudinal study of 3,272 patients of the Columbia Medical Plan's psychiatric department. They reported that data showing peaking effects subsequent to individuals being placed on the waiting list indicate that the decision to seek psychiatric care does not, by itself, begin the decline in medical utilization. (1982: 1220)

This finding, coupled with the customary interpretation that the utilization peak coincides with and is a reflection of the severity of distress the individual is suffering, implies that there are ethical considerations associated even with the use of a waiting list: while on the waiting list people grow more ill. Some analysts have argued that the offset may be more attributable to the patient's positive attitudinal predisposition toward psychotherapy (as evidenced by his or her act of actually seeking care) than to the psychotherapy treatment itself. Kessler and his associates, by contrast, strongly suggest that the causative agent in the offset effect is the treatment, implying that the self-selection bias is relatively minor.

To the extent that a self-selection bias is present, however, it confounds efforts to assess the offset effect. In order to gauge that effect, it is necessary to isolate these intervening effects of the self-selection process. Doing so requires introducing additional control variables which, in the context of a matched comparison group, means introducing additional criteria on which the researcher must match individuals in developing the experimental and control groups.

Undertaking this procedure, of course, begs a question: what criteria should be used to select control variables? Here is where the usefulness of a behavioral model becomes apparent in guiding the researcher. In this particular instance, variables that help to explain behavioral differences in predisposition toward the use of mental health services should be included (such as the particular mental health diagnosis, the severity of the mental disorder, the individual's attitude toward mental health and mental illness, and the availability and accessibility of mental health services).

The difference between mentally ill individuals who seek out and obtain mental health treatment, and those who do not, is not the only source of bias in offset studies. Most of the existing literature on offset is based on studies conducted in organized medical care settings (e.g., specific health facilities) and especially in large, prepaid group practices (health maintenance organizations—HMOs). To the likely extent that individuals select their particular facility or HMO based on the particular configuration of services it provides, such a restrictive sample contains a selection bias which undermines the external validity of the findings.

Similarly, insurance coverage is likely to be substantially self-selected: individuals who anticipate using mental health services (or more mental health services) are likely to choose insurance plans (or HMOs) with more generous mental health service benefits/coverage, or particular facilities with more and/ or better mental health services. The result is a selection bias which confounds the analysis and limits the generalizability of the findings. Higher rates of use may be a reflection of better insurance coverage or may be due to individuals with relatively poor mental health status who choose insurance plans with better mental health services or coverage.

Without additional information—which often may not be available—it cannot be determined whether the poorly insured (or uninsured) would have behaved in the same manner as did the better-insured. It cannot be determined whether those with relatively more, or with relatively less, or with no HMO-provided mental health services would have behaved in the same manner as did those in the HMOs studied. Thus, while it cannot be unimpeachably ascertained that these studies incorporate this (additional) self-selection bias, the probability that they do seems quite high.

Statistical Regression to the Mean

Early on, offset analysts became concerned that they might be stacking the deck for finding an offset. This became a major methodological issue in part because of interest in a tangentially related matter. As already noted, most (especially early) studies had recorded a decrease in the level of physical health service utilization following mental health treatment of nearly any duration and type (the so-called "peaking" phenomenon). As the issue of what constituted the appropriate observation time period for an offset study was debated, it came to light that researchers were individually analyzing study populations with a more or less common health service utilization pattern.

Just prior to the mental health intervention, when most researchers hypothesized that the severity of the mental disorder peaked, so too did physical health service utilization. After the onset of treatment, when (it was hypothesized) the severity of the mental disorder subsided, general health service utilization decreased to more normal levels. Because the start of psychotherapy was usually found to coincide with the expected reduction in the mentally ill individual's discomfort, amelioration of the illness was credited, at least initially, to the therapy.

An alternative explanation of this "improvement" is statistical regression; a movement toward the typical level of the (discomfort/distress) series will reliably follow the high or low points in a time series. If a control group is not matched for the "discomfort" variable with observations accumulated on a relative time base, there would be no comparable expectation for its values to regress toward the mean. (Mumford et al., 1981: 259)

This observation suggests that two essential—and perhaps the most important—characteristics on which to match comparison and study groups are, first, a qualitative indicator of mental disorder and, second, prior (to the mental health intervention) health service utilization. Such (at minimum) dual matchings on these variables, however, are relatively rare in the literature. In all fairness, it should be pointed out that the development of such a matched control group is by no means a simple matter. It would be a very expensive procedure and would require a very large pool of mentally ill persons from which to develop such a control group.

The health service usage peaking phenomenon has been widely observed. So much so, in fact, that it has given rise to considerable discussion of statistical regression to the mean, as well as considerable debate about how to control for it (altering the study design is most frequently suggested). The standard interpretation of the phenomenon—that it reflects the increasing severity of the mental disorder just prior to seeking care, and that it triggers the utilization of mental health services—is accepted by nearly all offset researchers. This explanation, however, is nothing more than a hypothesis—a hypothesis which has never been tested, though it is commonly accepted as fact.

Several studies that have longitudinally analyzed the utilization patterns of both a control and a study group before and after the mental health intervention have reported a similar peaking in the utilization rates of the control group (see, for example, Uris, 1974; Graves and Hastrup, 1978; Kogan et al., 1975; Rosen and Wiens, 1979; Kessler et al., 1982; Schlesinger et al., 1983; Hankin et al., 1983; Mumford et al., 1984; Borus et al., 1985). It is surprising that without exception these studies have not commented on this dualistic nature of the peaking phenomenon.

What might be the reason for a similar relationship being observed among the non-mentally ill? One possibility is that it is purely coincidental; another, especially among those not receiving any treatment, is that spontaneous remission occurs. Still another possibility—which does not preclude the possibility that the accepted hypothesis is accurate—is that there is some type of external contextual factor that is influencing the behavior of the study and control groups alike.

For example, it may be that after a secular increase in physical health service utilization there is a severe economic recession which increases unemployment and results in many individuals losing their employment-based group health insurance, which dampens the utilization of everyone: the mentally ill, the non-mentally ill, those with a mental health intervention, and those without one.

There are three lessons to be learned from recognition of the universality of the peaking phenomenon. First, it is important to take into account differences in the pre-mental health intervention level of general health service utilization. Second, rather than seeking to simply identify an offset, it would be preferable to seek to explain it. This may be done most accurately by specifying and estimating as full a behavioral model as possible. Third, a comparison group is exceedingly important, especially when no behavioral model is developed. With or without a comparison group, the customary practice is to credit any reduction in health service utilization to the mental health intervention.

In the case of a quasi-experimental design (for reasons already noted), this is likely to be inappropriate when the comparison group is not properly matched on known contributing factors—as has been the case in most offset research efforts to date. In the case of studies without a comparison group, given the analytical tools used to date, crediting the reduction of general health service usage to mental health intervention is even more problematic. Such studies (those with and those without a comparison group, but particularly the latter) are likely to be internally invalid. Since it has influenced research methodologies, the peaking phenomenon is an issue that should be empirically analyzed: to the extent possible, its cause should be empirically ascertained, and not presumed.

Time Dimension, Treatment Visits, and Functional Form

Some researchers have suggested that the offset effect is most importantly a function of time rather than the number of mental health treatment visits. Jones and Vischi, for instance, in reviewing the findings of the Puget Sound and Kaiser Permanente studies (Kogan et al., 1975, and Follette and Cummings, 1967, respectively) note that "the reduction in medical care utilization increases as the time after psychotherapy increases (Jones and Vischi, 1979: 4). In addition, it has been frequently noted in the literature that there is a lag between the initiation of a mental health intervention and the hypothesized occurrence of the offset. While there has been little speculation about why such a lagged relationship might exist, it is possible to investigate its existence with what is known as a distributed lag model (discussed in the appendix to this chapter).

In the offset research literature, there has also been considerable discussion about how to deal with the time period immediately following the initial mental health intervention, particularly in those studies which need to determine how and when to make comparisons with control groups. But, other than that issue, and beyond stating that longer is better, accounts of observed relationships of mental health treatment generally have not closely analyzed the time dimension of the relationship. The three specific techniques which are implicit in descriptive accounts of observed relationships are an arithmetic lag, a geometric lag, and a polynomial lag. Without any theoretical guidance, and in the dual interests of comparability and comprehensiveness, studies utilizing time series data would do well to explore each of these functional forms.

In contrast to those who contend that the time element is the primary causal factor in an offset, there are those who contend that instead it is the number and/or type of mental health treatments that are of pivotal importance. Some researchers have reported the perplexing finding that the duration and intensity of the mental health treatment seems to be irrelevant. Still others report an even more disconcerting finding: those with the least psychotherapy, and in some studies only a single session, realize the greatest offsets (Goldberg et al., 1970; Cummings, 1977; Jones and Vischi, 1979; Rosen and Wiens, 1979; Budman et al., 1982 and 1984).

Budman and colleagues (1982) have hypothesized that even with only a single session, "a reframing process begins...," and that "the patient's attendance at one or two meetings brings with it a ... message that 'some of your complaints and discomforts may NOT be physical in nature' " (Budman et al., 1982: 205). Budman and his associates have dubbed this phenomenon "psychotherapeutic insight," and, in one of the very few studies explicitly hypothesizing a behavioral relationship, speculate that

there are a number of ways in which psychotherapeutic insight might be assumed to affect excessive medical utilization:

1. The patient may learn that various types of feelings, symptoms, and internal experiences reflect particular psychological states rather than a physical illness. Thus, for example, a patient may come to recognize that he or she is depressed and not suffering from an illness-induced tiredness.

2. The patient may gain insight into his or her own illness behavior. For example, "I now realize that I came in frequently to see the doctor because I needed someone to talk with. I've been terribly lonely."

3. The patient may begin to link, monitor, and control the interplay between psychological-interpersonal factors and episodes of illness or physical symptoms. For example, "It is clear to me that I begin to have colon problems when I pressure myself too much at work. I've learned that I need to ease up on myself so that I don't get sick." (Budman et al., 1982: 354)

The early-into-treatment "insight" has implications for the specification of the mental health treatment—general health service utilization relationship. It suggests that the initial mental health treatment visit(s) produces the most pronounced offset effects. By implication, subsequent visits have a less dramatic impact. This can be demonstrated graphically in its several alternative forms, as shown in exhibit 3.1.

Panel A portrays the extreme case: a single mental health treatment visit results in a permanent reduction of general health service usage, but further mental health visits are ineffectual in enhancing the initial offset effect. Such a relationship has been discussed by Goldberg et al. (1970), Jones and Vischi (1979), and Rosen and Wiens (1979).

Panels B and C depict the offset as a more gradual, ongoing process, beginning with the initial mental health treatment, but continuing over the course of several mental health treatment visits. Beyond the transitional period, however, in this case five visits, mental health services are ineffectual in generating an additional offset. The endpoints of the payoff period are clearly demarcated, and the dynamic transverse itself may be a linear relationship (as depicted in panel B), or it might be concave from below (occurring at an accelerating rate until the effect is exhausted), or, what is most intuitively appealing, it might be convex from below (as shown in panel C). Initially the offset is great; and, while it continues thereafter, it does so at an ever-decelerating rate until the effect is exhausted.

The offset is thus a gradual and ongoing outcome of an ever-increasing number of mental health treatment visits. As in panels A and B, the major im-

Exhibit 3.1

Functional Forms of the Offset Effect

A) ONE-TIME OFFSET EFFECT (STEP FUNCTION)

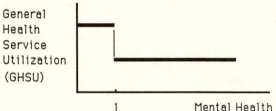

B) GRADUALLY DIMINISHING OFFSET EFFECT WITH LINEAR TRANSVERSE

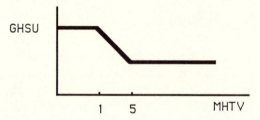

C) GRADUALLY DIMINISHING OFFSET EFFECT WITH CONVEX TRANSVERSE

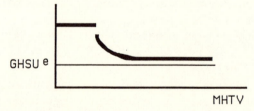

D) DUAL THRESHOLD OFFSET EFFECT

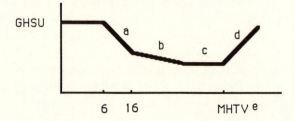

pact is associated with the initial mental health intervention, but the offset is not narrowly constrained to the first or the first few mental health treatment visits. The impact declines monotonically and asymptotically approaches a particular level, GHSU^e, of general health service use; it might, for example, approach the mean level of general health service utilization of the general population.

Other researchers have found just the opposite of an early-into-treatment insight. Panel D depicts a dual threshold cascading offset effect. This is the relationship described by Schlesinger et al. (1983), Mumford et al. (1984), and, with minor modifications, Goldberg et al. (1981). Schlesinger and his colleagues reported finding no relationship between mental health service utilization and mental health treatment visits until the latter exceeded six. Thereafter, as mental health visits continued to increase they recorded an offset effect until visits numbered sixteen. Beyond sixteen, however, they noted that the nature of the offset relationship changed: the magnitude of the offset realized with additional visits was less; the function flattened out—see segments "b" and "c" of the relationship in panel D.

Alternatively, rather than the relationship simply dissipating with increasing levels of mental health services being obtained, what might be observed is that the function acquires a positive slope, as it does in segment "d"; beyond MHTV^e, additional mental health visits actually encourage general health service utilization (and perhaps mental health service utilization as well). This turnaround may reflect having provided "so many" services as to have encouraged/cultivated a type of dependence on the health care delivery system. Such a possibility has been observed in two studies (Cummings, 1977; Goldberg et al., 1981).

Clearly the functional form of the relationship between mental health treatment visits and physical health care expenditures needs to be carefully examined in offset studies. In all of the still relatively few offset research efforts employing multiple regression analysis, a linear function is posited without comment. In the descriptive literature, on the other hand, we have discussed above the possibility of a non-linear relationship. Schlesinger and his associates (1983), for instance, have hypothesized that, rather than being linear, the relationship between general health service utilization and mental health treatment visits is a particular type of a reciprocal or a log-reciprocal function.

However, care must always be used in transferring these findings to other settings with different population characteristics, diagnoses, and provider types. Mumford et al. (1984), however, implicitly assumed that the specific characteristics of the treatment, the providers, and the clients are inconsequential to the process and outcome of psychotherapy, and that their findings have external validity. That is, they have assumed that they can legitimately transfer these results to another very different study, and they do so. Subsequently, in a study of individuals with unspecified diagnoses but at least seven mental health treatment visits (and with, again, unspecified treatments and providers), they write, "Previous work has shown a dose-response relationship for psychotherapy and medical care utilization, with a cost-offset becoming clear after about six psychotherapy visits" (Mumford et al., 1984: 1154).

The combination of (1) the mere repetition of the finding with its presumed but substantively unanalyzed universal applicability, coupled with (2) its implied nonlinear, functional form—itself a single empirical finding with no theoretical underpinning and a host of competing and equally plausible empirically derived functional relationships— together constitute practices which begin (in this case) the unwarranted accretionary process of developing a "conventional wisdom."

This type of practice has already been discussed. Offset researchers must be cognizant of such practices and avoid the snares they construct. Such practices again underscore the need (1) to develop a behavioral model to provide a framework within which to pursue the synthesizing of offset research findings, and by which to assess the external validity of any particular study's findings, and (2) to establish minimal "acceptable" reporting requirements concerning statistical procedures, their rationales, and results. In this way our knowledge of the effects of timing and functional form can better be assimilated.

Multiple Regression Techniques and Issues

From a practical perspective, the medical offset literature has taken the art of matched comparison groups about as far as it can be taken. Once a useful exploratory tool used alone, the technique has outlived its usefulness; it has become cumbersome, counterproductive, and, fortunately, unnecessary in its role as the solitary analytical device. Other more flexible statistical tools are now available and in order. Most importantly, multiple regression methods can and should be used to control for those variables already known (or plausibly hypothesized) to play an important role in the offset effect, as new variables and relationships are explored.

Multiple regression is not a panacea. It does, however, lend itself uniquely to the simultaneous solution of three of the most serious shortcomings pervading the offset literature: selection bias; statistical regression to the mean; and a greater degree of specificity with respect to the client, the provider, and the treatment. Notwithstanding, this technique does not provide a vehicle for unequivocally establishing causality. All it is able to do is establish the existence of correlations. Herein lies the importance of distinguishing between a descriptive and a causal or behavioral model: the more circumspect one is in constructing a model predicated on plausible, causal relationships which are explicitly hypothesized and posited, the greater the degree of confidence one may have in interpreting the results as representative of the expected causal— as opposed to simply a correlational—relationship.

Thus, failure to specify a behavioral model will continue to plague researchers even when using multiple regression analysis. Specifically, it may cause several methodological errors, which are summarized here and elaborated in greater technical detail in the appendix to this chapter. A specification error may occur when relevant variables are omitted from the equation, as we suggested earlier. As a result, the parameter estimates of the equation are biased, leading to possibly incorrect interpretation of the data with regard to an offset. Another familiar problem is that of multicollinearity. When two or more independent variables are highly correlated, it becomes difficult to distinguish the effects of one from the other. Indeed, when multicollinearity exists, independent variable parameter estimates may prove to be insignificant, even though the regression has high explanatory power. One solution used is to drop one or more of these highly correlated variables, but this becomes guesswork unless a behavioral model has been constructed to provide guidance.

Some statistical regression programs utilize stepwise regression (or forward inclusion/backward elimination) which entails adding independent variables to the equation in an order determined by their incremental contribution to the coefficient of determination (R^2). In some cases, variables are dropped by the program if their contribution to R^2 is too small. Thus the search for a high R^2 leads to the computer program specifying the relevant variables in the model, rather than a priori theorizing. This may result in a specification error, and is generally an inappropriate technique.

These and other issues in multiple regression analysis, including especially problems of autocorrelation, are covered in greater detail in the attached appendix. Applications of multiple regression analysis are still relatively uncommon in the offset literature. While the literature has been moving in this direction in recent years, there are a disturbing number of examples that suggest that another treadmill may be under construction; many researchers are again pursuing the hunt for statistically significant variables without having (yet) developed the context of a behavioral model within which to interpret and integrate new findings with what we already know.

Our stylized review of the medical offset literature has highlighted seven of the common methodological issues which have tended to divide the research community over the existence and the magnitude of the offset effect. Foremost among these was the absence of a behavioral model. In the following chapter we start the process of developing such a behavioral model of the offset effect.

APPENDIX 3.1: ADDITIONAL ISSUES IN MULTIPLE REGRESSION ANALYSIS

In this appendix we discuss some of the technical problems that arise in the use of multiple regression analysis, as well as the relevant offset studies using this technique. The topics covered are:

1. Stepwise Regression
2. Multicollinearity
3. Different Analytical Techniques and Inconsistent Findings
4. The Autoregressive Model and Autocorrelation
5. Heteroskedasticity

6. Specification Error
7. Time Dimension Modeling

STEPWISE REGRESSION

Several of the post-1980 offset research studies employing multiple regression techniques have used stepwise regression (cf. Goldberg et al., 1981; Kessler et al., 1982). The researcher using the stepwise method specifies the dependent variable and a list of possible explanatory variables. Most stepwise regression software packages then successively add variables to the model on the basis of their incremental contribution to the coefficient of determination, that is, R^2. Those which yield the greatest increase in R^2 are added first to the model. In some cases, a minimum number of variables to be included or a minimum value for a variable's contribution to the coefficient of determination is specified.

Following such rules, however, is often likely to lead to misspecification (the consequences of which will be discussed shortly). The coefficient of determination, it must be recalled, is sample-specific: it is determined by (1) the strength of the relationship between the individual exogenous variables and the dependent variable, (2) the inter-correlation among the exogenous variables, and (3) the variability of each of the exogenous variables. Because all three of these factors vary over samples taken from the same population, it is inappropriate to allow a causal model to be developed from generalizing to the entire population from any particular sample. Specification should, instead, be based on explicit a priori theorizing based on a behavioral model.

Moreover, the validity and reliability of stepwise regression models are further vitiated by recognition that the amount of variation attributable to any particular variable is dependent upon the order in which it is entered into the equation vis-à-vis other exogenous variables. Generally, the ordering of variables for entering into the equation is arbitrary and capricious, and not even alluded to in the methods section, adding to the probability that the model is misspecified.

An alternative method by which some researchers use stepwise regression to guide or determine the specification of the model involves a variable selection criterion based on the standard error of the variable. Quite simply, the rule followed is that significant variables are incorporated into the model, insignificant ones dropped. The finding that a particular variable is significantly contributing to the explained variation of an endogenous variable, however, is also a sample-specific phenomenon and (in the same manner as those techniques just noted) may result in serious misspecification of the model. Again, there is no substitution for a priori hypothesizing in the effort to develop a causal, behavioral model.

It may be further noted that if two or more exogenous variables are highly correlated, standard errors will be large. This, of course, reduces the size of the t-statistics, which decreases the likelihood of finding a statistically significant variable, and may misguide specification by encouraging the researcher to throw one or more variables out of the model. In other words, it may erroneously lead to acceptance of null hypotheses when statistical tests are applied to the corresponding coefficients (i.e., Type II errors). While a variable may be an important determinant of the offset effect, it may be rejected from the model because its inflated standard error is "too high" (or its t-statistic "too low").

The appropriate role of stepwise regression and similar techniques is in pioneering work wherein a researcher, exploring new terrain, has relatively little theoretical guidance. Such frontiers, of course, still exist within the medical offset field. Twenty years of research in this field, however, coupled with sophisticated and readily available analytical tools, have taken us beyond such problematic techniques in the general approach to further inquiries. The reliance upon these techniques, coupled with the legacy and still-extant practice of not conceptualizing or trying to specify a behavioral model, constitute the vicious cycle which is largely responsible for the previously expressed concern—that despite the arrival of potentially improved research methodologies to the offset field, a new research treadmill may be in the process of being constructed.

MULTICOLLINEARITY

Multicollinearity arises when two or more independent variables are highly correlated, so that it is difficult to separate the influence of one from the other. The regression estimates, while unbiased, will have larger variances and, thus, are likely to yield statistically insignificant results.

As the degree of multicollinearity increases, disentangling the individual effects of each independent variable becomes increasingly arbitrary and unreliable (Koutsoyiannis, 1977:235). Using stepwise regression (as well as other empirically led specifications) to guide theory and model building in such a context, is, therefore, likely to exacerbate the problems associated with those techniques.

At the very least, researchers need to explain their methodologies. For example, rather than simply presenting a model which contains only statistically significant variables (a common practice in the few offset studies using regression techniques), it is essential to present other estimated specifications and relevant statistics such as the correlation matrix, the standard error of the equation, both the residual and the explained sum of squares, the means of the variables, and the coefficients and their standard errors (or t-statistics).

The offset research community needs to develop a protocol governing the minimal acceptable reporting requirements of statistical analysis. Ideally, the reader should be presented with, or at least be given enough information to conduct, a rough-and-ready type of sensitivity analysis. In the twin interests of science and intellectual integrity, it is of critical importance to apprise readers, for example, that the results—the estimated coefficients—change dramatically if a single variable is included or excluded from the analysis. This would be a common symptom of multicollinearity.

Such sensitivity, it should be pointed out, is not uncommon. For instance, Goldberg and associates (1981) note (to their credit) that the addition to their model of a single variable (in this case, family size) results in more than half (three of five) of the previously significant variables becoming insignificant. Unfortunately, however, the authors do not speculate as to why this might have occurred; nor do they provide readers with adequate information to enable them to try to determine the cause of this instability. The result is that the reader cannot help but (and should) discount the findings of the study, and consider them, at best, suggestive or tentative.

DIFFERENT ANALYTICAL TECHNIQUES AND INCONSISTENT FINDINGS

Another closely related problem is found in many studies utilizing two different research techniques. In several instances, within a single study, the findings derived from application of more sophisticated techniques (most commonly analysis of variance and covariance—ANOVA and ANCOVA) have been inconsistent with those based on more traditional modes of analysis, such as juxtaposition of an experimental (or quasi-experimental) group's general medical care utilization changes, compared to that of a control group's. While both types of analyses and their respective results may be presented, to the extent that the less interesting (or, more troublingly, antithetical) finding of no offset is made, it is usually not discussed (cf. Hankin et al., 1983: 1108); or, to the extent that it is discussed, it is noted only briefly in passing with little or no comment (cf. Goldberg et al., 1981: 672), and generally conveniently disregarded in the "Discussion" or "Summary" sections. This does nothing to further the understanding of the medical offset effect. Again, a more complete presentation of the statistical analysis would encourage salubrious discussion of alternative interpretations and, more importantly, the advantages and disadvantages—the strengths and limitations—of alternative research methods.

THE AUTOREGRESSIVE MODEL AND AUTOCORRELATION

In regression analysis involving either cross-sectional or, especially, time series data, it is often hypothesized that the model contains one or more lagged values of the dependent variable among its explanatory variables. Such a model, referred to as an autoregressive model, may be represented (in its most simplistic form) as:

$$Y_t = a + bx_t + cY_{t-1} + u_t$$

In an offset model, Y_t might represent the utilization of general health services in time period "t"; x_t some type of variable reflecting the individual's predisposition toward care seeking, some measure of access to care, a measure of need, or a vector containing all such variables; and Y_{t-1}, the utilization of general health services in the previous time period.

It is plausible for offset researchers to posit such a model for several reasons. First, it is likely that the level of general health service utilization will vary across individuals in a persistent manner (i.e., over time) because of the individuals' differential and relatively unchanging (a) attitudes toward medical care utilization, (b) access to care, and (c) number of chronic conditions they may have (their longer-term health status). To the extent that these variables are important explanatory factors, they may all be simultaneously proxied for by a measure of the utilization of general health services in the previous period (i.e., the lagged value of the dependent variable). Also, controlling for prior utilization eliminates the problem of statistical regression to the mean.

While specifying this type of functional form may be acceptable for researchers interested in developing a predictive model, it is not ideal for those seeking, instead, to explain offset behavior; such an approach leaves many questions unanswered and unanswerable.

From a causal-behavioralist's perspective, the theoretical justification for specifying an autoregressive model is that he or she does not have better, more direct measures of the sundry behavioral influences proxied by the autoregressive term. A causal-behavioralist is likely to turn to such a model only when no other recourse exists, since he will find it irksome that in the likely event the lagged dependent variable is significant, he will not be able to ascertain which of the numerous competing, single-influence-specific, causal hypotheses are supported by this finding, and which are not.

Given this problem of interpretation, a preferred approach would be to measure directly the influence of the multifaceted (at least three) causal relationships proxied by the autoregressive term, such as predisposition toward care, access to care, and health status/need for care. It is important to note that if measures of some of these competing hypotheses are available, the inclusion of some of these relationships in the model does not preclude entering prior utilization. On the contrary, it is desirable to include them. Doing so will reduce the number of alternative possible explanations captured in the aggregative proxy variable, thereby enabling the testing of more detailed and specific hypotheses, and hence providing a better understanding of both the research findings and the offset process.

Like the use of multiple regression analysis in general, the first-order autoregressive model has recently come into vogue in offset research. First order autoregressive models have been posited in a large share of the relatively few regression analyses of the offset effect (Kessler, 1978; Kessler et al., 1982; Goldberg et al., 1981; Hankin et al., 1983). In all four of these studies, prior utilization accounts for an overwhelming share of the explained variation in general health service utilization. In the two studies which provide sufficient information for the interested reader to derive such figures, prior utilization accounts for 91 percent (Goldberg et al., 1981: 671) and 90 to 92 percent (Kessler et al., 1982: 1217) of total explained variation in general health service utilization.

There is another reason for specifying a more detailed version of the autoregressive model than has heretofore been employed: it is likely that the more simple, aggregative version violates the ordinary least squares (OLS) assumption of independence of the values of the residuals, thus leading to the problem known as autocorrelation (also known as serial correlation). Since many of the variables implicitly contained in the three sets of factors hypothesized to be captured in the prior utilization variable will themselves probably be autocorrelated, the residuals of the first order autoregressive model will also be autocorrelated.

Further heightening the probability of autocorrelation is the likely possibility that there are more than three such sets of factors which are captured by the prior utilization variable. In that event, it is possible that an autocorrelated variable has been excluded from the set of explanatory variables. Its influence, captured in the residual or error term (u_t in the equation above), will render them autocorrelated.

A third possible source of autocorrelation is misspecification of the mathematical form of the model. As previously discussed, mathematical form is very rarely an explicit topic of discourse in the offset research literature. This, in part, may be attributed to the relatively recent advent of the use of multiple regression analysis therein. Notwithstanding, it is a potential problem which warrants discussion.

If a mathematical form is specified which differs from the true form of the relationship, the error terms may be autocorrelated. If, for example, a linear form is specified to approximate a nonlinear relationship, there will be ranges of the independent variables where the fitted model consistently under- or over-estimates their true values. Consequently, the error terms for those observations (two for each individual in the first-order autoregressive case) will be systematically correlated. For instance, this is likely to be the case with the age–general health care utilization relationship. This relationship is widely recognized to be portrayed by an inverted U-shape.

Having established the likelihood that most of the few multivariate statistical analyses performed to date may be characterized by autocorrelation begs a question: So what? There are two relevant responses. First, that adequate information (particularly of a statistical nature) is generally not reported as a matter of course in many offset studies. All four of the offset studies specifying a autoregressive model may have tested for autocorrelation and found it not to be a concern, but there is no way to readily ascertain this from their presentations of methods or results. Offset researchers need to develop and adhere to uniform, minimum standards—a protocol—as to the types of statistical information which should be reported.

Second, and more specific to the issue at hand, with a lagged endogenous variable and autocorrelated residuals, the ordinary least squares estimates of the parameters will be biased (i.e., the size of the estimated coefficients will be too large or too small), and their variances are likely to be seriously underestimated. Underestimation of the variances increases the danger of incorrectly identifying a particular variable as significant when, in fact, it is not—a Type I error (Koutsoyiannis, 1977: 203–35). How important this may be depends, of course, on what the particular variable is, and its hypothesized role in the offset process. In the most dramatic case imaginable, the variable would be a measurement of the impact of the mental health intervention, and committing the Type I error would result in inferring the existence of an offset effect when one in fact did not exist.

The extent to which autocorrelation-related problems plague the four offset studies positing a first-order, autoregressive model is not possible to gauge without additional information which is not provided in their reports. The results of these studies, therefore, must be considered tentative, at least until one of the several tests which may be used to detect autocorrelation, such as the Durbin "h" test, are presented (see, for example, Gujarati, 1978: 269–70; Koutsoyiannis, 1977: 211–17; Judge et al., 1985: 319–30).

HETEROSKEDASTICITY

Another problem of empirical work concerns violating the ordinary least squares assumption that the residuals have a common variance. Violation of the assumption, known as heteroskedasticity, results in still unbiased but less reliable (that is, inefficient) parameter estimates. Most commonly, the true variance is underestimated, resulting in shorter confidence intervals. This, in turn, will result in more Type I errors in hypothesis testing, as discussed above (Maddala, 1977: 259–65).

Heteroskedasticity is more often encountered in cross-sectional data than in time-series data. In offset research it is very likely to be a problem because the tool most frequently to be used in multiple regression analysis of the offset effect is likely to be a regression of general health service utilization on mental health treatment visits (measured as either a dummy variable or a continuous one). It is probable that some of the variables that are omitted from the measure of general health service use (like mental health treatment visits) change in the same direction as general health service use, and thus cause an increase in the variation of the observation from the regression line.

Hence, attempting to explain changes in the pre- and post-mental health intervention levels of general health service usage by employing a multiple regression equation which excludes mental health service utilization as an explanatory variable (for example, Goldberg et al., 1981) are likely to be characterized by heteroskedastic residuals.

SPECIFICATION ERROR

Specification error or misspecification refers to the use of a wrong or inappropriate model. Specification errors include (1) the inclusion of an irrelevant variable, (2) the exclusion of a relevant variable, and (3) the use of an inappropriate functional form (usually applying a linear model to a nonlinear one, or vice versa).

A common problem characterizing much of the offset research literature has been the failure to include many of the variables which have already been shown to have an important impact on the offset effect. The omission of relevant variables results in biased parameter estimates. Hence, the actual role of the independent variables which are specified is different from that which might be inferred from the empirical "findings."

Specifically, in the case of ANCOVA, misspecification will result in a biased estimation of the common regression coefficient for the covariate(s) and, as a consequence, in the over- or under-adjustment of treatment means. This in turn is likely to produce a bias in the estimated effect of the treatment (which is the impact of the mental health intervention). Similarly, in regression analysis, misspecification results in coefficients which are either larger or smaller than their true value; consequently over- or understating the effect of the independent variables, including the mental health intervention (and thus the offset effect), on general health service use (the dependent variable).

What are the implications for specifying an offset model? As Hanushek and Jackson have explained,

in order to arrive at good estimates of the parameters of interest, it may be necessary to include other variables of lesser usefulness in the given problem. Recognition of the significance of a variable in a behavioral relationship does not necessarily imply that the analyst can or wishes to interpret its coefficient, only that one wishes to avoid biasing the coefficients of real interest (Hanushek and Jackson, 1977: 86).

The omission of relevant variables also results in overestimation of the residual variance. Thus, the standard errors of the coefficients are overestimated, and inferences about the coefficients of the included variables will be inaccurate. Overestimated standard errors result in smaller confidence intervals, that is, in conservative tests of significance (see, for example, Maddala, 1977: 155–57; Hanushek and Jackson, 1977: 79–86).

The solution, however, is not simply to include any variable. The inclusion of irrelevant variables is also problematic, though less so: while it does not introduce bias into the parameter estimates, it does introduce it into the variances (resulting in unbiased but inefficient estimates). Hence, if a researcher is uncertain about the relevance of a regressor, it is preferable to include it in the analysis. A behavioral model would be useful in this context: it would provide guidance to the analyst in identifying relevant variables that must be included if the estimates are to be as robust as possible.

Avoidance of specification problems may not be an easy task. The only way to be certain of the exact degree of misspecification is to juxtapose the parameter estimates of true or actual models and misspecified ones. The problem, of course, is that the true model is seldom, if ever, known. The researcher, therefore, is faced with the very difficult task of detecting and minimizing specification errors without knowing what the true model is. Obviously, therefore, although testing procedures exist for detecting some specification errors, there is no simple or entirely satisfactory solution to this dilemma. The researcher who is circumspect in hypothesizing and explicitly delineating the hypothesized theoretical foundations for the particular specification employed, however, is less likely to be at risk.

TIME DIMENSION MODELING

In contradistinction to the basic autoregressive model only recently introduced in the literature (which has empirically found prior utilization to be the most powerful variable in explaining the offset effect), some researchers have suggested that the offset is more importantly a function of time. Most of these same researchers further contend that the time dimension is even more important than the number of mental health treatment visits.

Another functional relationship frequently alluded to in the literature is that of a distributed lag model. Assuming that, ceteris paribus, the use of general health services is a function of whether or not a mental health intervention has occurred, or the number of mental health treatment visits over "s" periods, the model may be represented as a finite lag structure such as:

$$GHSU_t = a + b_0 MHT_t + b_1 MHT_{t-1} + \ldots + b_s MHT_{t-s} + u_t$$

Where, GHSU represents general health service utilization; the "t" subscripts denote the particular time period; "u_t" denotes the error term or residual; and MHT is the mental health treatment variable. Depending upon the particular hypothesis of interest, MHT could be constructed in two alternative ways. It could be a dichotomous variable equal to zero (0) if no mental health treatments were received in that particular time period, and one (1) if at least one mental health treatment were received in that particular time period. Alternatively, it could be a continuous variable, equal to the number of mental health treatment visits (or the cost of such visits) in the particular time period. In either of these specifications, such a model enables one to explore the time dimension of the offset impact (to the extent that it exists).

Two difficulties are generally encountered in attempts to estimate this type of model with OLS, however. First, if "s" is large—that is, the number of lags is large—and the sample size is small, there may not be adequate degrees of freedom to perform the traditional tests of statistical significance. Because these are relatively common characteristics of time-series data, this problem is frequently confronted. Second, since there is almost certain to be a strong correlation between the successive values of a particular variable, it is highly likely that multicollinearity will be a problem. As discussed earlier, if there is a high degree of multicollinearity the parameter estimates will be imprecise and inefficient, and may contribute to misspecification of the model by encouraging the dropping of important but seemingly (statistically) insignificant variables.

A variety of techniques have been developed to avoid these difficulties. These techniques all aim at reducing the number of lagged variables used in the estimation by some combination of (1) imposing restrictions on the coefficients of the lagged exogenous variables, and (2) constructing new variables from linear combinations of the lagged exogenous variables.

A BEHAVIORAL MODEL OF THE MEDICAL OFFSET EFFECT

4

The placebo is proof that there is no real separation between mind and body. Illness is always an interaction between both.
                    —Norman Cousins, *The Anatomy of a Disease*

... We are not ourselves
When nature, being oppress'd, commands the mind
To suffer with the body.
                    —William Shakespeare, *King Lear*

INTRODUCTION

As discussed in the previous chapter, the findings of virtually all medical offset studies have been vitiated by a variety of methodological shortcomings. Many of these shortcomings share a common etiology: the failure of researchers to explicitly either describe or analyze the behavioral foundations of the relationships they are trying to observe and measure. Research efforts have been largely devoted to identifying factors associated with the offset rather than explaining the offset; that is, description has superseded explanation.[1] Grappling with these issues is made more difficult when the participants lack a unifying behavioral model within which to synthesize and integrate the different components of health care behavior under investigation.

In this chapter we develop a behavioral model useful for explaining the medical offset and providing a priori justification for positing particular relationships and, concomitantly, selecting and analyzing particular variables for study. This approach will better enable future research to incrementally advance our knowledge and understanding of these complex behavioral processes.

BACKGROUND

Although a large share of the articles on the medical offset posit brief hypotheses about why the effect might be realized, rarely do the "methods" sections reflect the hypotheses discussed in the introductory sections. Instead, the focus of the analysis is simply to determine if an offset occurred, based on simple associations between two or three variables, or the cross-tabulation of a few variables with health services utilization.

The relationships so estimated are generally imprecise and often unreliable. They reflect not only the influence of the particular variables under study, but usually also the effects of excluded, but correlated, variables. For instance, suppose it is known that persons who have more social networks generally have a greater offset effect, and that those with more social networks are generally women. Now suppose further that a quasi experiment to measure the offset effect is conducted, and gender is controlled for, but the number of social networks an individual has is not. Finally, suppose that it is found that being female is associated with a greater offset effect. What has been learned?

Has it been learned that (1) females are more likely to experience an offset, or that (2) females have more values manifested in their behavioral patterns that encourage them to seek help/care, or that (3) gender has no direct role in explaining the effect, but rather is simply serving inadvertently as a proxy measure for the number of social networks? Generally the conclusion that would be reached would be the first one, that females are more likely to experience an offset (although the question of "Why?" remains unanswered). That purely descriptive analysis and "finding" would not be very useful in understanding the observed behavior.[2]

Methodological shortcomings such as these cannot be dismissed out of hand. They account for why, despite the voluminous upsurge in the quantity of studies of the offset effect, our understanding of the phenomenon remains at a low level—so low, in fact, that after two decades of study we are still uncertain of its existence. In essence, investigation of the offset effect has become stuck on a kind of research treadmill. Even when a variable is uncovered that is statistically significantly related to the offset effect, without adequate a priori hypothesizing about the behavior being modeled (and consequently not controlling for other variables known or plausibly hypothesized to impact the offset effect), additional research findings for the most part are unable to discount a host of competing hypothetical explanations. Given that, as Cook and Campbell have so succinctly put it, " ... the only process available for establishing a scientific theory is one of eliminating plausible rival hypotheses ... ," this is no minor flaw (1979: 25–26).

In this chapter we construct a causal behavioral model for investigating the medical offset effect. The model developed is something of an idealized one; it abstracts from considerations of data availability, accessibility, and cost, but nonetheless should prove useful in providing a benchmark for future empirical model-building efforts. The development of the model will proceed in two stages.

First, with a backdrop of relevant findings from offset research, the hypothetical relationships between mental and general health status and their interactions with mental and general health service utilization will be examined. This is the essence of this research note: it provides the wherewithal to synthesize and integrate the offset literature. But it is not the entire task set forth here.

Second, the offset model will be viewed within the more general theoretical framework of a behavioral model of health care service use. The modeling of medical care behavior, being a longer-standing, more sophisticated, and refined endeavor, will not be dealt with in detail. The discussion in this segment of the paper will seek merely to root the offset-specific considerations identified in the first portion of the discussion into a more general, better understood, and wholistic behavioral model framework.

BEHAVIORAL FOUNDATIONS OF THE OFFSET: HYPOTHETICAL LINKAGES BETWEEN MENTAL HEALTH STATUS AND GENERAL HEALTH CARE UTILIZATION

If it does exist, how can a medical offset be explained? To address this issue, it is necessary first to understand how mental health status might be related to health service utilization. There are various possible explanations.

The Link Between Mental Health Status and General Health Status

Numerous studies have found that persons with mental disorders have higher rates of physical disorders (Eastwood, 1975; Andrews et al., 1977; Houpt et al., 1979; Hankin and Oktay, 1979; Vaillant, 1979; Shepherd, 1980; Mechanic et al., 1982; Orleans et al., 1985), and even higher rates of mortality (Babigian and Odoroff, 1969; Sims, 1973; Tsuang and Woolson, 1977). In which direction, however, does causality run?

On the one hand, psychological and behavioral problems, in and of themselves, can cause poor health. The mentally disturbed are more likely to somatize their psychological problems (Hankin and Oktay, 1979: 32) and seek treatment for secondary physical symptoms. This is the causal relationship most commonly assumed by offset researchers, and portrayed by the paths labeled "4" and "7" in exhibit 4.1.

On the other hand, physical problems may cause psychological distress, leading to a rise in general health service utilization in three ways: (1) directly (path 7), whereby an individual seeks general health services in an effort to improve his low general health status; (2) indirectly (paths 5−4−7), whereby the secondary emotional reaction to the physical ailment reduces mental health status, which prompts individuals to seek care for derivative, mental-health-associated physical symptoms; and (3) indirectly (paths 5−6), whereby an individual seeks general health services for mental health problems because

Exhibit 4.1

Behavioral Foundations of the Medical Offset Effect

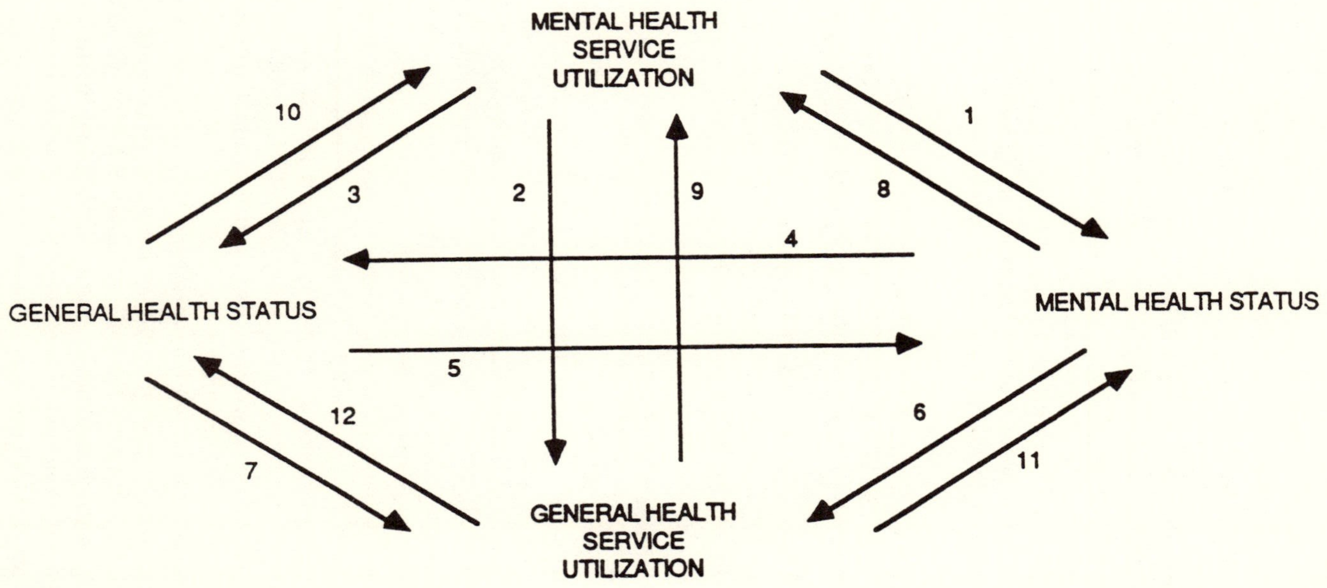

he seeks to avoid the stigma of using mental health services, and/or because general health services are relatively more accessible.

Yet another (the third) possible explanation of the coexistence of physical and psychological distress, and one that is rarely noted in the offset-specific literature, is what Hankin and Oktay term the "joint vulnerability theory": some individuals are more vulnerable to, and hence generally suffer, more physical as well as psychiatric ailments (Clyne, 1974; Cooper et al., 1969; Schwab, 1970; Reiser, 1975).

Joint vulnerability coupled with the observation that both psychological and physical conditions can serve as hidden causes or as complications of one another (Houpt et al., 1979; Shepherd et al., 1966), demonstrated by high and co-occurring levels of both physical and psychological distress, suggest that the psychiatrically ill may have even more physical problems than the general population. In eleven of the twelve studies reviewed by Hankin and Oktay (1979: 32), this was in fact found to be the case; the psychiatrically ill had more physical ailments. Moreover, at least one of these studies (Eastwood, 1975) found that this relationship persisted even after controlling for age, sex, marital status, and social class.[3]

The influence of other extraneous (not to imply unimportant) variables that jointly impact on mental and general health status and/or the possibility that particular individuals with particular types of characteristics are jointly vulnerable, however, suggest that the model of mental health status and health care utilization thus far developed is incomplete. The role of additional influences (exogenous variables) acting as conditioning and/or intervening factors will be investigated below.[4]

Potential Offset Effects

Within this context of the relationship between mental health status and general health status, what is it that mental health services can do to reduce general health service utilization? By reducing the severity of the level of distress in the mentally disordered, mental health treatment may reduce the somatization of their psychological problems and/or sever the linkages by which psychological and behavioral problems can lead to physical health problems (path 4).

Psychotherapy thus produces two positive health-enhancing effects. First, it results in the desirable primary effect of reduced mental distress; second, it produces the indirect, or secondary, effect of reducing physical discomfort— thereby reducing or eliminating the basis for seeking medical care via path 7. In addition, successful psychotherapy's positive impact on general health status (path 4) may feed back into mental health status (path 5); raising mental health status from an abnormally low level can, in effect, snowball, further enhancing mental health status. Viewed in this manner, the medical offset— to the extent that it exists—may be regarded as an outcome measure of psychotherapy. Other things being equal, the more effective the psychotherapy, the greater the offset.

This, in fact, is the perspective of most offset research. Note, however, that this model of behavior is consistent with only a portion of the behavioral model just developed. It is consistent with only two of the three just-discussed explanations of why individuals with mental disorders generally have physical distress as well. It is most compatible with the notion that psychological problems give rise to somatic ailments. To a lesser extent, it is also consistent with the joint vulnerability theory. In this instance, the (again, usually implicit) offset model posits that it is the use of mental health services that impacts upon general health service usage; the relationship is assumed to be unidirectional ("recursive" in the nomenclature of statistical modeling). This is portrayed by two different paths in exhibit 4.1: one consisting of arrows 1 and 6, the other of arrows 1, 4, and 7.

What, however, has happened to the third possible explanation of the coexistence of physical and psychological distress? The possibility that physical problems may cause psychological distress and mental illness has been ignored. Incorporating it necessarily complicates matters. This alternative explanation (which need not exist independently from either or both of the first two possible explanations) reverses the assumed causal relationship between general health service utilization and mental health service utilization: it is general health service use that now impacts on mental health service usage.[5]

Obviously, either one of these causal orderings, or both of them, might be occurring at any particular moment in time. The appropriate model to investigate the medical offset, therefore, should not preclude the possibility of this simultaneous (non-recursive) relationship by assumption.

Finally, mental health intervention may produce better general health status (and thus create an offset) in two other ways. Psychotherapy may encourage more rational behavior leading to a healthier lifestyle (path 3) or it may contribute to better general health service efficiency through greater compliance with medical advice (Cassell et al., 1972). Thus the offset would appear via paths 2–12.

The behavioral explanations of the offset effect thus far discussed share a common focus: the relationship between mental health status and physical health status. It has already been suggested that there are other exogenous variables, as yet not discussed, which also affect general health status and mental health status. So, too, there are other exogenous variables, as yet not discussed, that affect general health care utilization, mental health care utilization, and, very plausibly, by extension, the medical offset effect, as well.

Patient Characteristics and Medical Care Delivery Systems

In very broad, conceptual terms, these other factors are patient characteristics, characteristics of the medical care delivery system, and interactions between these two sets of variables. More specifically, they may be referred to as

(1) the patient's predisposition to seek help and of which kind, (2) patient compliance with medical advice, and (3) the provider's training and incentive structure. These possibilities warrant more detailed discussion than they have received in the literature to date.

The latter was discussed in detail in the previous chapter. With regard to patient compliance with medical advice, Schlesinger et al. (1983) have reasoned that psychotherapy may encourage more rational behavior including greater self-awareness, a healthier lifestyle, and closer adherence to medical advice. To the extent that psychotherapy does encourage a healthier lifestyle (the sixth possible explanation), it may improve health status (directly via path 3, or indirectly via path 1–4) and reduce the need for health services (via paths 7 and 6, respectively). To the extent that it encourages compliance with medical advice, psychotherapy may enhance the effectiveness of medical services, and thereby may result in a net reduction in the need for health services. Let us look at the role of a patient predisposition to care-seeking behavior in more detail.

Numerous studies have found that individuals with a mental disorder have a much higher rate of general health services utilization than other patients (Shepherd et al., 1966; Eastwood and Trevelyan, 1972; Cassell et al., 1972; Kogan et al., 1975; Mechanic, 1976; Tessler et al., 1976; Regier et al., 1980; Hoeper et al., 1980b; Goldberg et al., 1981; Kessler et al., 1982; Myers et al., 1984). Frequently the rate has been found to be more than double that of other patients (as in nine of the studies reviewed by Hankin and Oktay [1979], as well as in the studies reported in Eastwood and Trevelyan, 1972; Myers et al., 1984; Mechanic, 1972; Mechanic, 1978a).

Some analysts have tested specific hypotheses intended to sort out the extent to which this greater level of utilization might be at least partially attributable to the differences in physical health status—most notably Mechanic and associates (Mechanic, 1976; Mechanic, 1972; Mechanic, 1978a), but also Budman and his colleagues (Budman et al., 1982). That is, these researchers hypothesized that the mentally disordered have an enhanced predisposition to seeking care, and tested whether or not that factor alone (as opposed to their potentially greater physical health disorders) accounted for their relatively greater medical services utilization.

All of the studies investigating help or care-seeking behavior have found it to be a significant explanatory factor in the use of general health services. It may be that for the mentally distressed medical care utilization fulfills a variety of important, emotionally stabilizing functions (reassurance, social support, etc.), and that the actual source of care may be of secondary importance; they seek help "wherever" they can get it (Tessler et al., 1976; Regier et al., 1977; Shuval, 1970). Because there are factors encouraging individuals to enter the general health services sector (as opposed to the mental health specialty sector—most importantly differential insurance coverage and stigmatizing), this finding—a more specific behavioral/causal explanation—is suggestive of another line of inquiry. It implies that such individuals may be turning to a general physician—most likely their primary health care provider—for treatment of a mental disorder (path 6). It may also be that persons suffering psychological problems feel uncomfortable presenting psychiatric symptoms, and complain of one or more of a variety of minor acute ailments (Mechanic, 1972; Hankin and Shapiro, 1980; Balint, 1957). In these instances, depending upon a host of factors (including the individual patient's diagnosis, the severity of his disorder, his goals and expectations, his relationship with his provider, his provider's training, attitude, and caseload), this raises the specter of inappropriate utilization.[6]

Potential Offset Effects

Mental health intervention, as opposed to general health service use, more directly addresses the cause—rather than merely ameliorating the symptoms—of the mental problem. Mental health service utilization, therefore, may be substituted for general health service utilization, creating an offset; an increase in mental health service usage decreases the need for and use of general health service (path 6 is replaced by path 8). This substitution of mental health services for medical care service was the finding of Follette and Cummings (1967) in their landmark study.[7]

Several additional relationships need to be identified. Path 9 (like path 2) constitutes an efficiency-feedback loop, certainly a controversial one, in which non-mental health specialist providers might have an impact on mental health service utilization.

Finally, since there has been no claim in the literature that general health status directly affects mental health service utilization (i.e., no one has asserted that individuals in poor physical health seek care from mental health specialists for their physical health problems), and because there is no theoretical basis for such a direct relationship, path 10 is implausible and is not included in the model.[8]

Empirical research into the role and significance of help-seeking behavior has generally not focused on the potential offset effect. It is hardly surprising, therefore, that there have not been any efforts to integrate this line of inquiry and its fruits—the empirical findings and the behavioral model—with those of the more offset-specific literature. The time to do so, however, has come.

A GENERALIZED MODEL OF HEALTH SERVICE UTILIZATION

As noted in the previous section, various patient characteristics are important to consider. But further elaboration of the basic model thus far developed requires a more complex set of interrelationships than that heretofore considered. For the time being, to keep things from getting too complicated, it will be useful to simplistically conceptualize the model thus far developed and depicted in exhibit 4.1 in a slightly different, more aggregative manner. The two health status variables (mental and general) may alternatively be subsumed under the category "Patient Characteristics," as in exhibit 4.2. Similarly, the two types of health service utilization (mental and general) may be aggregated to comprise more simply undifferentiated "Utilization."

In this re-conceptualization of the model it is easy to see that one of the relationships earlier discussed, utilization as a function of health status, may now be recast as "Utilization" as a function of "Patient Characteristics." This relationship may be direct—as in the case of the patient's health status characteristics (path 2 in exhibit 4.2)—or it may be indirect. An individual's characteristics might indirectly affect his or her utilization by first affecting his or her perception of the need for, or the availability, acceptability, and affordability of health care services (as in paths 3 and 6). These indirect influences of patient characteristics on utilization are frequently lumped together and termed "access" considerations. Each of these considerations (need for, availability, acceptability, and affordability) constitutes a potential barrier to the use of services, and thereby constitutes a potential factor differentiating access to from utilization of services. Access and utilization, therefore, are different constructs, and are incorporated into the model as such.

It should be evident that access to medical care is not an either/or issue; it is a dialectical concept, a question of degrees. Differential access to either mental health services or general health services or both has not been adequately explored. It is possible that some, or all, of the variations in the levels of utilization between mentally ill persons with at least one mental health visit and those without one that have been reported in the quasi-experimental offset literature have very little or nothing to do with the psychotherapy received, but instead are attributable to variations in access to mental health care.

It is necessary, therefore, to incorporate access considerations into the behavioral model, and to investigate the role of potential obstacles to seeking and obtaining care (both mental health care and general health care). Such factors include: attitudes toward health and health care; whether or not the individual has a regular source of care; the individual's knowledge of the service characteristics of nearby care providers (types of specialties and treatments, hours of service, appointment time delays, in-office waiting time delays); confidence in the technical competence and the "humaneness" of the provider; and various dimensions of the affordability consideration (the individual's income, insurance coverage, the travel time to the provider, the travel distance, and the cost of care).

From this list it should be evident that access to care cannot be determined without joint consideration of characteristics of both the individual and of the health care delivery system. Access is not solely a function of the characteristics of the individual patient (or the potential patient). Those characteristics are only part of the picture and must be considered in combination with particular characteristics of the health care delivery system—specifically, individual provider and treatment characteristics. This joint determination of access

Exhibit 4.2

Constructing a Behavioral Model of the Medical Offset:
A Simplified View of the General Causal Model

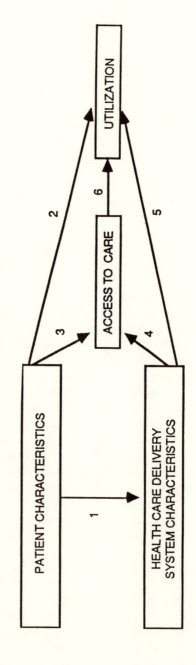

is schematically portrayed in exhibit 4.3 by the arrows running from "Patient Characteristics" and "Provider/Treatment Characteristics" to "Access," paths 3 and 4, respectively.

In addition, provider and/or treatment characteristics are likely to be a function of patient characteristics. Particular types of health problems require particular types of treatment regimens, and may require particular types of specialty providers. Thus "Patient Characteristics" may directly affect "Provider/Treatment Characteristics," as shown by path 1.

Furthermore, Lebow (1974) has hypothesized that patients shop around until they find a provider of whom they approve. This is less likely to be true of, or as important to, individuals who have more restricted choices, such as persons in small communities and rural areas, or persons enrolled in health maintenance organizations relative to those with standard insurance coverage. These relationships, too, are captured by path 1.

The remaining unexplained path in exhibit 4.2 is path 5. Independent of their effect on access, provider/treatment characteristics may have another, more direct, impact on utilization. Holding all access considerations constant, the perceived quality of care attributed to a particular provider (or provider organization), or associated with a particular treatment protocol, is likely to directly affect whether or not an individual even considers seeking care from that particular provider or accepting and adhering to a prescribed regimen.

In addition, health facilities that do not offer a relatively large number of services (or highly specialized medical care providers) are, by their nature, less likely to be capable of handling many different types of cases. Other things being equal, simply because of the particular characteristics of such facilities, organizations, and providers, an individual is less likely to turn to them for care; that is, utilization is a function directly related to their characteristics.

We are now in a position to integrate the two pieces of the behavioral model we have thus far developed independently. Re-extracting general and mental health status from "Patient Characteristics" and breaking utilization into its two component parts (general health service utilization and mental health service utilization), we now pool the relationships captured in exhibits 4.1 and 4.2 to obtain "A Behavioral Model of the Medical Offset Effect," shown in exhibit 4.3.

EMPIRICAL ESTIMATION: MODELING AND DATA CONSIDERATIONS

We have then a behavioral model that explains the utilization of general and mental health services, and the determination of general and mental health status. In its simplest form, such a model would consist of (at least) four dependent variables described by (at least) four equations:[9]

Exhibit 4.3

A Behavioral Model of the Offset Effect

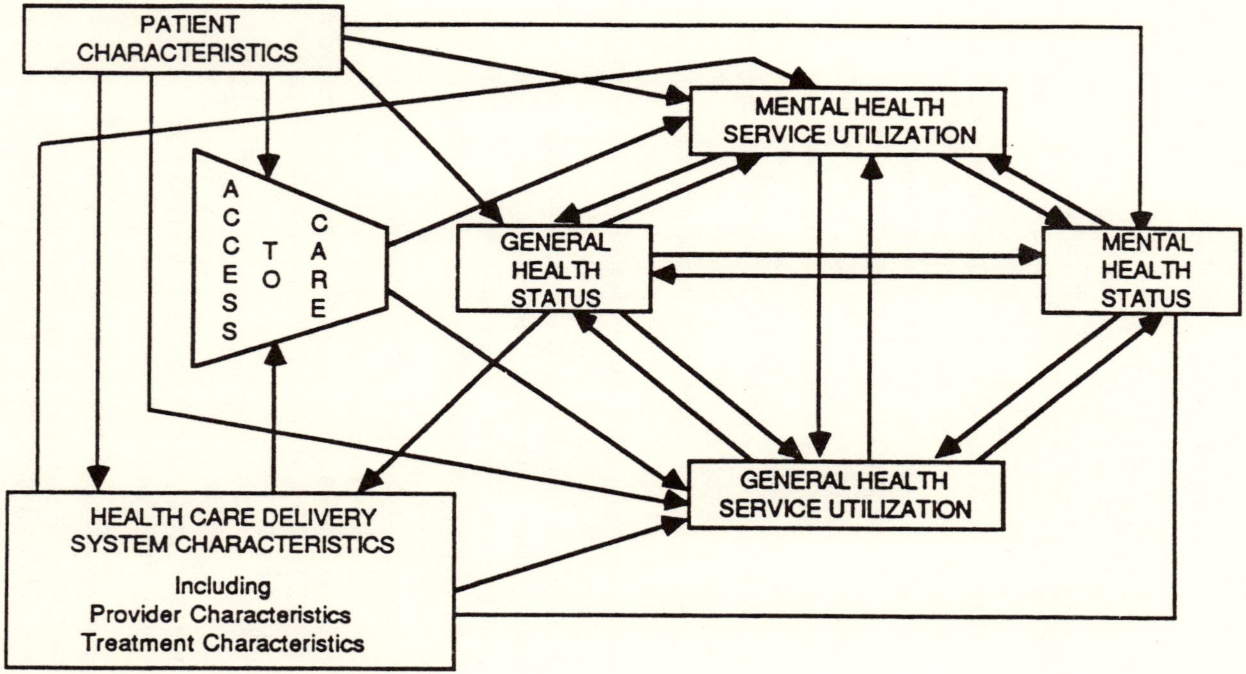

$$GHSU = f(GHS, MHS, MHSU, W)$$
$$MHSU = f(GHS, MHS, GHSU, X)$$
$$GHS = f(MHS, GHSU, MHSU, Y)$$
$$MHS = f(GHS, GHSU, MHSU, Z)$$

Where:

GHSU = General Health Service Utilization
MHSU = Mental Health Service Utilization
GHS = General Health Status
MHS = Mental Health Status
W, X, Y, Z = Vectors Containing All Other Relevant Considerations Including Patient Characteristics, Health Care Delivery System Characteristics, and Access to Care Considerations

This set of equations comprises a simultaneous equation model. At least initially the "simultaneous" characterization may be troubling; it may be more intuitive to conceptualize time-dependent causal orderings between (at least) some of the endogenous variables. For instance, it is likely (1) that it is an initial change in mental health status that gives rise to an encounter with a mental health specialty provider, rather than vice versa, or (2) that the change in mental health status and the utilization episode occur concurrently. Yet (following up on the same example), since the time it takes an initial change in mental health status to work its way back into another change in mental health status (while varying greatly by individual) is generally likely to be less than the time period between observations, the observed variables must be considered as occurring simultaneously—that is, they must be considered simultaneously related.[10]

As is evident in the preceding discussion (and as represented by the probably overlapping, yet distinct, vectors W, X, Y, and Z) there are a host of confounding influences that need to be controlled for and/or explored if the estimates of the offset are to be as accurate and robust as possible. As we noted in chapter 3, multiple regression lends itself uniquely to solving three of the most serious shortcomings pervading the offset literature: selection bias, statistical regression to the mean, and a greater degree of specificity with respect to the client, the provider, and the treatment. Nevertheless, it does not provide a vehicle for unequivocally establishing causality. All it is able to do is establish the existence of correlations. Herein lies the importance of distinguishing between a descriptive and a causal or behavioral model. The more circumspect one is in constructing a model based on plausible, causal relationships, explicitly hypothesized and posited, the greater the degree of confidence one may have in interpreting the results as representative of a causal, as opposed to simply a correlational, relationship.

The next step is to specify the model by developing explicit hypotheses concerning the causal relations (i.e., explaining each of the arrows in exhibit 4.3), and delineating the theoretical rationale for including (or excluding) particular variables from the analysis. Clearly, this hypothesizing cannot be undertaken in isolation from considerations of how the posited relationships might be measured, and whether or not the necessary data exist and are available.

The data requirements for testing the "full" behavioral model outlined are clearly prodigious. It is highly unlikely that any single data set will contain adequate measures of all of the necessary data elements. Since existing data sets contain different types of variables that reflect the different purposes for which they are collected, some data sets will be useful for addressing some of the hypotheses/issues related to the offset effect, but will be inadequate for others. Data availability and accessibility will not only largely determine the particular potential research issue menu, but will also largely circumscribe the particular analytical techniques that may be employed. These are salient issues molding the specific characteristics of the final model.

For purposes of elucidating the process of specifying this model, a sampling of the variables that might be analyzed (depending on data availability) is presented in exhibit 4.4.

CONCLUSION

Important though data considerations are in circumscribing the exact nature of the model that may be specified and estimated, they are secondary. The first step—the conceptualization, development, and use of a behavioral model benchmark—constitutes the framework within which to organize and pursue subsequent steps in the process of empirically operationalizing such a model. It is largely the failure to conceptualize, identify, and construct a behavioral model, a priori, that leaves many researchers working at cross purposes, and which too often serves only to further obfuscate the meaning of new findings and, concomitantly, what it is that we really know about the complex phenomenon known as the medical offset effect.

NOTES

1. This is not to belittle the efforts of those who have already conducted research in this area (as we noted in the preceding chapter).

2. Moreover, in the event that the analytical technique employed is multiple regression—as is increasingly the case—this failure results in what in statistical parlance is known as a "specification error." The omission of relevant variables results in estimated coefficients that will be either smaller or larger than their true values, and consequently either understate or overstate the offset effect. The omission of relevant variables also results in overestimating the residual variance. Hence, inferences about the confidence interval around the coefficients will be inaccurate (the probability of Type I errors will be increased).

Exhibit 4.4

Pertinent Variables for the Specification of a Behavioral
Model of Health Care Utilization

I. CHARACTERISTICS OF THE INDIVIDUAL

A. Predisposing Variables: Factors Hypothesized to Affect the Proclivity to Need/Use Health Care Services

1. Health and Utilization Attitudes and Values

(a) Perception of the value of health
(b) Definitions of health and illness
(c) Threshold(s) for reacting to illness(es)
(d) Coping styles
(e) Perception of appropriate help-seeking behavior
(f) Perception of available, relevant services
(g) Perception of the effectiveness of available, relevant treatments
(h) Perception of the technical competence of relevant providers
(i0 Perception of the humaneness of relevant providers
(j) Tendency to comply with provider's instructions

2. Individual and Family Characteristics

(a) Age
(b) Sex
(c) Family size
(d) Marital status

Exhibit 4.4 (Continued)

3. Social Structure

   (a) Race/culture
   (b) Education
   (c) Occupation
   (d) Religion
   (e) Social support network
   (f) Place of residence (rural vs urban)

B. Utilization Enabling Factors

   1. Income
   2. Insurance (quantity, quality and newness of coverage)
   3. Education
   4. Occupation
   5. Has a regular source of care
   6. Number of provider affiliations

C. Need for Services

   1. General health status
   2. Mental health status

II. CHARACTERISTICS OF THE HEALTH CARE DELIVERY SYSTEM

A. Resources

   1. Number, type, and capacity of providers/facilities
   2. Location of providers/facilities

B. Organization

  1. Entry

    (a) Distance to provider/facility
    (b) Transportation available to provider/facility
    (c) Usual appointment time delay
    (d) Usual travel time to provider/facility
    (e) Usual waiting time at provider/facility

  2. Structure

    (a) Comprehensiveness of services provided
    (b) Continuity of care provided

C. Individual Provider Characteristics

  1. Personal Characteristics

    (a) Age
    (b) Sex
    (c) Religion
    (d) Attitude towards mental illness and treatment

  2. Professional Characteristics

    (a) Type of Specialty
    (b) Diagnostic and Treatment Skills
    (c) Interpersonal Communication Skills ("bedside manner")
    (d) Referral Network

3. The various linkages between physical and mental health, in general, have enjoyed much greater recognition, and have been the focus of much research in recent years (e.g., Eisenberg, 1979; Burns et al., 1981). Increasingly, they are construed by the general public as scientific fact. Nevertheless, the exact linkage mechanisms are still not well understood. Some, for example, maintain that emotional difficulties increase susceptibility to germs and/or enhance accident-proneness (Broskowski and Baker, 1974; Jemmott and Locke, 1985; Romano and Turner, 1985). Yet the exact nature of the cause of this relationship has not, as yet, been definitively established. It may be that a complex constellation of causative factors—some or all of which may be necessary, but none of which in and of themselves may be sufficient—accounts for it. In that event, unequivocally establishing the relationship may be a long time (if ever) in coming.

4. An exogenous variable is one whose variation is assumed to be determined by causes external to the system or model. Such variables may be contrasted with an endogenous variable whose variability is assumed to be determined by variables that are exogenous to, or other endogenous variables of, the model.

5. This is the behavioral model that is both implicit and most evident in the psycho-educational-psychotherapy offset studies (see, for example, Schlesinger et al., 1983). Uniformly in these studies, the study population first experiences a physical health problem (most commonly undergoing a surgical procedure, or the onset of a particular chronic disease). Subsequently, the individual receives psychotherapy in the form of information and emotional support.

6. Other characteristics of the individual (e.g., the number and quality of his social networks) may, however, be the triggering device resulting in his turning to a general health, rather than a mental health, practitioner. This is the type of issue that can be raised and effectively addressed only with a behavioral model.

It is important to distinguish between these two different—though not mutually exclusive—explanations of the cause of the offset, because they represent two very different factors (perhaps characteristics of different people) and they both cause and affect other different behavioral factors. They are each subject to change, but by manipulation of different factors; which is to say, they have different policy implications.

7. They found, however, that when they added mental health service use to the postmental health intervention level of general medical service utilization, the offset effect vanished; the mental health services had, in effect, been substituted on nearly a one-for-one basis for the general health services.

Some offset researchers have argued that this is not always likely to be the case, and that Follette and Cummings's finding is an aberration. Their argument goes something like this: mental health service, being the more appropriate type of care, is more effective, and hence, if provided, results in a net reduction in the number of services needed to achieve a particular level of comfort, other things being equal. That is, the provision of more appropriate and effective mental health services results in an offset.

8. This is not to suggest that changes in general health status have absolutely no impact on mental health service usage. It is very likely—and has frequently been hypothesized—that they, in fact, do. The relationship, however, by all accounts, is construed to be an indirect one, with mental health status acting as an intervening/mediating factor; changes in general health status may affect mental health status, which, in turn, may affect mental health service utilization.

9. The most obvious additional endogenous variable that might be incorporated into the model is patient satisfaction. See Ross and Duff, 1982a; Ross and Duff, 1982b; Ross and Duff, 1982c) for examples of the development and estimation of a path-analytic model explaining general health status, general health service utilization, and patient satisfaction.

10. The assumptions of simultaneity do not preclude the possibility of there being (nor the investigation of) a concurrent lagged impact on one or more of the endogenous but (in this particular relationship) independent variables on one of the other endogenous but (in this instance) dependent variables. It is still possible to test the hypothesis—which several offset researchers have formulated—that the full impact of a mental health intervention may not be immediate, but might instead be of an enduring cumulative nature.

5

AN EMPIRICAL ANALYSIS OF THE MEDICAL OFFSET EFFECT

Sometimes it is more important to know what kind of a fellah has a germ than what kind of a germ has a fellah.
—Lemuel Shattuck (quoted in Gerald Kennedy, ed., *A Reader's Note-book*. New York: Harper and Brothers, 1953, p. 119)

'Tis not the body but the man is ill.
—Silas Weir Mitchell (ibid., p. 436)

INTRODUCTION

In the preceding chapters we have discussed many of the controversial issues which have challenged researchers in attempting to ascertain whether or not an offset effect exists. It is now time for us to look firsthand at how such estimates are made. In addition, we will address how the offset effect estimates may be sensitive to the particular institutional, sociological, political, or economic matrix from which the specific study population sample is taken. Since we anticipate that the minutiae of the econometrics may not interest some of our readers, we provide a preview and overview of our major findings in this and the next chapter (which is also largely devoted to empirical analysis).

In this chapter we present the results of our own estimates of the offset effect for Georgia Medicaid patients, over the period 1980–82. In the following chapter we compare and contrast these findings with estimates based on similar data from Michigan. For Georgia, we find a substantial and significant offset effect, and one that is "robust" (i.e., stable over the various subgroups we tested, as well as over the various specifications of the model used). In Michigan, too, we find a statistically significant offset, but only for a subgroup of that population. What accounts for the variation between these two states? Before proceeding with the empirical analysis, we turn first to a description of the data and the model.

THE DATA SOURCE AND MODEL

The Medicaid Program and the Tape-to-Tape Project

In 1965 the United States Congress passed Public Law 89-97 which amended the Social Security Act and created the Medicare (Title XVIII) and Medicaid (Title XIX) programs. Building upon the then-extant Medical Assistance for the Aged (or so-called Kerr-Mills) program, Medicaid was intended and designed to improve access to medical care for low-income persons who are aged, blind, disabled, or members of families with dependent children.[1]

Medicaid is the source of the data used in this study. Medicaid data—as we shall see—has many (at times, severe) limitations for both specifying and estimating an offset model. Medicaid data remains of interest, however, for two major reasons. First, Medicaid expenditures are of major significance in the budgets of the federal government, as well as in each of the fifty states. Second, the population is large enough and heterogeneous enough that it is less likely than most other available data sets to be distorted by demographic peculiarities.

Since its inception, Medicaid has been a decentralized program. While it is jointly financed by the states and the federal government, it is independently administered by the individual states. Although broad federal guidelines specify coverage provisions, mandatory services, and minimum administrative requirements, the states retain considerable latitude in establishing specific eligibility requirements and their particular administrative structures, as well as in determining the nature and duration of service coverage and the particular characteristics of their Medicaid Management Information Systems (MMISs).

Each MMIS has been designed by its own individual state bureaucracy with the principal aim of facilitating timely and accurate claims payment. Only as a secondary goal does it provide data for program monitoring and research endeavors. In all states the data are part of program administration activities, and are collected on an ongoing basis.

Despite their operational differences, all MMISs contain three basic data files:

- Enrollment files contain individual patient demographic information on race, date of birth, gender, basis of eligibility, and eligible/non-eligible days per month.
- Claims files contain data on actual health care encounters for all types of services for which a Medicaid claim was filed.
- Provider files contain data on provider type and location.

The patchwork of idiosyncratic differences in the state programs long precluded the development of detailed federal-level data. As a result, the federal government has had only limited ability to monitor performance and to measure, evaluate, and forecast the implications of program changes, both real and potential. As a specific response to this problem, the Health Care Financing Administration (HCFA) initiated a project known as the Tape-to-Tape Project, which extracts person-level, episode-specific, medical care data from existing state MMISs to generate "uniform" inter-state/federal data sets.[2] During its initial phase, the 1980–84 period, the project was implemented in the states of New York, California, Michigan, Georgia, and Tennessee.

The Study Sample

The data used for this study were extracted from the Medicaid Tape-to-Tape enrollment and claims files for Georgia and Michigan for three years: 1980, 1981, and 1982. The study group is a small sample of each state's total Medicaid population during this period. The criteria and definitions used in the development of the study group are summarized below. Data refinement procedures and data element definitions are elaborated in appendix 5.1.

In each state's total claims files, individuals who were enrolled continuously (at least 350 days per year) from January 1, 1980 through December 31, 1982 were identified. From this group, individuals were selected who: (1) had no mental-health-diagnosis-related outpatient-only claims in quarters 1 and 2 of this twelve-quarter period, but (2) did have such a claim and (3) were treated in quarter 3 by a mental health specialist (identified by five database elements, defined as psychiatrist, psychologist, hospital-based mental health clinic, community mental health clinic, and mental institution). Only three mental health specialists/institutions were identified as having treated members of the study sample in Georgia: psychiatrists, psychologists, and community mental health clinics. The mental health diagnoses included were ICDA-9-CM codes 290, 293-302, and 305-316; that is, all mental-health-related illnesses exclusive of alcohol- and drug-related illnesses.[3] Implementing this selection process in Georgia yielded an outpatient file of 59,560 Medicaid claims and a drug file of 61,098 Medicaid claims during the three-year period 1980–82.

To the extent that it exists, the offset effect is an individual-specific phenomenon; namely, it is the reduced medical care expenses incurred by a person following his/her receiving mental health services. As such, for most types of analyses, and, in particular, for the main analytical tool used in this study (multiple regression), an individual-specific data set is required. Accordingly, the Tape-to-Tape Project files were restructured from claim-specific to individual-specific files, and merged with demographic data developed from a third Tape-to-Tape file, the enrollment file. The resulting file for Georgia (following some additional housekeeping described in appendix 5.1) consists of 411 individuals or cases.

Specification of the Multiple Regression Model

As detailed in chapter 4's discussion about the process of constructing the behavioral model, general physical health service utilization depends interactively on a host of factors: patient physical health status, patient mental health status, other patient characteristics, patient access, health care delivery system characteristics, and—most importantly from this study's perspective—mental health service utilization.

A medical offset would occur if a patient used physical health services as an inappropriate substitute for mental health services, and the subsequent provision of mental health care reduced physical health charges (by reducing the severity of a physical health problem caused by mental illness). While there are a host of possible explanations as to why this might occur (see chapter 4), the most common are: (1) the patient's ignorance that the physical symptoms suffered are derivative of a mental health problem; (2) the desire to avoid the stigma of being treated by a mental health specialist and being dubbed "mentally ill"; or (3) health insurance covers mental health services less adequately than it does general physical health services. More appropriate and effective treatment for the root problem can be provided by mental health specialists. Such treatment, it is hypothesized, will improve mental health which, in turn, will improve physical health and thereby reduce physical health service expenditures.[4]

It is useful to dissect the potential generation of an offset effect into its two related yet distinct component issues. The first issue concerns the quality of care provided, and the efficiency with which a mental health problem is treated. A separate issue is whether the costs of mental health treatment would be more than offset by any savings in physical health service utilization (e.g., the mental health intervention expense would actually reduce "total" medical expenses). There is no reason, a priori, to expect total medical expenses to fall; the elasticities of supply and demand for mental relative to physical health care are probably very different, and are likely to vary by the particular population studied. Consequently any offset of mental health care for physical health care might actually raise total expenses.

The extent to which mental health treatment visits (MHTV) reduce expenses for physical health care may be viewed as a necessary, but not sufficient, condition for a "total" offset effect to exist. Our model is designed to address these two offset issues independently. First, we will investigate whether or not the pre-condition is found to be satisfied. If it is, the next research question is whether the mental health intervention is cost-effective. (If the pre-condition is not met, of course, there is no such second step.)

In our model, therefore, we seek to determine the extent to which mental health treatment visits reduce expenses for physical health care expenses in quarters 3 to 12 (LNET3–12), controlling for other factors such as patient health status and other patient characteristics (PC), patient access to health care (PA), and health care delivery system characteristics (HCDS), and allowing for a random error term (e):

$$LNET3-12 = f(MHTV, PC, PA, HCDS, e)$$

Dependent variable: (LNET3-12)

The net charge for medical care exclusive of mental health treatment charges in quarters 3–12 is calculated as the log of the difference between total health care treatment costs minus mental health care treatment costs. This variable, LNET3–12, measures the expenditures for the treatment of physical ailments in the ten quarters during and following the initial mental health treatment intervention (July 1, 1980 through December 31, 1982).

To measure expenditures in constant dollars (in other words, to control for the influence of medical care inflation), each quarter's total charges have been adjusted so as to make them equal to the value of the medical care dollar in quarter 12.[5]

Independent Variables and Functional Form: Offset Variables

The independent offset variable is the number of mental health treatment visits (MHTV) to one of three mental health specialists/institutions in quarters 3 to 12 (inclusive).[6] Mental health treatment visits are reported in the data set as per each billable meeting between patient and practitioner. The length of each visit is not recorded. Our selection and use of MHTV (as opposed to the charges for care provided) as the independent variable is justified on the theoretical grounds that it is the encounter itself which is the relevant variable, and not the associated charges (which may vary dramatically by provider for a single treatment). Whether this encounter lasts forty-five minutes or sixty minutes, or whether the individual is charged $50 or $125, is not as pertinent as the fact that an encounter or session has occurred.

As we noted in chapter 3, there is substantial evidence suggesting that, if an offset exists, it may not be simply a linear relationship between mental health treatment visits and net physical health charges. Accordingly, we explore several different plausible relationships by specifying alternative functional forms: (1) the semi-log linear form, wherein the number of mental health treatment visits (MHTV) is the independent variable;[7] (2) a semi-log quadratic specification, which adds the square of MHTV (MHTVSQ) to the MHTV term (still) in the equation; (3) the reciprocal of MHTV (RECIPMHT); and (4) the natural logarithm of MHTV (LMHTV).

All of these functional forms allow for a non-linear relationship, specifically allowing for a diminishing effect of mental health treatment visits on physical health charges.[8] That is, it is hypothesized that additional mental health treatment visits lower physical health charges, but at a diminishing rate. In the quadratic specification, moreover, physical health charges are hypothesized first to decrease with more MHTVs, but then, beyond some point, to increase (i.e., eventually there can be "too many" mental health treatment visits from the perspective of generating the offset effect).[9] There are several theoretical reasons why such a reversal might occur. Some analysts have maintained that mental health treatment could result in the increased use of health services because the mentally ill may have less access to general health services prior to mental health treatment intervention. After a certain level of mental health treatment visits, the patient's emotional and psychological barriers to services may have crumbled (as a result of, for example, learning from experience); this increase in the patient's access to care is likely to contribute to greater use of services.

Other analysts note that if the mentally ill are self-neglectful or self-destructive (and purposely avoid use of needed health services prior to intervention), a psychotherapeutic intervention will likely increase utilization. Again, it may be necessary for some individuals to receive several treatments before they become motivated enough to change to their general health care utilization with the aim of addressing the results of their long neglect and trying to "get back on their feet again." Or, it could be that "so many" mental health services have been provided that a dependence on health care providers develops (on either or both mental and physical providers).[10]

If this hypothesis about the reversal of the relationship is accurate, the eventually increasing level of physical health utilization associated with additional mental health visits will map out a parabola (U-shaped curve) and the quadratic functional form will be the most appropriate. In this instance, it is expected that the MHTV coefficient will be negative, while that for the quadratic term (MHTVSQ) will be positive.[11]

Specification of the semi-log linear (MHTV), the reciprocal of MHTV (RECIPMHT), or the natural log of MHTV (LMHTV), on the other hand, hypothesize a monotonically decreasing function and one which decreases at a decreasing rate. This indicates a continuously diminishing effect of mental health treatment visits on physical health charges; with increasing numbers of mental health visits there is a reduction in physical health charges, but the size of that reduction decreases (eventually approaching zero) as mental health visits continue to increase. The hypothesized sign for MHTV is negative, that for RECIPMHT is positive, and that for LMHTV is negative.

We also disaggregate the MHTV variable to analyze the offset associated with specific provider types. The variables PSY, CMH, and MD represent the number of visits in quarters 3 to 12 (inclusive) to a psychologist, a community mental health center, and a psychiatrist, respectively.

Additional independent variables were selected (based in part on data availability) to control for patient characteristics, patient access to care, and provider characteristics.

Gender

There is a general consensus that important differences exist between men and women with respect to (1) prevalence of mental illness in general, and of particular mental health problems,[12] (2) utilization rates of physical and mental health services,[13] and (3) the rate of successful psychotherapeutic outcome.[14] However, there is considerable controversy over the causes of these differences (e.g., constitutional vulnerability, environmental vulnerability, and socialization processes, to name a few hypotheses).

Unfortunately the detailed data necessary to ascertain why these differences exist are not available in this data set. Consequently, the GENDER variable is simultaneously controlling for a variety of conditioning factors and behavioral processes; and it is impossible to determine unambiguously which of these factors, or combinations thereof, is being captured by the GENDER variable. Hence, it is impossible to predict confidently the sign of the variable.[15] As a dummy variable, GENDER was set to a value of 1 for males and 0 for females.

Race

RACE, like the GENDER variable, acts as a composite proxy variable to control for differences in general and mental health status,[16] tastes and attitudes toward health care utilization,[17] and access and utilization of care[18] between whites and non-whites. It may also reflect the indirect effects of discrimination in the treatment provided. Whites have the race variable set to 1; nonwhites have it set to 0. There is no hypothesized sign.

Age

It is recognized that there is a U-shaped relationship between age and the use of medical services (Aday and Eichhorn, 1972; Guzick, 1978). The shape of this relationship is largely accounted for by a paralleling U-shaped curve relating the frequency of illness episodes and age; that is, utilization is largely a function of "need," or health status.

In the mental health arena, on the other hand, the parabolic relationship between utilization and age is turned on its head, due to the inverted U-shaped relationship between mental health status and age (Shapiro et al., 1984); the incidence of psychiatric disorders is relatively low for the very young, increases more or less continually until approximately age 45, after which it drops off sharply (Myers et al., 1984).

This suggests that there is a tension between general health status and mental health status in terms of their impact on the general health service utilization–age relationship.[19] During those years of life when general health status is generally relatively good—from early adulthood to about the onset of middle age (i.e., from approximately eighteen to forty-five years of age)—general health service utilization is likely to be relatively low. But it is during these same years that mental health status is likely to be relatively poor, and acting (inappropriately) to increase general health service utilization.

The combined impact of general and mental health status on total health service use is the result of the interplay of these two countervailing forces. Although much of the relationship between age and general health service utilization may be explained by incorporating general health status and mental health status variables into the equation (as we do), the age variable remains useful for providing insight into the intensity of the general illnesses and the mental illnesses a person experiences.

We constructed four dummy variables to represent five age groups, with ages 0–17 as the reference group: AGE1 (18–24), AGE2 (25–44), AGE3 (45–64), AGE4 (65 and older). Accordingly, we hypothesize that the signs of AGE1 and AGE2 are indeterminate, and that those of AGE3 and AGE4 are positive.

Physical Health Status

Other things being equal, a person with a history of physical health problems or diagnoses is more predisposed to be physically ill. Moreover, a person who is ill, other things being equal, is more likely to seek health care. Hence it is important to include some measure of health status as a covariate to control for the individual's "need" for health services.

In addition, it is essential to try to obtain some measure of an individual's predisposition toward the use of medical care, and the degree of access thereto. As already noted, we have several composite variables (AGE, RACE, and GENDER) which could capture or reflect a number of different possible effects—general health status, mental health status, access to care, predisposition to using health services—depending upon what is included in the equation (controlled for) simultaneously. This is another rationale for including some measure of health status in the equation: to be better able to disentangle the rival hypotheses of different factors contributing to utilization which are embodied in the composite proxy variables.

It would be ideal to have some measure of longer-term, or permanent, physical health status, as well as short-term (study period) deviations. Such measures, unfortunately, are not available. The best we can do is to develop and employ two (crude) proxy measures: the individual's number of different pre- and post-mental health intervention physical diagnoses (NPREDX and Q312NDX, respectively). We use both of these measures to calibrate the offset as precisely as possible, while simultaneously eschewing one of the more common pitfalls of offset research, namely, not controlling for the peaking phenomenon.

Severity of Mental and Physical Illnesses

Patients with different types of mental illness have been found to have different offset responses (Borus et al., 1985; Kessler et al., 1982). The data file contained seven different patient mental health diagnoses, which we classified as either "mild" or "severe."[20] It is hypothesized that mental health treatment produces the greatest offset in situational, transitory, or other mild mental health situations. Those suffering from severe mental health problems are hypothesized not to experience as large an offset (if any).

Accordingly, we control for patient mental health diagnosis in the regression equation via a "dummy" variable SEVERE, and an interactive offset variable SEVMHTV, which is the product of SEVERE and MHTV. The intercept term SEVERE captures whether overall physical health charges for the more severely mentally ill are significantly different from all others. While on the surface one might anticipate that the severely mentally ill would be physically sicker than the rest of the population, and thereby experience higher levels of physical health care utilization, it may also be the case that, while these patients are physically sicker, they may not seek care. That is, the most severely mentally ill may be unaware of their physical health problems, may feel they do not warrant treatment, or may seek to resist obtaining any kind of treatment. The anticipated sign of SEVERE, therefore, is uncertain.

The "slope" term SEVMHT is of greater interest for the offset estimation because it captures whether additional mental health treatment visits affect the physical health charges of the severely mentally ill differently than those with milder symptoms. Our hypothesis is that the sign of SEVMHT will be positive; that is, since the offset variable MHTV will be *negative* if there is an offset, a positive coefficient for SEVMHT implies a lesser offset (if any) for the more severely mentally ill.

We also controlled for the severity of physical health by Q312DAYG, which is the number of days in quarters 3–12 which the patient spent as an inpatient receiving physical health treatment. It is expected that those with inpatient treatments face generally more severe physical health problems than those receiving outpatient treatments, and will have significantly higher charges for utilization; a positive sign is therefore expected for Q312DAYG.

Patient Attitudes and Access

Holding physical health status constant (through the proxies NPREDX and Q312NDX), and controlling for mental and physical health severity (via SEVERE and Q312DAYS), individuals who have a positive attitude toward the value of medical care will consume more, as will those with greater access. We use as a proxy for these attitudes and access LPREGHSU, the natural logarithm of the total general health care charges in the period prior to mental health intervention (adjusted for inflation). Individuals with greater levels of LPREGHSU are assumed to have greater access to care and more positive attitudes about the use of medical care and the value of health, and to be more predisposed to help-seeking behavior. This variable has an expected sign which is positive.

The psychological obstacles to seeking and obtaining medical care are likely to be greatest for persons without a regular source of care. Individuals with a more regular provider have been shown to have greater access to medical care (Aday, 1975), greater utilization of care (Luft et al., 1976), and more satisfaction with the care they receive (Aday and Andersen, 1975). Holding other factors constant, we hypothesize that persons with a larger number of providers over a given period of time have the least continuity of care and, hence, the greatest psychological obstacles to care and the greatest time costs in obtaining care. In short, they have the least access to care.

In addition, individuals with less continuity of care are likely to obtain a lower quality of care, both because the provider is not as familiar with the individual and because the individual patient, not being familiar with the provider, may have a greater tendency to disregard the provider's medical advice. Care from a regular provider is likely to be more timely, since there are fewer search costs and other barriers, and a regular provider is likely to charge less, since the visit can be shorter with a regular patient.[21] Controlling for health status, the variable NPRO3–12 (the number of different providers from quarters 3–12) measures the individual's regular source of, and continuity of, care. The expected sign of the coefficient is positive.

Finally, note that as the number of diagnoses increases (Q3–12NDX), the number of specialist health care providers is also expected to increase (NPRO3–12). We control for this possible multicollinearity via an interactive variable NPRONDX, which is the product of Q3–12NDX and NPRO3–12.

A summary of these variables, their definitions, and expected signs are found in exhibit 5.1. Appendix 5.2 contains the means and standard deviations, while appendix 5.3 presents the correlation matrix.

EMPIRICAL RESULTS

As already noted, due primarily to the limited types of data available in Medicaid claims file-based data sets, nothing very closely approaching a full behavioral or causal model can be estimated. The results, therefore, should be interpreted conservatively, and should not be regarded as definitive. Alternative specifications and estimations are employed in the analysis to better gauge the confidence which may be placed in the results.

The discussion of the multiple regression findings for Georgia begins with the most aggregated results and proceeds to the more detailed, disaggregated results. The basic offset model seeks to explain variations in physical health care charges in the quarters during and following the initial mental health treatment intervention (LNET3–12) as a function of the number of mental health treatment visits (MHTV), while controlling for patient characteristics and other intervening variables.

Approximately one-half (49 percent) of our sample experienced inpatient treatments for physical health ailments over quarters 3–12. The segment of the population with inpatient treatments for physical illnesses had significantly more providers and diagnoses, along with significantly higher previous and current charges for utilization, and was made up of significantly more females than those with no inpatient treatments. Before proceeding with the regressions, we analyzed whether it was appropriate to "lump together" the data of patients who had received inpatient treatments with those who had

Exhibit 5.1

Variable Definitions and Expected Signs

DEPENDENT VARIABLE

LNET3-12   Non-mental health treatment costs in quarters 3-12 (inclusive), calculated as the natural log of the difference between total health treatment costs and mental health treatment costs. All costs are in constant dollars of 1980.

INDEPENDENT VARIABLES (Expected Sign)

A) OFFSET VARIABLES

MHTV (-)   The total number of mental health treatment visits the individual made to any mental health specialist in quarters 3-12.

MHTVSQ (+)   MHTV squared.

PSY (-)   The total number of mental health treatment visits made to a psychologist in quarters 3-12.

CMH (-)   The total number of mental health treatment visits made to a community mental health center in quarters 3-12.

MD (-)   The total number of mental health treatment visits made to a psychiatrist in quarters 3-12.

SEVMHTV (+)   An interactive offset variable calculated as the product of SEVERE and MHTV.

Exhibit 5.1 (Continued)

B) PATIENT CHARACTERISTICS, ATTITUDES, AND ACCESS VARIABLES

GENDER (?)   Sex of the patient. (1 for males and 0 for females.)

RACE (?)   Race of the patient. (1 for whites and 0 for non-whites.)

AGE (+)   The patient's age, measured in years, in 1980. There are also five breakdowns of age: AGE1 18-24, AGE2 25-44, AGE3 45-64, and AGE4 65 and older.

NPREDX (+)   The natural log of the number of different diagnoses prior to mental health intervention (proxy for general level of health).

Q3-12NDX (+)   The natural log of the number of different diagnoses in quarters 3-12, after mental health intervention.

PREGHSU (+)   The natural logarithm of the inflation-adjusted total general health care charges in the period prior to mental health intervention.

NPRO3-12 (+)   The natural log of the number of different providers the individual visited after the mental health intervention in quarters 3-12.

Q312DAYG (+)   The number of days inpatient for physical health treatment in quarters 3-12.

Q312DAYM (+)   The number of days inpatient for mental health treatment in quarters 3-12.

SEVERE (?)   Mental health diagnosis. (1 for severe, 0 for mild.)

NPRONDX (?)   An interactive control variable calculated as the product of the number of different providers frequented (NPRO3-12) and the number of different diagnoses received (NDX3-12).

not; that is, we asked the question, would the estimated regression coefficients be "stable" across these two groups? The results of a Chow Test indicated not—that it would be inappropriate to regress these two different groups together.[22] Consequently, the offset responses of these two groups need to be examined independently.

Exhibit 5.2 presents the empirical results obtained from different specifications of the population. Equation #1 presents the results of those with no inpatient care for physical health, while equation #2 specifies those with some inpatient care. Both equations do a good job of fitting the data. Adjusted for degrees of freedom, the regression models explain 64 and 70 percent, respectively, of total variation in net general health service charges, and both are significant at well beyond the 99.9 percent level. As discussed in chapter 3's section on evaluating alternative methodological approaches, to judge the adequacy of any particular regression specification requires assessing the extent to which the data and the fitted model conform to the assumptions underlying the regression mode. We find that the model conforms reasonably well to these assumptions (as shown in appendix 5.4).

Empirical Findings

The variables of primary interest, of course, are MHTV, MHTVSQ, and the mental illness severity interactive term SEVMHTV. In both regressions we find that the coefficient of MHTV is negative and significant at least the 1 percent confidence level, demonstrating that an offset effect does exist; mental health treatment visits significantly lower physical health care charges in the ten quarters following the initial mental health intervention in both of these Georgia study populations.

In regression #1 we also find that the quadratic term MHTVSQ is not significant, indicating that the offset effect, while diminishing with more visits, does not turn upward for this population group.[23] For those with inpatient treatment, however, we find that the quadratic term MHTVSQ is significant, indicating that physical health charges eventually begin to rise with more mental health treatment visits.

The size of the offset also varies by severity of mental illness, at least for those with no inpatient treatments; those diagnosed with severe mental health problems in regression #1 experienced a smaller offset effect (since the interactive term SEVMHTV is positive and significant, counteracting the negative effect of MHTV), which is as anticipated. Since the coefficient for SEVMHTV is not significant in regression #2, however, we cannot infer this for the population which had received inpatient physical health treatments.

In summary, these findings should be intuitive to offset researchers—that *while an offset effect exists, its magnitude varies by the severity of physical and mental illnesses which individuals suffer.*

Exhibit 5.2

Multiple Regression Results (Georgia)

Dependent Variable	All Cases (N=411)		#1 No Inpatients (N=208)		#2 Inpatients (N=203)	
	LNET3-12		LNET3-12		LNET3-12	
MHTV/100	-2.122**	(2.95)	-2.529**	(2.39)	-1.798*	(2.31)
MHTVSQ/100	0.021*	(2.10)	0.023	(1.64)	0.021*	(1.93)
SEVERE	-0.243	(1.71)	-0.330	(1.55)	0.041	(0.27)
SEVMHTV	0.881	(1.62)	1.377*	(1.71)	-0.329	(0.55)
Q312DAYG	0.009**	(3.56)			0.013**	(6.52)
GENDER	-0.163	(1.53)	-0.205	(1.40)	-0.017	(0.14)
AGE 1	0.086	(0.35)	0.095	(0.26)	-0.128	(0.50)
AGE 2	-0.023	(0.13)	-0.027	(0.09)	0.016	(0.09)

	(1)		(2)		(3)	
AGE 3	0.322*	(1.79)	0.371	(1.33)	0.270	(1.49)
AGE 4	0.997**	(4.44)	1.116**	(3.54)	0.540*	(1.86)
RACE	0.111	(1.13)	0.109	(0.73)	-0.045	(0.42)
NPRO3_12	0.572**	(7.05)	0.621**	(5.96)	0.337**	(3.05)
Q3_12NDX	-0.456	(5.22)	-0.110	(0.71)	-0.251	(2.21)
NPREGHSU	0.272**	(4.13)	0.203*	(1.99)	0.104	(1.47)
NPREDX	-0.221	(2.92)	0.094	(0.65)	-0.192	(2.63)
NPRONDX	0.748**	(11.55)	0.505**	(4.50)	0.508**	(7.06)
Constant	2.706**	(7.02)	2.297**	(3.91)	5.234**	(11.28)
R Squared	0.692		0.639		0.699	
Std Error	0.940		0.966		0.690	

Notes: Absolute Value of t-statistic in parentheses
  *Significant at the 5% level
  **Significant at the 1% level

The Magnitude of the Offset Effect

Holding other factors constant, an additional mental health treatment visit results in a reduction in net general health service charges. Quantifying the impact of a single mental health treatment, however (what we shall term the incremental or marginal offset effect), is not a simple or straightforward task. Its magnitude depends on the simultaneous consideration of several factors, including the severity of physical and mental illness, the number of mental health treatment visits made, and the level of net physical health care charges over the ten quarters following the mental health intervention (NET3–12).[24]

MARGINAL OFFSET EFFECT

No Inpatient Treatment
Only Mild Mental Health $= [-.02529]$ NET3–12
Diagnoses (Regression #1)

No Inpatient Treatment
Severe Mental Health $= [-.02529 + \underline{.01377}]$ NET3–12
Diagnoses (Regression #1)
                            $= [-.01152]$ NET3–12

Inpatient Treatment
Both Severe and Mild $= [-.01798 + 2(.00021)\text{MHTV}]$ NET3–12
Diagnoses (Regression #2)

The offset for the patients with more severe mental illnesses is smaller (i.e., less negative); the underlined number is the estimated coefficient for the severe interaction term (SEVMHTV).

Exhibit 5.3 presents the marginal, average, and cumulative offset estimates for patients without any inpatient physical health treatment, calculated using the predicted values of physical health charges over quarters 3–12 (NET3–12), generated by regression #1.[25] As shown, there is a diminishing marginal offset effect for each additional mental health treatment obtained, and this marginal effect will asymptotically approach zero. The first mental health treatment visit results in savings in physical health charges of almost $33 for those with mild diagnoses, and $15 for those with severe diagnoses. By the thirtieth visit these savings drop to less than $16 for those with mild diagnoses and less than $11 for those with severe diagnoses.

From a public policy point of view, these results are somewhat disquieting; they imply that in order to achieve a larger offset, mental health resources should be channeled toward those who are only mildly mentally ill! The severely ill, by contrast, who presumably "need" more treatment from both a clinical as well as a social perspective, do not promise much of a payout in terms of an offset. This is an important issue that we address further in chapter 7.

Exhibit 5.4 presents the offset calculations for patients with inpatient care for physical illness, calculated from regression #2; as shown, the initial MHTV results in a substantial offset of almost $124.[26] In light of the relatively comparable offset coefficients in the two regressions, the much larger initial offset for those with inpatient treatments is the result of this group having much higher treatment charges to begin with; because these charges are substantially higher, much larger savings can be generated via an offset. Because of the significant quadratic term (MHTVSQ), however, these savings fall off very rapidly, so that by the thirtieth visit the incremental savings are $27, and, after the forty-second visit, are totally exhausted. Any additional mental health treatments beyond the forty-second will actually cause physical health charges to rise. One possible reason for this, as discussed earlier, may be that patients with too many visits become overly dependent on care providers of both mental and physical health care.

Thus, in summary, individuals suffering from mental illness who also have severe enough physical health problems to be admitted inpatient for treatment provide the greatest vehicle for saving physical health treatment dollars via the offset effect. This finding is intuitively appealing. While those in this population have a lower offset savings rate than those with no inpatient treatment (i.e., a smaller estimated coefficient for MHTV in regression #2 than #1), they have a much greater offset potential since these individuals are using up the lion's share of physical care resources—$11,391 on average over the ten-quarter period, compared to $2,574 for those with no inpatient physical health treatment.

In terms of policy, this suggests that patients who are undergoing surgery or other relatively traumatic medical treatment (such that they require inpatient care) can indeed benefit from mental health treatment visits, and in a very demonstrable way. These findings corroborate what is known of the importance played by a patient's motivation and psychological outlook in terms of recovery from illness and surgery. Patients with more mental health treatments (controlling for severity and other characteristics) are able to reduce their physical health charges below those of patients who have fewer mental health treatments.

These findings also underscore the need to recognize the differential impact of and the fundamentally different role of mental health care in the treatment of different types of physical and mental disorders, as well as the differential impact of mental health care on different types of physical health care utilization. As we have empirically found here, it also underscores the need to recognize and analyze these subsets of the mentally ill as manifesting distinct behavioral processes, which it is inappropriate to aggregate. As noted in the literature review of chapter 3, disaggregated analyses of the offset effect have generally been the exception.

Exhibit 5.3

The Estimated Size of the Offset Effect for Georgia:

No Inpatient Files

MHTV	--------MILD--------			--------SEVERE--------		
	MARGINAL	AVERAGE	CUMULATIVE	MARGINAL	AVERAGE	CUMULATIVE
1	-32.80	-32.80	-32.80	-15.15	-15.15	-15.15
2	-31.98	-32.39	-64.77	-14.97	-15.06	-30.12
3	-31.18	-31.99	-95.96	-14.80	-14.97	-44.92
4	-30.40	-31.59	-126.36	-14.63	-14.89	-59.55
5	-29.65	-31.20	-156.01	-14.46	-14.80	-74.02
6	-28.91	-30.82	-184.92	-14.30	-14.72	-88.32
7	-28.19	-30.44	-213.10	-14.14	-14.64	-102.45
8	-27.49	-30.07	-240.59	-13.97	-14.55	-116.43
9	-26.80	-29.71	-267.39	-13.82	-14.47	-130.24
10	-26.13	-29.35	-293.52	-13.66	-14.39	-143.90
11	-25.48	-29.00	-319.01	-13.50	-14.31	-157.40
12	-24.85	-28.65	-343.85	-13.35	-14.23	-170.75
13	-24.23	-28.31	-368.08	-13.19	-14.15	-183.94
14	-23.62	-27.98	-391.71	-13.04	-14.07	-196.98
15	-23.04	-27.65	-414.74	-12.89	-13.99	-209.88
16	-22.46	-27.33	-437.21	-12.75	-13.91	-222.63
17	-21.90	-27.01	-459.11	-12.60	-13.84	-235.23
18	-21.36	-26.69	-480.47	-12.46	-13.76	-247.69
19	-20.82	-26.38	-501.29	-12.32	-13.68	-260.00
20	-20.31	-26.08	-521.60	-12.17	-13.61	-272.18

21	-19.80	-25.78	-541.40	-12.04	-13.53	-284.21
22	-19.31	-25.49	-560.70	-11.90	-13.46	-296.11
23	-18.83	-25.20	-579.53	-11.76	-13.39	-307.87
24	-18.36	-24.91	-597.89	-11.63	-13.31	-319.50
25	-17.90	-24.63	-615.79	-11.49	-13.24	-330.99
26	-17.45	-24.36	-633.24	-11.36	-13.17	-342.36
27	-17.02	-24.08	-650.26	-11.23	-13.10	-353.59
28	-16.59	-23.82	-666.85	-11.11	-13.02	-364.69
29	-16.18	-23.55	-683.03	-10.98	-12.95	-375.67
30	-15.78	-23.29	-698.81	-10.85	-12.88	-386.52
31	-15.38	-23.04	-714.20	-10.73	-12.81	-397.25
32	-15.00	-22.79	-729.20	-10.61	-12.75	-407.86
33	-14.63	-22.54	-743.83	-10.48	-12.68	-418.34
34	-14.26	-22.30	-758.09	-10.37	-12.61	-428.71
35	-13.91	-22.06	-772.00	-10.25	-12.54	-438.96
36	-13.56	-21.82	-785.56	-10.13	-12.47	-449.09
37	-13.22	-21.59	-798.78	-10.01	-12.41	-459.10
38	-12.89	-21.36	-811.68	-9.90	-12.34	-469.00
39	-12.57	-21.13	-824.25	-9.79	-12.28	-478.78
40	-12.26	-20.91	-836.51	-9.67	-12.21	-488.46

*Cases for which there is no inpatient treatment for a physical health illness (N = 208), based on regression #1. "Mild" and "severe" refer to the mental health diagnosis.

Exhibit 5.4

The Estimated Size of the Offset Effect for Georgia Inpatients*

MHTV	MARGINAL	AVERAGE	CUMULATIVE
1	-123.84	-123.84	-123.84
2	-118.80	-121.32	-242.64
3	-113.95	-118.86	-356.59
4	-109.27	-116.47	-465.87
5	-104.76	-114.13	-570.63
6	-100.41	-111.84	-671.04
7	-96.21	-109.61	-767.25
8	-92.15	-107.42	-859.39
9	-88.22	-105.29	-947.62
10	-84.43	-103.20	-1032.04
11	-80.75	-101.16	-1112.80
12	-77.19	-99.17	-1189.99
13	-73.75	-97.21	-1263.74
14	-70.40	-95.30	-1334.14
15	-67.16	-93.42	-1401.30
16	-64.01	-91.58	-1465.31
17	-60.94	-89.78	-1526.25
18	-57.96	-88.01	-1584.21
19	-55.06	-86.28	-1639.28
20	-52.24	-84.58	-1691.52
21	-49.48	-82.90	-1741.00
22	-46.80	-81.26	-1787.79
23	-44.17	-79.65	-1831.96
24	-41.60	-78.07	-1873.56
25	-39.09	-76.51	-1912.65
26	-36.63	-74.97	-1949.28
27	-34.21	-73.46	-1983.49
28	-31.84	-71.98	-2015.34
29	-29.52	-70.51	-2044.85
30	-27.23	-69.07	-2072.08
31	-24.97	-67.65	-2097.05
32	-22.75	-66.24	-2119.80
33	-20.56	-64.86	-2140.36
34	-18.39	-63.49	-2158.75
35	-16.24	-62.14	-2174.99
36	-14.12	-60.81	-2189.11
37	-12.02	-59.49	-2201.13
38	-9.93	-58.19	-2211.06
39	-7.85	-56.89	-2218.90
40	-5.78	-55.62	-2224.68

* Cases with inpatient treatment for physical illnesses. Since the severity interactive term SEVMHTV was not significant in regression # 2, the offset is calculated to be the same for those with mild or severe mental health diagnoses.

Exhibit 5.5

Marginal Offset Effect Estimates for Georgia

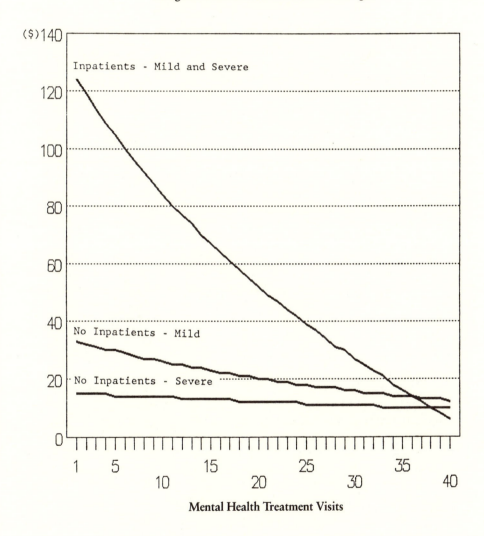

Mental Health Treatment Visits

The average number of mental health treatment visits in our sample for those patients with no inpatient treatment was 17.6, with a breakdown of mild and severe diagnoses of 13.9 and 21.7, respectively. The average Georgian non-inpatient in our sample who was treated exclusively on an ambulatory basis had physical health charges over this two-and-a-half-year period that were cumulatively lower (i.e., offset) by approximately $392 for mild patients and approximately $296 for severe patients as a result of mental health treatments. Those having inpatient physical health treatment, on the other hand, had an average of 16.4 mental health treatments (15.0 for mild and 19.2 for severe) over this period, and experienced cumulative savings amounting to about $1,465 as a result of mental health treatments.

In the aggregate, if similar offset savings were generated per individual treated for a mental disorder throughout the country, the savings would be substantial. More than fifty-six million Americans obtained mental health services in 1980. If each of these individuals experienced the same offset effect (which, as we will discuss, is unlikely), total savings in physical health care services for the entire nation would exceed $20 billion a year.[27] While this sum may seem too large to be plausible, readers should recall that U.S. expenditures on health care goods and services amounted to $237 billion in 1980. Is it unrealistic to think that expenditures might have been around 8 percent higher in the absence of mental health treatment?

It is important to underscore the crude nature of these projections, which are offered only to provide a reference point. These empirical results provide no clues as to their external validity; that is, as to whether the observed offset effect actually does occur in the same magnitude, or even if it exists at all, in the Medicaid populations of other states, or in the population in general. We return to the issue of external validity (i.e., the generalizability of the results) in chapter 6.

Is Mental Health Treatment Cost Effective?

A significant offset effect (as we define it) does exist; that is, there is a reduction in physical health charges attributable to the provision of mental health treatment services to the diagnosed mentally ill. An issue of obvious interest is whether the savings in physical health charges would be enough to completely pay for these mental health treatment visits; that is, is mental health treatment cost-effective?[28]

Since the estimated average offset benefit for those with no inpatient treatment (starting at $33.80 and declining steadily) is less than the average cost of the mental health treatment in this sample ($62.88), this suggests that insurance firms would not offer any mental health services if they were motivated exclusively by the desire to garner offset-generated monetary gains. It is evident that a "total" offset does not exist for those clients with no inpatient treatment; that is, the charges incurred by obtaining the incremental mental health treatment visit more than outweigh any reduction that occurs in physical health care charges, as estimated by Equation #1.

The situation for clients with inpatient treatment for physical illness is quite different. The average offset saving was approximately $91.58 (with 16.4 mental health treatment visits), compared to the average costs of only $62.88, thus yielding a "total" offset for this subgroup. The cost of the mental health treatment visits are more than paid for by the savings in physical health care expenditures.

Given these results, why wouldn't insurance companies rush to increase mental health treatment provisions? Insurance companies never know in advance which patients will require inpatient treatments and which will not. The latter group, recall, did not exhibit a total offset. Firms must weigh the risk of liberalizing mental health benefits for the entire group, hoping that the offset generated by inpatients will cover the losses incurred by non-inpatients. Firms deciding on general policy, therefore, may not anticipate or wish to risk there being a total offset for the entire group of current or potential subscribers.

In our sample population, there indeed is not a total offset for the entire group, as shown in exhibit 5.6. While the 203 clients with inpatient treatments had a net reduction in total health care expenditures (physical plus mental) by an average of $473, the 208 clients without inpatient treatment had a weighted average net increase in health expenditures of $763 per person. For the entire sample of 411 cases, the weighted average results in a net increase in total health care expenditures of around $153 per person. In other words, mental health treatment visits cost $153 more on average than the benefits generated by the offset effect in lowered physical health charges.[29]

Abstracting from legal mandates and marketing strategies, these considerations may mean that medical insurers will only provide mental health coverage if premiums can be and are raised to pay for this service, since overall medical care utilization (mental plus physical) may rise. With a rising standard of living, many individuals find that indeed their desire (willingness and ability) to purchase mental health services rises disproportionately faster than their rise in income.[30] In chapter 7 we return to this issue by arguing that there are indeed other salient points to be raised in favor of mental health treatment over and above any offset benefits.

When Is the Offset Exhausted?

The offset diminishes with more mental health treatment visits. Is it ever completely exhausted (or reversed)? For those with no inpatient treatment, the answer is no; eventually it asymptotically approaches zero. For those with inpatient visits, we find that eventually the offset does become zero; taking the first derivative of physical health charges with respect to MHTV in equation #2 and setting the result equal to zero yields a value of forty-two visits. This is the number of treatment visits which maximizes the offset effect; expanding

Exhibit 5.6

Estimated Changes
in Health Care Expenditures

	N	Ave. MHTVs	Per Person Estimated Changes in Health Care Expenditures		
			Physical ($)	Mental ($)	Net ($)
No Inpatient Treatment					
Mild Diagnosis	109	14	-392	+868	+476
Severe Diagnosis	99	22	-296	+1364	+1068
No Inpatient Treatment	208	18	(Weighted Average)		+763
Inpatient Treatment	203	16	-1465	+992	-473
Overall	411	17	(Weighted Average)		+153

the number of visits beyond this level actually results in an increase in physical health care charges.[31]

As discussed earlier, there are several possible theories to explain ultimately rising health charges. One is that a very large number of mental health treatment visits, such as might occur for long-term personality reconstruction, is not conducive to an offset effect.[32] Or, mental health treatments beyond some point act to break down real and perceived barriers and resistance to access and utilization, thereby increasing all types of utilization—including that of physical health care.

Analysis of Other Independent Variables.

The other independent variables' results in equations #1 and #2 contain no surprises, and generally support the predictions of the model. There is a strong (and statistically significant) relationship between the number of different providers the individual visits following the mental health intervention (NPRO3−12) and the level of general health service charges he/she incurs. Having controlled for health status (specifically, Q3−12NDX, the number of different diagnoses the individual had during this same time period), this finding suggests that persons with relatively low levels of continuity of care will have significantly greater levels of utilization, thereby raising physical health care expenditures (as was hypothesized). NPRONDX, the interactive term of providers and diagnoses, was statistically significant as well.

Although the number of different diagnoses prior to mental health intervention diagnoses, NPREDX, is not statistically significant, the pre-mental health intervention level of the log of physical health service charges, LPREGHSU, is significant for those with no inpatient treatment. As noted in the specification section, since the Medicaid population is relatively homogenous in terms of income and insurance coverage, LPREGHSU is primarily capturing variability due to access (differential travel and waiting time costs), the severity of the physical ailment, and—probably most importantly—individual proclivity to use medical care. We find that for every 10 percent increase in the pre-intervention level of physical health charges, there is a 2.0 percent increase in the post-mental health intervention level of physical health charges. Not surprisingly, the variable Q312DAYG is also significant, demonstrating that inpatient length of stay is a determining factor in physical health care expenditures.

None of the age variables except AGE4 proved to be statistically significant.[33] From AGE1, AGE2, and AGE3's insignificance, it may be inferred that the general health service utilization behavior of individuals aged 18 to 64 does not vary systematically from that of those less than 18, holding other factors constant. The relationship between AGE4 and net general health service charges mapped out by the remaining age variables is a direct one. These findings are only partially consistent with the age-related hypotheses noted in the specification section.

The other independent variables GENDER, RACE, and SEVERE have estimated coefficients which are not significantly different from zero.

Comparison with the Control Group

In the best of all worlds, one would like to compare the changes in physical
health charges of our study group (which received treatment for mental illness) against changes in physical health charges of a control group, made up
of the mentally ill who did not receive mental health treatment, though suffering from mental illness. In addition, one would randomly select which mentally ill individuals received treatment and which did not. Our data sets, obviously, do not come close to approaching this ideal. For one thing, our
patients self-selected to receive treatment for physical as well as mental illness;
and the withholding of treatment from those in need is clearly not desirable or
possible.

We do, however, have baseline data on the physical health charges of a random sample of Medicaid patients in Georgia who did not receive mental
health treatments over the period 1980–82. We adjusted these expenditures
to control for inflation as we did with the study group, and then calculated a
trend line based on quarterly charges. We found a statistically significant upward trend in charges over this period, of approximately $3.50 per quarter.[34]

There are a variety of explanations for such an upward trend. Most importantly, as we will discuss in chapter 6, there were a number of institutional
changes which positively affected access to treatment over this period. In addition, attitudes about care might have changed; during this period the national economy went in and out of a recession and back into a steep recession,
leading to fluctuations in unemployment rates which might be expected to influence the need for, and decision to seek, care.[35] Finally, this trend might simply be the result of poorly measured variables.[36]

How might this secular upward trend in physical health charges be affecting
our estimate of the offset? While the quarterly charges for the control group
were rising over this period, the quarterly charges for those in the study group
were falling from the third quarter on—that is, we experienced an offset as
the result of mental health treatment. If our study group was similarly experiencing an upward trend in access and utilization, however, then the physical
health charges for the study are higher than they would have been in the absence of this trend. In other words, if access and utilization rate considerations
were held constant, physical health charges for the study group would be falling even more, on a quarterly basis, than our data show them to be.

In order to calculate how this would affect the offset, we de-trended physical health charges in the study group on a quarterly basis using the trend estimate obtained from the control group. Then we reestimated the offset
regressions and found that the offset parameters MHTV and MHTVSQ were
statistically significant and larger in absolute value than before:[37]

| | New Estimate | |
	No Inpatient	Inpatient
Coefficient of MHTV:	− 3.978*	− 2.143*
	(2.18)	(1.94)
Coefficient of MHTVSQ:	0.045*	0.028*
	(1.86)	(1.78)

While the offset parameters are slightly larger (in absolute value) in the new estimate, they must be multiplied times the (now smaller) total physical health charges to calculate the offset savings. Consequently, the offset calculation has remained about the same. Thus while the rate of savings in physical health charges has increased, the total physical health charges have diminished; hence the dollar value of the savings is approximately the same.

The control group analysis, while hampered by the factors outlined above, thus serves as an additional means by which our offset findings may be verified via a sensitivity analysis.

CONCLUSION

This empirical chapter has been intended as a preliminary foray into a research area in which multiple regression analysis—explicitly controlling for confounding variables—has been relatively rare to date. The dearth of multivariate analyses of the offset may be due to the data problems typically confronting offset researchers. The data set used here, while similarly limited, can provide insights into the medical offset issue.

Our results indicate that a statistically significant offset effect does exist for this sample of Georgians continuously enrolled in the Medicaid program over the 1980–82 period. Significant differences were found between those patients having no inpatient treatment for physical illnesses and those having such treatment. Mental health treatment visits significantly lowered physical health charges in the former group by an average of $392 for patients diagnosed as having "mild" disorders, and by $296 for those diagnosed as having "severe" disorders. For the second group—which did have inpatient treatments for physical illness—not only was an offset apparent, but it also resulted in a "total" offset. The average savings of $1,465 in physical health care expenses over the two-and-a-half-year period more than compensated for the cost of providing the mental health treatment visits.

This offset, however, was not enough to recover the full cost of the mental health treatment visits provided for those who had no inpatient treatment. Thus mental health treatment, while fulfilling an important role in improving the quality of life for those suffering from mental illness, did not reduce overall expenditures for health care services (physical plus mental) in this group; rather, it increased overall expenditures.

These results have important policy implications for the provision and financing of mental health services. Most importantly, the advocacy of increasing mental health service provision and/or its financing must be justified primarily on its own merits rather than on the merits of any total offset, or cost, savings. While an offset exists, it is not an overall total offset; it is not enough to pay for all the mental health treatment provided.

Evaluated from a societal perspective, however, any estimate of the offset would also need to include external benefits, such as the economic benefits derived from a healthier work force (improved productivity, lower turnover, fewer missed days, etc.), and the psychosocial benefits to family members and others affected adversely by the mental illness of a relative, friend, or associate. This fuller picture, however, is not the one viewed by private actors, particularly health insurance companies. It is, however, or should be, the relevant domain of public policymakers (see chapter 7).

An additional policy conundrum is that those most in need of mental health services are the ones who generate the smallest offset effect; other things being equal, it is (overall) more costly to provide the identical mental health services (in terms of number of visits and provider type) to someone with a severe diagnosis than to someone with a mild diagnosis. Taking into account diagnoses thus underscores the intractable conflict between, on the one hand, providing the most appropriate type and level of care to the mentally ill, and, on the other hand, minimizing financial outlays and the risks to so doing. We shall explore the insurance policy implications of our findings in chapter 7.

There are several important qualifications to these preliminary results. The most important is the very limited nature of the data. Since claim files are maintained primarily to monitor expenses, they lack the detailed information (itemized in exhibit 4.4 of chapter 4) that are necessary to more accurately model utilization behavior and to estimate an offset effect. For example, an important piece of information that is lacking is whether these individuals had a history of mental illness preceding the start of the study period, and whether the mental health treatment received covered one "episode" of illness or several. In addition, there are only a few demographic factors which can be used to control for a host of influences. We would like to know, for instance, whether other sources of informal care—for example, church and/or family— were utilized and, if so, how often? These are important areas about which the application of the behavioral model developed in this study to a more complete and detailed data set will have much to tell us.

We return to this issue in the next chapter when we discuss the "external validity" of these findings by juxtaposing results from a Michigan Medicaid population sample population—a state with institutional and population characteristics substantially different from those of the Georgia sample. In addition, we explore other policy-relevant issues relating to the offset.

APPENDIX 5.1: CHECK FOR THE ACCURACY OF THE DATA

Payment and charge data from the state Medicaid management information systems data are sometimes not available at the level of the individual service.

As a result, some data on total charges (data element 010) and/or on the amount paid by Medicaid (data element 013) need not be for only the particular service and claim they are indicated on. They may, for instance, (1) include other additional claims; or (2) they may be included on other claims; or (3) it may not be known/indicated what the amount charged or (Medicaid) paid has covered. Such inconsistencies may result in the systematic over- or understatement of the charges made to, or the Medicaid amount paid for, an individual's medical service claims.

Since the accuracy of the analysis of the medical offset effect is predicated on (among other things) the accuracy of these totals, it is important to assess the possible bias(es) this might introduce into the study. As part of the Tape-to-Tape Project, SysteMetrics has constructed two variables to eliminate ambiguities with respect to the level of expenditures. Both of these variables—the "charge indicator" and "Medicaid paid indicator" variables (data elements 010 and 013, respectively)—were examined, revealing that an overwhelming share of both the total charges and the amounts paid by Medicaid were dollar totals for only the particular claim on which they were recorded. In the case of Georgia, for instance, this was true of 94.5 to 98.5 percent of all claims in the drug and outpatient files of both the study group and the control groups. Those cases in which this was not the case (i.e.,those in which the indicator fields were not coded "1") were excluded from the analysis. This, of course, reduced both the number of claims and the number of individuals contained in the final data set.

Appendix 5.2

Means and Standard Deviations—Georgia

Variable	Mean	Std Dev
LNET3_12	7.794	1.659
MHTV	17.007	17.735
MHTVSQ	603.022	1229.203
PSYCHIAA	3.642	8.274
CMHCALL	9.487	17.186
PSYCHOGA	3.878	7.397
SEVMHTV	8.321	15.825
SEVERE	.401	.491
Q312DAYM	2.978	10.467
Q312DAYG	10.032	24.937
GENDER	.333	.472
AGE	44.148	19.621
RACE	.557	.497
NPRO3_12	4.047	3.102
Q3_12NDX	4.219	3.197
LPREGHSU	6.156	1.482
NPREDX	2.803	1.377
NPRONDX	4.709	1.251

N of Cases = 411

Appendix 5.3

Correlation Matrix—Georgia

	LNET3_12	MHTV	MHTVSQ	PSYCHIAA	CMHCALL	PSYCHOGA	SEVMHTV	SEVERE	Q312DAYM	Q312DAYG	GENDER	AGE	RACE
LNET3_12	1.000	-.020	.027	.235	-.106	-.063	-.052	-.092	.257	.532	-.228	.068	.176
MHTV	-.020	1.000	.919	.306	.829	.130	.634	.172	.142	.025	.133	.026	.054
MHTVSQ	.027	.919	1.000	.240	.833	.001	.585	.128	.093	.045	.108	-.023	.034
PSYCHIAA	.235	.306	.240	1.000	-.100	-.153	.042	-.064	.355	.297	-.065	-.088	-.088
CMHCALL	-.106	.829	.833	-.100	1.000	-.223	.568	.160	.018	-.068	.152	-.039	.103
PSYCHOGA	-.063	.130	.001	-.153	-.223	1.000	.154	.114	-.097	-.114	.038	.251	-.009
SEVMHTV	-.052	.634	.585	.042	.568	.154	1.000	.643	.055	-.058	.104	.073	-.007
SEVERE	-.092	.172	.128	-.064	.160	.114	.643	1.000	.048	-.100	.095	.198	-.079
Q312DAYM	.257	.142	.093	.355	.018	-.097	.055	.048	1.000	.132	-.123	.009	-.036
Q312DAYG	.532	.025	.045	.297	-.068	-.114	-.058	-.100	.132	1.000	-.078	-.070	.123
GENDER	-.228	.133	.108	.065	.152	.038	.104	.095	-.123	-.078	1.000	-.027	.059
AGE	.068	.026	-.023	-.088	-.039	.251	.073	.198	.009	-.070	-.027	1.000	.102
RACE	.176	.054	.034	-.088	.103	-.009	-.007	-.079	-.036	.123	.059	.102	1.000
NPRO3_12	.711	.059	.066	.345	-.063	-.110	-.007	-.063	.313	.699	.145	-.059	-.150
Q3_12NDX	.675	.074	.074	.370	-.053	-.147	-.018	-.098	.323	.706	-.169	-.149	.127
LPREGHSU	.470	.144	.190	.179	.136	-.171	-.001	-.127	.110	.401	-.135	-.113	-.106
NPREDX	.469	.089	.129	.197	.067	-.161	-.032	-.133	.144	.473	-.163	-.110	.070
NPRONDX	.659	.017	.046	.321	.061	-.177	.066	-.135	.244	.490	-.274	.276	.087

Appendix 5.3 (Continued)

	NPRO3_12	Q3_12NDX	LPREGHSU	NPREDX	NPRONDX
LNET3_12	.711	.675	.470	.469	.659
MHTV	.054	.059	.144	.089	.017
MHTVSQ	.066	.074	.190	.129	.046
PSYCHIAA	.345	.370	.179	.197	.321
CMHCALL	-.063	-.053	.136	.067	-.061
PSYCHOGA	-.110	-.147	-.171	-.161	-.177
SEVMHTV	-.007	-.018	-.001	-.032	-.066
SEVERE	-.063	-.098	-.127	-.133	-.135
Q312DAYM	.313	.323	.110	.144	.244
Q312DAYG	.699	.706	.401	.473	.490
GENDER	-.145	-.169	-.135	-.163	-.274
AGE	-.059	-.149	-.113	-.110	-.276
RACE	.150	.127	-.106	.070	.087
NPRO3_12	1.000	.972	.472	.575	.678
Q3_12NDX	.972	1.000	.464	.593	.755
LPREGHSU	.472	.464	1.000	.862	.422
NPREDX	.575	.593	.862	1.000	.524
NPRONDX	.678	.755	.422	.524	1.000

APPENDIX 5.4: REGRESSION DIAGNOSTICS

As discussed in chapter 3's section on evaluating alternative methodological approaches, the adequacy of any particular regression specification requires assessing the extent to which the data and the fitted model conform to the assumptions underlying the regression model. Although the study population will be segmented and analyzed in several different ways in this study, the regression diagnostics presented here will be limited to application of the most general model to the entire study population.

Initially, we should note why we used the logarithm of physical health charges as the dependent variable. The reason for this is that the unadjusted distribution of health service charges (total and net) are highly skewed toward the right—that is, toward high levels of charges. Many individuals use few or no health resources during some time periods, but very large amounts of resources in other time periods. Untreated, this skewness violates the ordinary least squares (OLS) assumption that the residuals are normally distributed. Although the F tests used in regression hypothesis testing are generally relatively insensitive to minor and even moderate departures from normality, the precision of the estimated parameters will be greater the closer the residuals conform to this assumption.

To correct for this in our regression runs, we took the natural logarithm of net general health care expenditures. The resulting equation is thus in semi-log form, since the MHTV variable was not transformed by the logarithm. A normal plot of the residuals of the log transformation of net general health care charges shows clearly how this transformation has nearly eliminated the undesired skewness. A histogram of the standardized residuals and a plot of the normal curve reveal that, with the exception of some clustering toward the center, the residuals are (now) approximately normally distributed.

Another important assumption underlying the regression model is that the residuals are homoscedastic, that is, of equal variance. The scatterplot of the studentized residuals, plotted against the predicted values of Q3–12NET, suggests that the residuals conform reasonably well to this assumption.

In light of the fact that the quadratic and simple linear MHTV terms are highly collinear (from Appendix 5.3, rho = .919), this is encouraging; despite having introduced multicollinearity into the original linear equation via the inclusion of the MHTVSQ term, the behavior of all of the other variables—in terms of the signs of their coefficients, their sizes, and their levels of significance—are nearly identical in the two equations.

This model—being relatively insensitive to minor changes in specification—is what is termed "robust." Robustness—while obviously a relative issue (i.e., a matter of degrees)—is clearly a desirable property. The more robust a model, the greater confidence the analyst may have in the model's ability to accurately represent or portray the particular complex, real-world behavioral phenomenon being studied. Alterations in the specification of the age variable similarly yielded only very minor changes in the estimated equations; for example, excluding those over sixty-four years of age—or excluding those under eighteen years of age—had no significant effects on the estimated coefficients, again manifesting the robust nature of the basic model.

NOTES

1. This section draws extensively from Margaret O'Brien and John Savich, "Initial Findings from the Medicaid Tape-to-Tape Project: Tennessee and Georgia, 1980," SysteMetrics, Inc., Bethesda Md. (no date).

2. For a fuller discussion of differences likely to exist between a given state's own Medicaid data and its Tape-to-Tape counterpart, and of related issues, consult the six-volume *Administrative Manual for the Tape-to-Tape Files*, SysteMetrics, Inc., Bethesda Md., October 1985.

3. As we mentioned in the introductory chapter, we are excluding these categories to create a more homogeneous study population.

4. Note that this is only a partial equilibrium model, however, since causality also runs in the opposite direction. Mental health treatment visits are also a function of physical health, since physical distress may produce mental distress (particularly in those undergoing a surgical procedure or experiencing the onset of a chronic disease).

5. This process consisted of multiplying the quarter totals by the relative medical care price index component of the consumer price index. In the case of Georgia, the medical care price index used in the adjustment was the one computed by the Department of Labor for Atlanta, Georgia, statewide indices not being readily available. Similarly, for Michigan, the Detroit-specific index was employed. These relative price indices were constructed from information contained in the United States Department of Labor, Bureau of Labor Statistics monthly publication, *CPI Detailed Reports*, various issues, 1980–83.

6. The specialists are psychiatrists, psychologists, and community mental health centers.

7. This is semi-log form, since the dependent variable is in log form, while the independent MHTV variable is not. Analysis of the residuals showed that the log form of the dependent variable more closely conformed to the assumptions of the regression procedure.

8. See the graphical representations of each of these functional forms in chapter 3.

9. It is imperative to note that additional mental health treatments might still be desirable in light of the patient's mental health status. However, it is possible that too many mental health treatments might create a dependency on the provider with spillover dependencies on physical health services as well. In other words, patients become "addicted" to getting treatment (attention) from mental and physical health providers, thereby increasing physical health charges.

10. Empirically, McHugh and his colleagues (1977) have found evidence supportive of the former scenario. They recorded a 72 percent increase in medical encounters among a previously underutilizing population of Mexican-Americans following the establishment of a community mental health center that markedly enhanced access to services. Two other studies (both of which were offset studies) have also uncovered this

positive relationship between mental health treatment visits and the level of general health service utilization.

11. Alternatively, the quadratic might reveal that initially, as the number of MHTVs increases, net physical health charges increase; but that beyond some minimal threshold level of visits (à la Mumford, Schlesinger, and Glass) net medical expenditures fall.

12. For instance, it is generally recognized that women have a higher reported incidence of minor psychiatric disorders—particularly depression—while men have a higher incidence of alcoholism and other drug-related psychiatric disorders (Shapiro et al., 1984; Jenkins, 1985).

13. A large number of studies have found that females are more likely than men to use mental health services (Andersen et al., 1977; Williams, 1979; Russo and Sobel, 1981; Shapiro et al., 1984; and Horgan, 1985).

14. Lantz and her colleagues (1983), however, found that females showed no significantly greater probability of successful treatment outcomes as measured by their levels of functioning.

15. Inclusion of other variables in the regression equation, however, does help to provide insight into which of these competing possibilities is more (or less) likely to be reflected in the estimated coefficient. For instance, if (as in our estimated equation) physical and mental health status are controlled for, GENDER differences in the level of physical health service charges following mental health intervention may be interpreted as representing primarily differences in abilities to obtain and tendencies to seek care (i.e., differences in access to care and utilization of care).

16. "Social alienation" and "fatalism" have been identified as characteristics both of lower socioeconomic classes and, more specifically, Hispanic culture; and they have been shown to contribute both directly and indirectly to higher distress levels, that is, to more mental illness (Ross and Duff, 1982a; Sharp et al., 1983).

17. Williams et al. (1979) reported that whites have a much higher level of mental health service use than non-whites.

18. Aday and Andersen (1984) have shown that non-whites (blacks and Hispanics) have significantly less access to general health services than whites.

19. As discussed in detail in chapters 2 and 3, the mentally ill have been found to make relatively greater use of general health services than the population in general.

20. Those classified as MILD were those whose initial quarter 3 mental health diagnosis was "neurosis," "special symptom," "transient, situational," or "personality disorder." Those classified as SEVERE were those whose initial quarter 3 mental health diagnosis was "psychosis," "organic brain disorder," or "schizophrenia."

21. See Muller, 1978: 539.

22. The F-value was calculated to be 5.83, with degrees of freedom 17, 379. The critical F-value is approximately 1.67. For further discussion of the Chow Test, see Maddala, 1977: 200.

23. Recall that the semi-log linear regression, by itself, allows for a diminishing offset effect.

24. In semi-log form, the calculus is:

$$\ln NET = B_1 MHTV + B_2 MHTV^2$$
$$d(\ln NET)/d(MHTV) = B_1 + 2B_2 MHTV$$

Since $d(\ln NET)/d(NET) = 1/NET$, therefore $d(\ln NET) = (1/NET)d(NET)$... Thus, by substitution,

$$d(NET)/d(MHTV) = [B_1 + 2B_2 MHTV]NET$$

25. The calculation is based on the average values for all independent variables except MHTV, MHTVSQ, and SEVMHTV, which vary according to the number of mental health treatment visits. These calculations assume that mental health treatment visits are not correlated systematically with any of the other independent variables in the regression.

26. Since the severity interactive term, SEVMHTV, was not significant in regression #2, these calculations are done based on the average number of inpatients who had severe and mild diagnoses.

27. This also assumes that the inpatient-outpatient split that we observed in our sample (49 percent with inpatient treatment) is the same as that observed nationally. Our estimates do not include monetary equivalent benefits to these individuals as a result of improved mental health, nor do we account for savings accruing to society as a result of fewer sick days, increased worker productivity, reduced worker turnover, etc., which might occur because of a physically more healthy society (see chapter 7 for a further discussion and estimates of these savings).

28. Standard neoclassical economic theory suggests that (in the short run) a profit-maximizing health insurance company would provide mental health treatment visits up until the point at which the marginal benefit equals the marginal cost of providing the mental health treatment service, assuming that all variable costs are covered in the process. This is the "optimal" number of treatment visits (as compared to the average).

29. Note also that inpatient charges are highly correlated with length of stay (in our sample 0.69). With the greater pressure on hospitals to reduce lengths of stay and overall inpatient charges, inpatient offset benefits would no doubt be substantially smaller in the late 1980s and 1990s than they were in the pre-DRG days of the early 1980s. Another possible reason why insurance companies may not accept the offset findings is that these results, for a specific population at a specific time and place, may not be generalizable to the entire population (an issue discussed at greater length in chapter 6).

30. In the parlance of economists, there is a high income elasticity of demand for mental health services.

31. This is not the optimum number of mental health treatment visits, however, since one must consider also the cost of providing these treatments. As noted earlier, the optimum number of treatments (from a private insurer's point of view) is where the marginal benefit equals marginal cost of these visits.

32. This suggests that the existence of a diminishing effect of the offset (as captured by the MHTVSQ variable) might vary by mental illness diagnosis. A different regression equation (not shown) attempted to measure any changes in the diminishing effect between the two diagnosis groups we developed (mild and severe) by introducing an additional interactive variable which was the square of SEVMHTV. Unfortunately, this produced severe multicollinearity in the regression, thus lowering t-values and yielding a statistically significant regression but insignificant coefficients. It was thus not possible to separate out these different elements without creating insurmountable methodological problems.

33. The AGE variable is broken into five categories with four corresponding dummy variables, 0–17 years (the reference group), 18–24 (AGE1), 25–44 (AGE2), 45–64 (AGE3), and 65 or older (AGE4). The five AGE dummy variable groups seek to determine whether individuals' responses vary systematically by the different age categories.

34. The regression calculation of charges against quarters (Q) yielded:

$$\text{CHARGES} = 159.68 + 3.45Q$$
$$(19.8) \quad (3.15)$$

with $N = 701$, and an adjusted R-squared of .49. T-statistics are shown in parentheses, indicating that both coefficients are statistically significant.

35. Since the individuals in this control group were on Medicaid for this entire period, this implies that they were not in the labor force. Nevertheless, the changes in the macroeconomy may have changed perceptions about the possibility of finding work (the so-called "discouraged worker"), thus leading to less physical activity, lower self-esteem, and perhaps greater physical distress leading to higher physical health charges.

36. If, for example, the true inflation in physical health charges in the sample over 1980–82 exceeds the medical care inflation index for Atlanta used to deflate these charges, then this upward trend could simply be a reflection of unadjusted inflation.

37. The new regression has an adjusted R-squared of 0.56 and a standard error of 1.39. All of the variables which were significant in equation #2 are similarly so in this regression, with the exception that the SEVMHTV interactive term is not significant here.

6

THE MEDICAL OFFSET EFFECT: POLICY CONSIDERATIONS AND IMPLICATIONS

My mind is troubled, like a fountain stirr'd;
And I myself see not the bottom of it.
— William Shakespeare, *Troilus and Cressida*

In this chapter we further explore several policy-relevant issues related to the offset. Specifically, we examine whether a "peaking" phenomenon exists, whether there is a "threshold" of required mental health treatment visits which must be crossed before an offset effect is realized, and whether the offset differs according to mental health provider types; and we investigate whether the offset findings for Georgia have external validity, by comparing them to results from the Michigan Medicaid sample population.

TIME FRAME OF ANALYSIS AND THE "PEAKING" PHENOMENON

A series of major and still-unresolved questions that pervade the offset research literature involves the appropriate time frame within which to measure the offset effect. At what moment in time is the offset-producing impact of the mental health treatment the greatest? Does it die out quickly after its moment of maximum intensity?

Some researchers maintain that the time period in which the first mental health treatment is sought should be eliminated from the analysis to avoid a spurious finding in favor of the offset (which, in fact, would be largely attributable to regression to the mean). This contention is based on what has come to be termed the "peaking phenomenon": most researchers agree that the severity of mental distress peaks just prior to mental health intervention. Patients may return to a lower "normal" level of distress following the peak, with or without the aid of mental health treatment.

Because individuals usually enter psychotherapy (especially for the first time) near the height of their distress, the initiation of psychotherapeutic treatment is frequently found to coincide with the onset of falling levels of distress.

Hence, the therapy might be credited with ameliorating the illness when in fact it is due entirely to a return to a typical level of distress, with all its attendant manifestations—including lower, more common levels of general health care utilization. This phenomenon of abnormal behavioral patterns—we are particularly interested in the abnormally high levels of general health care use associated with episodes of abnormally intense distress—generally is referred to as "statistical regression to the mean."

In order to test whether this "peaking" phenomenon—with statistical regression to the mean—is biasing the results in favor of finding an offset, we excluded quarter 3 from the regression. As can be seen in exhibit 6.1, regressions #3-A and #3-B, the results with LNET4–12 as the dependent variable are very similar to those of LNET3–12. The coefficients of primary interest MHTV, MHTVSQ are nearly identical compared to the initial results presented in chapter 5, indicating that the offset effect is insensitive to this change in the time domain.[1] Consequently, it may be inferred that the offset effect is generated overwhelmingly in the periods after quarter 3, and that the "peaking" phenomenon is not biasing the results in favor of finding the offset.

Recall, it was our concern about the possibility of the peaking phenomenon biasing our empirical estimates in favor of finding an offset effect which prompted us to include the individual's pre-mental health treatment intervention level of general health care utilization in the regression model. That technique, coupled with the finding that most of the offset is produced after quarter 3, makes us confident that the peaking phenomenon has not tainted our finding of an offset effect.

THE THRESHOLD EFFECT ISSUE

Emily Mumford and her colleagues (1984) maintain that there is a minimum threshold of mental health treatment visits which must be crossed before a medical offset effect is generated. They have empirically—as distinguished from theoretically—identified seven treatments as the minimally required dose to achieve an offset response.

To test for this relationship, the Georgia study group was segmented into (1) those with fewer than seven mental health treatment visits, and (2) those with at least seven visits (see regressions #4 and #5 in exhibit 6.1). The sample with less than seven treatment visits did not produce a statistically significant offset effect, lending support to the threshold theory. However, no offset was found in the group with seven or more mental health treatment visits either; clearly some other factors are at work. It is likely that, within these population segments, the functional form of the relationship between mental health treatment and general health care utilization is different from what it is when they are aggregated. However, neither semi-log linear nor semi-log quadratic specifications proved successful in uncovering what that different

Exhibit 6.1

Multiple Regression Results Continued (Georgia)

Regression	MHTV/100	MHTVSQ/100	SEVMHT/100	N	R^2
#3 LNET4-12					
A NO INPATIENT	-2.468*	0.022	1.320	208	.65
B INPATIENT	-2.369***	0.027*	-0.864	203	.67
#4 MHTV >= 7					
A NO INPATIENT	.0.379	-0.006	-0.915	129	.65
B INPATIENT	-0.846	0.010	-0.039	121	.70
#5 MHTV < 7					
A NO INPATIENT	16.292	-2.487	-2.658	79	.72
B INPATIENT	10.217	-1.938	-1.199	82	.74
#6 MHTV >= 3					
A NO INPATIENT	-2.114*	0.017	1.708*	175	.65
B INPATIENT	-1.899***	0.022*	-0.172	162	.72

Exhibit 6.1 (Continued)

#7 PROVIDERS	CMHC	CMSQ	PSY	PSYSQ	MD	MDSQ	N	R^2
A NO INP	-3.905**	0.04**	-2.72	0.10	-0.45	0.03	208	.66
B INPAT	-1.398	0.023	-1.70	-0.01	-3.19**	0.04*	203	.71

#8 RECIPROCAL FORM	RECIPMHT/100	N	R^2
A NO INPATIENTS	0.005*	208	.63
B INPATIENTS	0.003*	203	.70

#9 LOG FORM	LMHTV/100	N	R^2
A NO INPATIENTS	-0.192**	208	.64
B INPATIENTS	-0.101*	203	.70

Note: *Significant at the 5% level
      **Significant at the 1% level

functional form might be (only the quadratic specifications are shown in exhibit 6.1).

Let us summarize our findings to this point. The results suggest that for the Georgia sample, a threshold may exist, but our data do not help to more definitively prove or disprove its existence. This issue of a dose-response relationship and the appropriate number of mental health visits is an exceedingly contentious one for mental health care providers, health insurance companies, and public policymakers, and is a topic that we shall return to in the next chapter.

DISAGGREGATING THE OFFSET EFFECT BY PROVIDER TYPES

Are there differences in the size of the offset effect produced by different mental health providers? Addressing this issue requires disaggregating the mental health treatment variable.[2]

Exhibit 6.2 presents a detailed look at the utilization of the three mental health specialists frequented by the study population. Over the ten quarters studied, there were 6,990 visits to mental health care providers, the vast majority of which were to community mental health centers. Row 1 contains summary data on visits to psychiatrists, row 2 contains such data for psychologists, and row 3 contains such data for community mental health centers. For instance, in column I of the first row it may be seen that 1,497 visits were made to psychiatrists. Column II of row 1 shows that the 194 persons who had at least one visit to a psychiatrist had 17.5 mental health visits on average, independent of the specialist seen. Of these 17.5 visits, 7.7 were to a psychiatrist, 1.8 were to a psychologist, and 8.0 were to a community mental health center. Column III specifies that out of these 194 persons, 119 individuals used a psychiatrist on a "regular" basis—defined here as the provider seen most frequently.

Of those who regularly visited a psychiatrist, the average number of visits to a psychiatrist was 10.6, the average number of visits to a psychologist was 0.6, and the average number of visits to a community mental health center was 0.8. Finally, column IV isolates those individuals who used a psychiatrist exclusively. From column IV of row 1, we see that 89 individuals received mental health treatment from only a psychiatrist, and on average had 9.5 visits.

From examining exhibit 6.2, it is readily apparent that community mental health centers provided most of the mental health services to the study population—over half of the total. The average number of visits to a community mental health center by those with at least one was twenty-two visits, roughly three times the corresponding level for psychiatrists and psychologists alike.

It may also be seen from exhibit 6.2 that about two-thirds of all individuals in the study group obtain their mental health treatment exclusively from one provider type. Of these 279 persons, 32 percent turned to psychologists, 42

Exhibit 6.2

Mental Health Service Utilization
by Provider Type

MENTAL HEALTH PROVIDER/ TYPE	I. TOTAL NO. OF VISITS (%)	II. PERSONS WITH AT LEAST ONE VISIT TO:					III. PERSONS WHO REGULARLY GO TO THIS PROVIDER TYPE:					IV. PERSONS WHO RECEIVE THEIR MENTAL HEALTH TREATMENT EXCLUSIVELY FROM THIS PROVIDER TYPE	
		NUMBER OF PERSONS	MEAN UTILIZATION (STAN.DEV.)				NUMBER OF PERSONS	MEAN UTILIZATION (STAN.DEV.)				NUMBER OF PERSONS	MEAN UTILIZATION (STAN.DEV.)
			TOTAL	PSYCHIA	PSYCHO	CMHC		TOTAL	PSYCHIA	PSYCHO	CMHC		
(1)Psychiatrist	1,497 (21.4%)	194	17.5 (18.6)	7.7 (10.7)	1.8 (5.1)	8.0 (16.4)	119	11.9 (13.4)	10.6 (12.4)	0.6 (2.2)	0.8 (2.4)	89	9.5 (12.7)
(2)Psychologist	1,594 (22.8%)	190	12.9 (12.5)	1.7 (5.8)	8.4 (9.0)	2.8 (7.5)	146	10.3 (10.4)	0.3 (0.7)	9.6 (9.6)	0.4 (2.0)	118	9.1 (9.6)
(3)CMHC	3,899 (55.8%)	174	26.3 (20.3)	2.3 (4.9)	1.6 (4.5)	22.4 (20.2)	174	28.9 (21.1)	1.37 (3.5)	0.8 (2.6)	26.7 (20.2)	72	27.9 (20.7)
TOTALS	6,990 (100%)											279	

percent to psychiatrists, and 26 percent to community mental health centers. Persons who had at least one treatment at a community mental health center were far more likely to have had some treatment from at least one other specialist/facility type. At the other extreme, the clientele of psychologists were the most likely to obtain all of their care from a psychologist. Finally, it is readily apparent that all users of community health centers had a significantly higher number of mental health treatments than those using psychiatrists or psychologists exclusively.

How might these differences be explained? The available data set does not provide many tools by which to address this question. No information is available, for instance, about the preferred modality, treatment approach, case load, or the relative accessibility of each provider type to this Medicaid population. We were able to compare the characteristics of patients seeing the different provider types, however, which yielded some interesting findings. First, as noted earlier, we categorized patient diagnoses as either MILD or SEVERE.[3] Using two-tailed t-tests, it was found that, at a 95 percent significance level, the diagnoses of patients visiting the three provider types did not differ significantly from the sample as a whole.[4]

While no consistent differences in mental health diagnoses existed between patients visiting different providers, differences were detected on the basis of physical health. Those patients who had received at least one treatment, or exclusive treatment, from a psychiatrist had a significantly higher number of different diagnoses both before and after the mental health intervention (NPREDX and Q3–12NDX, respectively), while those who had visited psychologists had significantly lower numbers of diagnoses both before and after intervention.

In addition, clients seeing psychiatrists, both occasionally as well as exclusively, had a significantly higher level of fragmentation in the provision of services, as measured by the number of providers (NPRO3–12). In part, this may be attributable to the significantly greater number of different health problems (i.e., diagnoses) which psychiatrist-users have, relative to the rest of the study population. As a consequence, it is not surprising that these same patients had significantly higher levels of physical health care utilization in quarters 3 to 12 (LNET3–12)—almost $800 more on average for those who saw a psychiatrist at least once.

Individuals who sought care from psychiatrists were the least healthy physically.[5] In light of the fact that psychiatrists are the only provider type capable of treating both physical and mental illness (they are medical doctors), this finding is not surprising. While the data set contains no information on specific treatment modalities, we do know that by virtue of training, medical practice, and law, psychiatrists have a wider assortment of treatment methods at their disposal than other providers; specifically, the ability to prescribe psychotropic drugs. In addition, because of their medical training, psychiatrists are more likely to be more knowledgeable about physical health conditions and the mental-physical health/illness nexus. Thus, they may have a greater proclivity to employ different treatment methods relative to other providers who are trained only in clinical psychology.

These results suggest that, at least for this study group, psychiatrists are relatively less likely to generate a medical offset effect; clientele such as theirs may be expected to have and to maintain relatively high levels of general health care utilization. And, even more importantly for the offset, the dynamics of changing health status of these persons do not auger well. Still, there are other considerations to take into account, and, reconciled with those mentioned here before, a final accounting can be made.

Further analysis of the t-tests performed on the different clientele of different provider types reveals that the patients of psychiatrists were, on average, more likely to be female, and were, on average, younger than the rest of the population. Patients of psychologists also tended to be younger on average than the rest of the sample, and had significantly better health status (as measured by diagnoses and lower physical health charges prior to intervention). Patients of community mental health centers, in contrast, were more likely to be male, and had physical health treatment charges which statistically were not significantly different from the rest of the group prior to intervention. After the initial intervention, however, in quarters 3–12, these charges were smaller on average than charges for patients who saw psychiatrists and psychologists exclusively.

With an understanding of differences in provider clientele, we are now in a better position to interpret the findings of the next regression, which disaggregates mental health treatment visits by psychologists (PSY), psychiatrists (MD), and community mental health centers (CMH). As shown in equations #7-A and #7-B in exhibit 6.1, both the semi-log linear and quadratic terms for the provider types were specified (CMSQ for community mental health centers, MDSQ for psychiatrists, and PSYSQ for psychologists); and again the time period analyzed is the entire two-and-one-half-year post-intervention period.

The results for those with no inpatient physical health treatment indicate that only community mental health centers show a significant offset effect. The estimated coefficients of both the semi-log linear and quadratic terms are of the expected signs, and the magnitude of the community mental health centers' coefficient is similar to the aggregated mental health treatment visits' coefficients estimated in chapter 5. The estimated parameters for other independent variables are also very similar, again providing evidence of the robust nature of the basic model. The patients of psychiatrists and psychologists show no statistically significant offset effect for this subset with no inpatient physical health treatment.

A possible explanation as to why the patients of psychiatrists do not exhibit a significant offset is that the very nature of their treatment (which may include and in fact emphasize use of psychotropic drugs) may reduce psychological stress but may not lead to reduced physical health charges—due to side effects of these drugs and/or the fact that the drugs are generally not curing the mental illness. This factor is likely to be compounded by patient severity/patient responsiveness considerations; in multiprovider settings often psychiatrists are viewed as the "pill pushers," "on the periphery as pharmacologic experts, treating only the most severely mentally ill who do not respond to the ministrations of non-medical mental health professionals" (Beigel, 1984: 1116).

For those who have experienced inpatient treatment for physical illness, however, the story is very different (regression #7-B). In this subset of the study population, it is the psychiatrists who generate an offset effect, while community mental health centers and psychologists show no offset. These results confirm what we might expect; that the more severely physically ill who also have a mental health problem systematically select (or their referring physicians select) psychiatrists as providers.[6]

OTHER FUNCTIONAL FORMS

Researchers may be curious as to how the estimate of the offset might be affected by using functional forms other than the semi-log linear and quadratic specifications. The two other functional forms that we considered were the reciprocal (1/MHTV) and the logarithmic (natural log of MHTV). Each of these forms also allows for a diminishing offset effect. We ran these regressions (the offset coefficients are reported in #8 and #9 in exhibit 6.1), and found that both of these specifications also identified an offset effect. The coefficients of the reciprocal and log forms were statistically significant and of the expected signs. The other independent variables were very similar in sign and size, relative to our basic equation of chapter 5, thereby demonstrating the robust nature of the estimates. Because the semi-log quadratic specification of chapter 5 conforms more closely both to the assumptions of our theoretical behavioral model and to those of the regression model, we selected it as the main equation—the one upon which we have based the bulk of our discussion.

THE MICHIGAN MEDICAL OFFSET FINDINGS

We have analyzed Georgia Medicaid data and found that a significant offset effect exists. Do these findings have external validity? That is, can they be generalized to Medicaid populations of other states, or, more broadly, to the general population? Conversely, to what extent are these results likely to be the product of a unique set of conditions and circumstances?

Intuitively, it would seem as though the presumption (the null hypothesis) should be that offset findings as a rule do not have great external validity. There is often, after all, great variability across states in terms of a number of characteristics which have been shown to affect whether or not there is a medical offset effect: states have their own distinct Medicaid programs (in terms of eligibility, benefit levels, and types of providers covered); they have different absolute and relative supplies of mental health providers, different institutional settings, and varying cultural attitudes about mental illness and its treatment—all of which are likely to be reflected in public and private policies, as well as individuals' behavior patterns as they relate to the offset effect.

In this section we analyze a Michigan Medicaid population during the (same) three-year period, 1980–82, and juxtapose the results with those from Georgia to investigate whether a similar offset exists in this very different state. Before proceeding to the analysis, it is useful to identify some of the characteristics that distinguish the Michigan Medicaid study sample from its Georgia counterpart.

DIFFERENCES BETWEEN THE GEORGIA AND MICHIGAN SAMPLES

Our Michigan sample was drawn in an identical manner as the Georgia population sample, and yielded a group of 331 cases.[7] Demographic characteristics of the Michigan sample group are displayed in exhibit 6.3, and that of the Georgia sample group in exhibit 6.4.

The most striking differences between these two populations is in inpatient mental health treatment. Throughout the study period, the Georgia Medicaid program did not provide inpatient mental health treatment coverage (SysteMetrics, 1985: VII–26) hence, all inpatient care provided was physical health care in nature. In Michigan, by contrast, 15 percent of the study population has at least one day of mental health inpatient care, and on average had 5.3 days of inpatient mental health care over the two-and-one-half-year time period we are considering.

Georgians were far more likely to utilize inpatient physical health care services. Forty-nine percent of Georgians had at least one inpatient day for general health care in sharp contrast to 17 percent for all Michiganders. Furthermore, in contrast to the Michigan average of 7.0 days for physical health inpatient care, Georgians averaged 15.4.

The two states' study populations vary by demographic characteristics as well. The Georgia group has a slightly lower percentage of females than males (67 percent to 70 percent). As with Michigan, females had higher physical health charges over the twelve quarters than did men; however, in Georgia, whites (especially white women) had higher average charges for physical health care than did non-whites. Mental health charges, as well as the number of visits, for patients under eighteen years of age and those over sixty-four years of age were significantly below other groups. This is as expected given the evidence about the age-distribution of mental illness.

In order to determine if the sample populations of Georgia and Michigan are significantly different from each other, two-tailed t-tests were performed

Exhibit 6.3

Michigan—Sample Population Characteristics

	N (%)	MEAN AGE (s.d.)	MEAN MHTV (s.d.)	PHYSICAL HEALTH CHARGES (Constant $ of 1980)			MENTAL HEALTH CHARGES (1980$)	TOTAL HEALTH CARE CHARGES (1980$)
				MEAN Q1-2 (s.d.)	MEAN Q3-12 (s.d.)	MEAN Q1-12 (s.d.)	MEAN Q3-12 (s.d.)	MEAN Q1-12 (s.d.)
OVERALL	331 (.)	32.2 (14.6)	6.1 (6.9)	1,250 (2,953)	6,393 (9,330)	7,643 (10,707)	1,964 (10,986)	9,608 (16,019)
MALE	99 (30)	26.5 (15.1)	6.4 (7.5)	1,098 (4,151)	3,926 (4,694)	5,024 (6,958)	3,533 (18,099)	8,557 (21,299)
FEMALE	232 (70)	34.6 (13.7)	6.0 (6.6)	1,315 (2,265)	7,446 (10,550)	8,761 (11,880)	1,295 (5,654)	10,057 (13,171)
WHITE	156 (47)	33.1 (16.6)	5.4 (6.7)	1,135 (3,345)	5,150 (7,951)	6,285 (9,446)	489 (4,303)	6,774 (10,285)
NON-WHITE	175 (53)	31.4 (12.5)	6.7 (7.0)	1,353 (2,559)	7,502 (10,304)	8,854 (11,612)	3,280 (14,448)	12,135 (19,463)
WHITE MALE	47 (14)	25.6 (17.0)	5.0 (6.7)	1,385 (5,500)	2,565 (2,798)	3,950 (6,028)	271 (2,924)	4,222 (7,017)
WHITE FEMALE	109 (33)	36.3 (15.5)	5.6 (6.8)	1,028 (1,771)	6,264 (9,123)	7,292 (10,450)	583 (4,785)	7,874 (11,260)
NON-WHT MALE	52 (16)	27.4 (13.2)	7.7 (8.0)	839 (2,385)	5,155 (5,659)	5,994 (6,991)	6,481 (24,558)	12,475 (28,182)
NON-WHT FMALE	123 (37)	33.0 (11.9)	6.3 (6.4)	1,569 (2,608)	8,494 (11,606)	10,063 (12,919)	1,927 (6,277)	11,991 (14,428)
AGE 0 - 17	48 (15)	9.9 (4.0)	3.3 (3.4)	1,206 (5,451)	4,048 (9,745)	5,254 (11,318)	2,946 (11,936)	8,200 (16,945)
AGE 18 - 24	51 (15)	21.6 (2.0)	6.3 (9.0)	900 (1,318)	5,736 (5,448)	6,636 (5,808)	5,984 (23,316)	12,620 (26,318)
AGE 25 - 44	166 (50)	33.0 (5.5)	6.6 (7.0)	1,133 (1,934)	6,780 (9,444)	7,913 (10,595)	1,143 (4,893)	9,056 (12,255)
AGE 45 - 64	66 (20)	54.6 (5.1)	6.9 (6.3)	1,848 (3,384)	7,635 (10,849)	9,482 (13,037)	211 (3,557)	9,694 (13,107)

Exhibit 6.4

Georgia—Sample Population Characteristics

	N (%)	MEAN AGE (s.d.)	MEAN MHTV (s.d.)	PHYSICAL HEALTH CHARGES (Constant $ of 1980)			MENTAL HEALTH CHARGES (1980$)	TOTAL HEALTH CARE CHARGES (1980$)
				MEAN Q1-2 (s.d.)	MEAN Q3-12 (s.d.)	MEAN Q1-12 (s.d.)	MEAN Q3-12 (s.d.)	MEAN Q1-12 (s.d.)
OVERALL	441	44.2	17.0	1,542	6,928	8,470	1,069	9,540
	(19.6)	(17.7)	(3,444)	(11,800)	(14,019)	(2,167)	(14,444)
MALE	137	43.4	20.3	1,394	4,827	6,220	1,043	7,263
	(33)	(21.9)	(19.5)	(4,219)	(9,602)	(12,416)	(1,870)	(13,017)
FEMALE	274	44.5	15.3	1,616	7,980	9,596	1,081	10,678
	(67)	(18.4)	(16.6)	(2,987)	(12,644)	(14,647)	(2,305)	(15,001)
WHITE	229	45.9	17.9	1,802	8,179	9,981	1,158	11,139
	(56)	(19.9)	(18.0)	(4,093)	(12,889)	(15,483)	(2,514)	(16,017)
NON-WHITE	182	41.9	15.9	1,216	5,356	6,571	956	7,527
	(44)	(19.1)	(17.4)	(2,360)	(10,084)	(11,692)	(1,629)	(11,921)
WHITE MALE	82	44.2	21.7	1,848	5,889	7,737	1,215	8,952
	(20)	(21.8)	(19.2)	(5,319)	(10,542)	(14,437)	(1,875)	(15,366)
WHITE FEMALE	147	46.9	15.8	1,776	9,456	11,232	1,127	12,359
	(36)	(18.8)	(16.9)	(3,234)	(13,899)	(15,947)	(2,814)	(16,293)
NON-WHT MALE	55	42.2	18.4	717	3,242	3,960	786	4,746
	(13)	(22.2)	(19.9)	(1,274)	(7,825)	(8,179)	(1,849)	(7,861)
NON-WHT FMALE	127	41.8	14.9	1,432	6,271	7,702	1,030	8,732
	(31)	(17.7)	(16.2)	(2,673)	(10,819)	(12,784)	(1,526)	(13,146)
AGE 0 - 17	40	10.2	7.8	660	4,004	4,664	575	5,238
	(10)	(4.7)	(8.8)	(920)	(6,623)	(6,789)	(570)	(6,662)
AGE 18 - 24	27	21.7	20.0	2,431	6,621	9,052	1,157	10,209
	(7)	(1.8)	(23.8)	(2,436)	(11,967)	(13,671)	(1,362)	(13,766)
AGE 25 - 44	137	34.0	19.7	2,268	8,969	11,237	1,192	12,429
	(33)	(5.8)	(19.6)	(5,180)	(15,943)	(19,508)	(1,943)	(19,845)
AGE 45 - 64	148	54.7	18.1	1,142	6,790	7,932	1,358	9,290
	(36)	(5.7)	(17.7)	(1,985)	(9,905)	(10,971)	(2,941)	(11,741)
AGE 65 and older	59	74.6	12.9	1,056	4,663	5,714	354	6,068
	(14)	(6.7)	(11.1)	(845)	(2,488)	(3,181)	(667)	(3,417)

on demographic and other characteristics. The results reveal that there are in-deed significant differences. While the sex ratio of both states is similar, the Georgia group has a significantly higher percentage of whites than does Mich-igan. The Georgia sample is also significantly older than the Michigan group, by, on average, twelve years—forty-four as compared with thirty-two.

In terms of their physical health status, Michigan patients had significantly fewer diagnoses prior to mental health intervention (quarters 1 and 2), but significantly more diagnoses and significantly more providers following the in-itial intervention. We surmise that Michigan patients avoid treatment (or have higher search or other barriers to seeking treatment, i.e., less access to care) and, when they finally do enter treatment, their previous neglect has resulted in a multitude of illnesses which require treatment by a variety of providers.[8] Since we control for the number of different diagnoses, a larger number of providers is an indicator of less continuity of care. As we explained in chapter 3, less continuity of care (having a less regular source of care) is expected to result in more expensive—and perhaps lower-quality—care, other things being equal. It is not surprising, therefore, that we find physical health care charges in Michigan in quarters 3 through 12 to be roughly equal to those of Georgians—$6,393 versus $6,928, respectively—despite the fact that Geor-gians had an average number of physical health care inpatient days, more than twice that of Michiganders (15.4 versus 7.0, respectively).

PATTERNS OF MENTAL HEALTH TREATMENT: INTER-STATE VARIATIONS IN NUMBER OF CONTACTS, DURATION, AND CONTINUITY OF CARE

Very different numbers of mental health treatment visits were recorded by patients in Georgia relative to those in Michigan. Georgia patients had an av-erage of seventeen mental health treatment visits in quarters 3 through 12, compared with just six for Michigan patients over the same period. These av-erages (means) are statistically significantly different at the 99 percent confi-dence level.[9]

Furthermore, there were great differences in the duration and continuity of outpatient treatment. (Because of the non-comparability of the two states with regard to Medicaid-covered inpatient care—mental health inpatient care was not being observed in Georgia—Michigan's inpatient care patterns are shown in appendix 6.1.) As indicated in the accompanying exhibits 6.5 and 6.6, most Michigan clients received the majority of their mental health treat-ments in the last two quarters of 1980; for 59 percent of the Michigan sample, these were the only mental health treatments made during the study period (i.e., through 1982). Of those who continued in treatment, 46 percent (i.e., 19 percent of the total sample) returned for visits only in 1981. Another 8 percent of the total sample had interrupted care, or what we might term two episodes of care: they had no mental health treatment visits in 1981, but returned for

Exhibit 6.5

Outpatient Mental Health Treatment Duration and Continuity

--------MICHIGAN--------

At Least One Treatment Visit in Year(s)	N (%)	Mean Mental Health Treatment Visits				Mean Age
		Total	1980*	1981	1982	
1980 only	196 (59)	3.0	3.0	0	0	30
1980 and 1981 only	62 (19)	9.0	5.0	4.0	0	36
1980 and 1982 only	25 (08)	6.9	3.0	0	3.9	31
1980, 1981, and 1982	48 (15)	14.8	3.8	5.9	5.0	38
All Cases	331 (100)	6.1	3.5	1.6	1.0	32

--------GEORGIA--------

N (%)	Mean Mental Health Treatment Visits				Mean Age
	Total	1980*	1981	1982	
97 (24)	2.8	2.8	0	0	40
74 (18)	10.4	5.7	4.7	0	47
21 (06)	9.2	4.6	0	4.7	42
219 (66)	26.3	6.0	10.3	9.6	46
411 (100)	17.0	5.3	6.4	5.3	44

Note: *Last two quarters only.

132

Exhibit 6.6

Outpatient Mental Health Treatment Visits by Year

-------------------MICHIGAN-------------------

Year	Mean	High	Low	S.D.	% Of Sample With NO Visit That Year
1980	3.5	33	1	3.5	0%
1981	1.6	23	0	3.4	67%
1982	1.0	19	0	2.7	78%
1980-82	6.1	42	1	6.9	--

-------------------GEORGIA-------------------

Year	Mean	High	Low	S.D.	% Of Sample With NO Visit That Year
1980	5.3	42	1	5.5	0%
1981	6.4	43	0	7.8	29%
1982	5.3	50	0	8.4	42%
1980-82	17.0	98	1	17.7	--

an average of nearly four visits in 1982. Only 15 percent of the sample received continuous treatment in all three years, with an average of 3.8 visits in 1980, 5.9 visits in 1981, and 5.0 visits in 1982.

Except for the group which received interrupted treatment, mean age rose as treatment was extended from 1980 to 1982. Those who had a single mental health episode (1980 only) were slightly younger than the rest of the sample population, with an average age of thirty years. Those who sought and obtained continued assistance in 1981, on the other hand, were six years older on average, while those who continued in treatment in 1981 and 1982 were eight years older on average. Without further information, which is not available in this data set, it is impossible to refine this analysis; we do not know whether those who received what we refer to as continuous treatment were suffering from a single, prolonged bout of mental illness, or a series of episodes over the three-year period.

The Georgia group, by contrast, exhibited a very different frequency, duration, and continuity of care. As shown in exhibit 6.5, two-thirds of the Georgia sample population received continuous mental health treatment over the years 1980–82, in stark contrast to the 15 percent of the Michigan sample.[10] The Georgia group that received continuous care had 180 percent more visits on average than the Michigan group over the study period: 86 percent more in 1980, 300 percent more in 1981, and 430 percent more in 1982.

These profiles of treatment reveal that variations in the intensity, the duration, and the continuity of mental health care all contribute to the average Georgia patient's ambulatory mental health charges being almost twice those of the average Michigan patient's, $1,069 versus $573. But recall, however, that only Michiganders had inpatient mental health treatment. When inpatient charges are added in, the relative ratios of total (inpatient plus outpatient) mental health charges are reversed. Seventy-one percent of Michigan patients' total mental health care charges per person over this two-and-one-half-year period were comprised of inpatient care. Adding them to the outpatient total boosts the mental health care charges per capita in Michigan to $1,964, compared with (still) $1,069 for the Georgians.

The relatively higher charges in Michigan are also probably attributable in part to higher medical fees in Michigan compared with Georgia. Another partial explanation is that the source of care was different and more expensive in Michigan; the bulk of the Medicaid patients in our sample received ambulatory mental health treatment from hospital outpatient units. Only a very small share received treatment from community mental health centers, which were the provider-type workhorse of the Georgia Medicaid sample population.

THE CHOW TEST FOR AGGREGATION

The results of the t-tests noted above revealed considerable differences in the two states' sample populations in terms of demographic characteristics and treatment regimens. Are the behavioral processes of these two populations so different that they should not be aggregated? We addressed this important question by performing a Chow Test, and found that the coefficients are indeed unstable across these groups.[11] Hence it is inappropriate to aggregate the Michigan and Georgia data files. This finding empirically validates our caveat that offset estimations should be generalized only with great care; offset estimates will necessarily be very dependent on the institutional and cultural milieu and other specific characteristics of the group. In short, the external validity of offset studies cannot and should not be presumed. Accordingly, we analyze the Michigan data independently in the next section, contrasting it with our Georgia findings.

EMPIRICAL FINDINGS FOR THE MICHIGAN SAMPLE

We performed a Chow Test to determine if it would be appropriate to aggregate those with at least one inpatient day (for either mental or physical health care) with those with only outpatient mental health treatment. The test yielded a calculated F statistic of 3.09, which (with a critical F value of 1.83) indicated rejection of the null hypothesis that the estimated coefficients were stable across the two groups. Hence, the groups are sufficiently disparate to require that they be disaggregated in order to enable the estimation of more stable and more precise coefficients, and to better understand these statistically significantly different behavioral processes.

Next, we disaggregated mental health inpatient from general health inpatient care, and performed two more Chow Tests to determine whether either of these inpatient groups could be aggregated with the mental health outpatient-only group. The general health inpatient care Chow Test F statistic was 2.63; the mental health inpatient care calculated F was 2.30 (critical F values were 1.74 with 13/305 degrees of freedom). Thus we could not aggregate individuals with inpatient care—be it mental or physical health inpatient care. Consequently, we had to analyze three subsamples: persons with some general but no mental health inpatient care (n = 57); those with some mental but no general health inpatient care (n = 30)—individuals in both groups had some outpatient care; and those with exclusively ambulatory mental health care (n = 244).[12]

Results for Those Without Any General Health Inpatient Care

Exhibit 6.7 presents the regression results for different subpopulations. Regression diagnostics revealed that the fitted equations conformed reasonably well to the assumptions underlying the technique of ordinary least squares.[13] Adjusted for degrees of freedom, equation #1 explains approximately 70 percent of the variation in physical health charges over quarters 3

Exhibit 6.7

Multiple Regression Results for Michigan

(Absolute Value of t-statistics in parentheses)

Dependent Variable	LNET 3-12		LNET 3-12		LNET 3-12		LNET 3-12	
Independent Variables	Unrestricted MHTV, Q312DAYG=0, Q312DAYM=0 #10		MHTV>3, Q312DAYG=0 and Q312DAYM>0 #11		Q312DAYG>0 and Q312DAYM=0 #12		Q312DAYG>0, Q312DAYM=0 and MHTV>4 #13	
MHTV / 100	-.342	(.235)	-4.228	(1.98)*				
MHTVSQ / 100	.037	(.845)	.118	(2.10)*				
RECIPMT / 100					.027	(.182)	3.369	(1.87)
AGE 1	.226	(8.48)**	.484	(2.10)*	.549	(2.41)*	1.993	(1.83)
AGE 2	.216	(1.97)*	.315	(1.71)	.308	(1.66)	1.819	(1.64)
AGE 3	.393	(3.06)**	.395	(1.99)*	.302	(1.43)	1.963	(1.68)
GENDER	-.066	(.795)	.195	(1.78)	.187	(1.35)	.243	(1.00)
RACE	-.124	(1.69)	-.026	(.262)	-.223	(2.08)*	-.221	(1.12)
LPREGHSU	.035	(2.43)**	.027	(1.44)	-.009	(.256)	-.138	(1.43)
NPRO3-12	.702	(8.48)**	.310	(4.71)**	.209	(4.15)**	.232	(2.41)*
Q3-12NDX	.327	(6.62)**	.458	(11.1)**	-.208	(3.42)**	.336	(3.35)**
NPREDX	-.017	(.361)	.008	(.013)	.104	(1.31)	.229	(1.60)
NPRONDX	-.033	(2.34)**	-.027	(3.64)**	-.036	(4.98)**	-.030	(2.23)*
Q312DAYM / 100			.028	(1.04)				
Q312DAYG / 100					1.551	(6.39)**	.010	(.176)
CONSTANT	4.593	(25.4)**	5.224	(17.3)**	6.70	(18.8)**	4.683	(4.53)**
Adjusted R-Square	.723		.675		.808		.794	
S.E.	.557		.537		.341		.349	
N	244		140		57		29	

* Significant at the 5% level.
** Significant at the 1% level.

S.E.: Standard Error
N: Number of Observations

through 12, and is significant at well beyond the 99.9 percent level of confidence.

As may be seen in regression #10 (which employs a semi-logarithmic, quadratic specification), mental health treatment does not generate an offset effect in the Michigan sample. Although, as anticipated, the coefficient for mental health treatment visits (MHTV) is negative and its quadratic term (MHTVSQ) is positive, neither coefficient is significant. The medical offset effect cannot be said to be different from zero for the portion of the study group which has no inpatient treatment of any kind; that is, no offset exists.[14]

All of the variables which are significant have their predicted signs, including NPRO3–12 (the number of providers in quarters 3 to 12), Q3–12NDX (the number of diagnoses in quarters 3 to 12), and NPRONDX (the interaction term of these two variables). In addition, several demographic variables are significant. The AGE1, AGE2, and AGE3 variables are positive and significant; each of these subgroups has higher net physical health charges than the reference group which is comprised of individuals less than eighteen years of age.

We explored the possibility that a few extreme cases (i.e., outliers) might be distorting the results with regard to an offset. It could be that a small number of individuals with very severe or intractable psychosomatic problems were incurring very large physical health charges and/or receiving very large numbers of mental health treatment visits, and thereby distorting the aggregated relationship. To control for outliers we sublet the subsamples, eliminating those cases which were more than two standard deviations away from the mean in terms of mental health treatment visits or physical health charges. In none of these generated subsets was there a significant offset finding. While this series of regressions did not uncover a significant offset effect, it did demonstrate the robustness of the model, as significant coefficients were very stable over the different subsamples and specifications.

Mental Health Treatment Continuity and Threshold

A substantial proportion of the Michiganders had very few visits; in fact, a quarter of them had but a single visit. In addition, almost 60 percent of the Michigan sample had no treatment beyond the first six months (i.e., they did not have treatment beyond 1980). In Georgia, by contrast, more than 90 percent of the sample had more than one mental health treatment visit, and in excess of 75 percent continued treatment beyond the first six months. These observations led us to hypothesize that if some type of threshold of treatment existed in Michigan, the aggregation of all of the Michiganders (within each subsample) might result in the "masking" or "drowning out" of any offset effect which might have been experienced by those patients who had "enough" visits and/or those who had "adequate" continuity or intensity of care.

To explore this hypothesis, we segmented the entire Michigan sample (n = 331), subletting for further analysis only those persons who had more than a single mental health treatment visit (n = 252). We again performed two Chow Tests to determine if it were possible to aggregate those receiving some mental or physical inpatient care with those receiving exclusively outpatient mental and physical care. Again we found that it was necessary to (continue to) analyze those with some physical health inpatient care separately from the rest of the sample (the calculated Chow Test F statistic was 3.59, with a critical F value of 1.79 and 13/226 degrees of freedom). But it was now possible to aggregate persons with inpatient mental health care with individuals who had had exclusively ambulatory care (the calculated Chow Test F statistic was 1.69).

We then reestimated the basic regression for those with more than one, those with more than two, those with more than three, and those with at least four mental health visits, for (1) those receiving mental health care (regardless of its setting) but no physical inpatient care (what we shall term subsample A), and (2) those with some physical inpatient care and only ambulatory mental health care (what we shall refer to as subsample B).

Persons in subsample A experienced an offset effect if they received more than three ambulatory mental health treatments (equation #11 of exhibit 6.7). For those with more than just a single visit (results not shown), the MHTV coefficient is significant at only the 85 percent confidence level, and MHTVSQ at the 92 percent level. In the more-than-two-visits equation (also not shown), both coefficients decrease slightly in absolute magnitude, while their levels of significance rise to 92 percent and more than 95 percent, respectively. Then, in the more-than-three-visits equation—equation #11 of exhibit 6.7—both MHTV and MHTVSQ's coefficients again decrease slightly in absolute magnitude from the previous equation, and cross the threshold into what is commonly regarded as being "statistically significant"; that is, the null hypothesis of the coefficients being equal to zero is rejected at the 95 percent confidence level. Both coefficients are of the hypothesized signs. The inpatient mental health treatment (Q312DAYM) did not achieve statistical significance in any of the fitted equations.[15]

The MHTV coefficient is about twice the absolute magnitude of its Georgia analog. However, we hasten to add, the dollar estimate of the marginal, average, and cumulative offset effects depend not only on the magnitude of the two estimated coefficients, but also upon the dollar level of net physical health services (see chapter 5 for a detailed discussion). With its larger (in absolute terms) MHTV coefficient—coupled with the higher average treatment costs in Michigan—the Michigan offset, shown in exhibit 6.8, consequently, is quite different: it takes more care to generate (at least three visits are required); is initially larger (the initial visit produces an average offset of $127.09); and it is exhausted earlier (the marginal offset of the eighteenth visit is zero).[16] Furthermore, beyond eighteen visits, mental health treatment of the Michigan Medicaid population actually adds to net physical health care charges. In Georgia, on the other hand, with increasing numbers of treatment

Exhibit 6.8

The Estimated Size of the Offset Effect for Michigan

Subsample of Those with
No Physical Health Inpatient Treatment and MHTV > 3

MHTV	MARGINAL	AVERAGE	CUMULATIVE
1	-127.09	-127.09	-127.09
2	-115.06	-121.08	-242.15
3	-104.00	-115.39	-346.16
4	-93.81	-109.99	-439.96
5	-84.37	-104.87	-524.34
6	-75.61	-99.99	-599.95
7	-67.45	-95.34	-667.40
8	-59.80	-90.90	-727.20
9	-52.61	-86.65	-779.82
10	-45.82	-82.56	-825.63
11	-39.36	-78.64	-864.99
12	-33.19	-74.85	-898.18
13	-27.26	-71.19	-925.44
14	-21.53	-67.64	-946.98
15	-15.95	-64.20	-962.93
16	-10.49	-60.84	-973.41
17	-5.10	-57.56	-978.51
18	0.26	-54.35	-978.25
19	5.61	-51.19	-972.64
20	11.01	-48.08	-961.63
21	16.48	-45.01	-945.14
22	22.08	-41.96	-923.07
23	27.82	-38.92	-895.24
24	33.77	-35.89	-861.47
25	39.97	-32.86	-821.50
26	46.46	-29.81	-775.04
27	53.29	-26.73	-721.76
28	60.52	-23.62	-661.24
29	68.21	-20.45	-593.02
30	76.43	-17.22	-516.59
31	85.25	-13.91	-431.34
32	94.76	-10.52	-336.58
33	105.03	-7.02	-231.55
34	116.18	-3.39	-115.37
35	128.31	0.37	12.94
36	141.55	4.29	154.49
37	156.05	8.39	310.54
38	171.96	12.70	482.51
39	189.47	17.23	671.98
40	208.78	22.02	880.76

visits the marginal effect approached zero, but did so asymptotically, that is, never quite reaching zero.

For this segment of the Michigan sample with more than three visits, the average number of mental health treatment visits was 10.0. Hence, the average cumulative offset effect amounted to approximately $825.63 per capita over the two-and-a-half-year period. In contrast, Georgians' average offset was $903 (this figure is the weighted average—weighted by their respective share of the total Georgia sample population—of the average of each of the three different subsamples for which we estimated an offset).

Results for Those with Some General Health Inpatient Care

Finally, we fitted the basic model to the second Michigan subsample, those with at least one day of physical health inpatient care in quarters 3 through 12. In the unrestricted subsample B (equation #12 of exhibit 6.7), we found no offset. We again explored alternative specifications of the mental health treatment variable, and examined different segments of this subsample. We found that the reciprocal of the number of mental health treatments generally fit the data better than the semi-logarithmic quadratic form. We also found that, as we increasingly restricted the sample to those with some minimal number of mental health visits, the degree of significance of the mental health treatment variable approached an acceptable degree of significance (91 percent), although it never attained the 95 percent level (see equation #13 of exhibit 6.7). The relatively few degrees of freedom characterizing this subsample make it of less general interest.[17]

INSTITUTIONAL AND SUPPLY CONSIDERATIONS

The general patterns of care provided in Georgia and Michigan are very different. Outpatient Medicaid mental health treatment was not utilized very intensively nor very continuously in Michigan during the study period, in comparison with Georgia. The average number of mental health treatment visits over the three-year period in Michigan is a low 6.1. Moreover, a majority of the sample population never returned for follow-up treatment in subsequent years. In part, these differences may be explained by the states' different institutional and mental health industry contexts and their different cultural norms. Exhibit 6.9 presents portraits of the very different mental health provider/facility supply constellations which existed in the two states during this era, and which gave rise to the states' very different utilization and expenditure patterns in the two states during this era.

As may be seen in exhibit 6.9, although Michigan's total mental health care expenditures in 1981 (from all sources, not solely Medicaid) were nearly 70 percent greater than those in Georgia, on a per capita basis they were roughly equivalent (and both exceeded the nationwide average). The composition of those expenditures, however, was very different. Historically, mental health treatment in both states (as throughout the nation) was largely confined to psychiatric care in state psychiatric hospitals. Federal Medicaid law, however, specifically disallowed reimbursement for inpatient mental health care in institutions for mental diseases (to persons between the ages of twenty-two and sixty-four). By 1981, consequently, Michigan had developed a relatively much more diversified mental health treatment infrastructure.[18]

Georgia, meanwhile, lagged behind both Michigan and the rest of the nation in this trend of deinstitutionalization. In 1982, Georgia had a mental health care inpatient bed per 100,000 (civilian population) rate nearly one-quarter greater than that of the nation as a whole, and nearly 40 percent greater than Michigan's. Moreover, two-thirds of its 7,303 beds were (still) in state and county mental hospitals. These institutions, in contrast, accounted for only slightly more than half of all psychiatric beds in Michigan.

For the most part, expenditure patterns in the two states mirrored their different facilities and providers mixes, as shown in exhibit 6.9. In 1981, less than 40 percent of Michigan's total expenditures were made on care provided in state and county mental hospitals, in comparison with Georgia's 56.5 percent. Moreover, a larger proportion of Michigan's total expenditures was made for outpatient (relative to inpatient) care than in Georgia. In Georgia, nearly 80 percent of all expenditures in 1981 were made for inpatient services; in Michigan the proportion was slightly less than 70 percent.

While both the number of beds and the number of inpatient days per 1,000 population in Georgia exceed their Michigan counterpart rates by 40 percent, the number of inpatient episodes per 100,000 population in Georgia is more than 80 percent greater than in Michigan. In addition, the margin by which Georgia's inpatient episode rate exceeds Michigan's varies markedly by type of organization. Georgia's state and county mental hospitals have an inpatient episode rate that is more than three times (336 percent) greater than Michigan's. Even when inpatient episodes at these facility types are standardized by their respective bed-population ratios in each state, Georgia's inpatient episode per bed ratio remains twice that of Michigan.[19]

Given that the occupancy rates of these facilities in both states is roughly equal (their inpatient day–population rates are approximately equal to their number of inpatient bed–population rates), it may be inferred that the average length of stay in Georgia is much shorter than in Michigan. In other words, hospitalization was a much more common component of treatment of the mentally ill in Georgia than it was in Michigan in the early 1980s. We cannot be certain whether this is the result of distinct variations in practice patterns, average utilization rates (specifically a mental health care delivery system characterized by excess demand relative to its capacity), or the incidence of mental illness. Nor can we ascertain whether these variations are a response to the types of resources available or a reflection of the differences in cultural norms (concerning the recognition (definition) of mental illness and/or proclivities to seek care). It is clear, however, that those who are severely mentally

Exhibit 6.9

Mental Health Treatment Characteristics in Georgia, Michigan, and the Nation,
by Type of Mental Health Organization

Type of Organization

A. Expenditures, 1981

	Total	Per Capita	State & County Mental Hospitals	Private Psychiatric Hospitals	Non-Federal Gen. Hosp. Psychiatric Services	Residential Treatment Centers	Free Standing Clinics
					% of Total Expenditures		
Total U.S.	$10,685	$46.94	42.1	10.4	19.0	5.0	14.5
Georgia	287	52.03	56.5	16.0	7.3	0.3	10.2
Michigan	476	51.74	39.7	9.1	20.5	5.7	18.5

B. Inpatient Beds, 1982

                                                                              ---All Other---

	Number	Rate*	Number	Rate	Number	Rate	Number	Rate	Number	Rate
Total U.S.	247,312	108.1	140,140	61.2	19,001	8.3	36,525	16.0	51,636	22.6
Georgia	7,303	131.8	4,810	86.8	1,132	20.4	614	11.1	747	13.5
Michigan	8,726	95.4	4,602	50.3	789	8.6	1,421	15.5	1,914	20.9

C. Inpatient Days and Episodes, 1981

	Days*	Episodes*	Days	Epis.	Days	Epis.	Days	Epis.	Days	Episodes
Total U.S.	338.5	755.7	195.7	219.3	24.5	77.5	47.1	297.3	71.1	161.5
Georgia	411.1	1,159.2	278.0	604.1	64.1	144.8	26.9	233.0	42.1	177.2
Michigan	294.1	640.7	156.6	179.6	27.1	91.9	45.8	266.3	64.6	102.8

Source: *NIMH, Mental Health, U.S., 1985*

* Rate per 100,000 civilian population.

143

ill in Georgia are probably more likely to be admitted to a hospital during the course of their illness.

This suggests several things with regard to our offset finding in Georgia relative to Michigan. First, it lends support (as did the Chow Test) to our hypothesis that the Medicaid sample populations in Georgia and Michigan are markedly different—that in Georgia our sample of outpatients is more likely to be made up of people with fairly mild symptoms, since the more severe cases were treated inpatient. Recall that this is indeed the very type of group in which one is more likely to find an offset, for reasons discussed in chapter 3 and corroborated empirically by results of the study in Georgia (chapter 5). In Michigan, by contrast, the effects of deinstitutionalization were much more pronounced, implying that patients with more severe symptoms or diagnoses were not institutionalized, but were more likely to be treated on an outpatient basis. We conjecture that for a given diagnosis the average Michigan Medicaid beneficiary is more ill than his or her Georgia counterpart.

Second, this suggests that our outpatient Medicaid sample population is probably not representative of the mentally ill in Georgia, implying (of course) that the general offset for the entire Georgia population of mentally ill is likely to be different—a point we have underscored previously when discussing the external validity of offset findings.

These factors, in combination with our findings on the duration and continuity of care, may explain why we observe an offset for the entire Georgia study population, but in Michigan only for a more restrictive group—only for those Michiganders with at least three ambulatory mental health visits. There are other issues that affect this outcome, however.

Despite the rapid outflow of patients from psychiatric hospitals in Michigan, outpatient services were very limited prior to 1983. During the period of this study, 1980–82, limited outpatient services were being provided by psychiatric units of hospitals, while mental health clinics played a negligible part in Medicaid benefit payments. Moreover, outpatients covered under Medicaid were limited to (1) psychiatric testing and (2) five therapy sessions with a physician, *or* ten therapy sessions with a psychiatrist. Even these low limits were not reached on average in Michigan, suggesting that other factors were also at work. Waiting lists, co-payment requirements, and other institutional barriers to access may have acted to limit the number of mental health treatment visits over the study period. For example, long waiting periods for appointments at crowded hospital outpatient departments may have discouraged would-be users.

Since 1983 there has been a dramatic change in Medicaid payments to mental health clinics (including disability) in Michigan, rising from negligible amounts in 1981–82 to $3 million in 1983, and a staggering $24.8 million in 1984. By 1985 this figure had climbed to $27.2 million. Thus there has been a focusing of attention on outpatients receiving treatment from clinics. Private hospital psychiatric units also saw Medicaid payments rise from $2.2 million in 1983 to $4.6 million in 1985.

By comparison, by fiscal year 1980 Georgia's mental health clinic programs received Medicaid benefit payments of $6.3 million (Department of Medical Assistance, State of Georgia, 1983). In addition, Medicaid also paid additional sums to psychologists and psychiatrists (unfortunately separate breakdowns were unavailable). In fiscal year 1981 payments to mental health clinics in Georgia jumped 50 percent to $9.4 million. This, along with rapidly rising Medicaid expenses in all expenditure categories (not only mental health), prompted cost-containment measures to be instituted in November 1981. Among other things, these changes mandated that recipients must be referred by a physician or social service agency, and limited mental health therapy and/ or evaluation and testing to five hours per calendar year per recipient. In addition, physician visits were limited to twelve per year per recipient. At least among the study population, however, average utilization levels were not noticeably affected by this cap.

Our data set, therefore, is not very representative of Georgia's mentally ill. Despite the fact that Georgia continued to rely on institutionalizing the mentally ill to a much greater extent than Michigan (and indeed the nation)—see exhibit 6.9—as we have already noted, throughout the three-year study period, 1980–1982, Georgia's Medicaid program did not cover inpatient mental health care. The bulk of the funding for inpatient care came from other sources (and thus is not contained in our data set). In fiscal year 1981, the State Mental Health Agency of Georgia (which obtains more than three-quarters of its budget from the Georgia state government) spent 91 percent of its budget on state mental hospital programs—the highest proportion of any state mental health agency in the country (IHPP, (8)1984: 2). Hence, it is likely that our Medicaid data cover the less severely ill. In light of the fact that we found the offset to be substantially greater for those with less severe mental diagnoses in Georgia, our estimates would probably overstate the magnitude of the offset if we attempted to extrapolate our findings to the rest of the state's mentally ill population. We can only speculate about how much the offset would be overstated.

EXTERNAL VALIDITY

As has become evident in the course of this analysis, it is essential to be cautious in generalizing these—or any—offset results and their policy implications to all populations and all insurance policies. It has not been shown that these results have external validity beyond the population sample and time period covered. In fact, as we just noted, it is highly probable that even within the state of Georgia these findings are of dubious external validity with regard to the non-Medicaid covered mentally ill. Why is the generalizability of findings likely to be a recurring problem in virtually all offset studies?

It is almost unavoidable that estimates of the offset will differ depending on the study population, the time period, the provider type, the treatment modality, the institutional structure, the provider incentive structure, the insurance coverage, and so on. For example, our study population is very (economically) poor. It is likely that a member of this subgroup of the population would have very different attitudes about following the advice of a mental health specialist (who is probably of a different socioeconomic class) than would a member of a middle-class group. Similarly, rural attitudes about independence, and the availability of traditional and informal care (the church and extended family), are likely to affect receptivity to mental health treatment by a specialist—and, consequently, the offset. These are just two of many possible reasons why estimates of the offset, even supposing that all data and methodological problems have been overcome, would probably continue to show significant differences between different population groups over different time periods of analysis.

Our sample in particular, as we noted earlier, provides information on only a subset of the Medicaid mentally ill in Georgia; it does not include persons diagnosed as suffering from alcohol- or drug-related problems. We narrowed the focus of the analysis to this subset for a very important reason: most data sets (including our own) lack the necessary detail to include a number of important variables which probably influence the offset. Consequently, it is preferable methodologically to exclude (as in our case) alcohol- and drug-related cases to provide a more homogeneous sample. Thus one cannot even be sure that the Medicaid mentally ill in Georgia or Michigan as a whole behave as do those individuals included in our sample.

Another relevant consideration is the welfare dependency status of our study groups in both states. Although to our knowledge no Georgia- or Michigan-specific welfare dependency studies have been conducted, national, multiyear, longitudinal studies have consistently found that about one-half of persons ever dependent on Medicaid are recipients for at most two years (Boskin and Nold, 1975; Harrison, 1979; Coe, 1982). This suggests that our study population, all of whom—in both states—were not only Medicaid recipients in each of the three years 1980-1982, but were continuously enrolled in Medicaid programs throughout those years, are among the most destitute and welfare-dependent of Medicaid recipients. Whether they were so because of mental illness, or whether mental illness was a major causal factor in their welfare status, or whether the relationship between their poverty and mental illness is largely coincidental, are intriguing questions we have no way of addressing.

Since our study groups are somewhat unrepresentative samples of their respective states' Medicaid populations, there is a presumption that our findings have limited generalizability to non-Medicaid populations. There is a modicum of evidence by which to gauge the accuracy of this presumption. Perhaps the most telling of the few relevant studies is the 1986 study of Taube and Rupp. They found that the poor and near-poor with continuous Medicaid coverage had almost double the probability of use of ambulatory mental health care compared with the poor/near-poor not enrolled in Medicaid, although the level of use per user in the two groups was not significantly different.

Coupled with other findings on the demand for mental health care (reviewed in chapter 3)—that the income elasticity of demand is high; that price elasticity is greater for low-income groups; and that, once individuals have received some mental health treatment, there is a tendency for their level of use to increase over time—it is likely that our findings cannot be extended to short-term Medicaid enrollees, and even less so to low-income non-Medicaid populations.

While our discussion has centered on differences between Georgia and Michigan samples, exhibit 6.10 suggests that these two states (regions) might actually be closer in terms of treatment modalities than other regions in the country. Recall also that the Chow Test found that aggregation of data was not appropriate between Georgia and Michigan; thus, the substantial differences found to exist between Georgia and Michigan are probably dwarfed by the even greater differences between Georgia, Michigan, and the rest of the nation.

It must be concluded therefore that the offset effect is largely an idiosyncratic, person-specific phenomenon conditioned by a number of factors—of which only some are amenable to alteration by public or private policies. Consequently, from the strictly private, profit-maximizing economic perspective of an insurance company, mental health insurance policies should be individual- (or experience-) based. Just as it would be foolhardy for an auto insurance company to set national rates based on a sample of claims for one city or state, so too would it be foolhardy for administrators to set insurance policies based on offset findings from just one population group within one state for just one time period. In other words, offset studies must be done on a local and routine basis for different population groups, as the conditions which mold behaviors important to the offset evolve, if they are to provide accurate, detailed policy-relevant findings.

SUMMARY AND CONCLUSIONS

In this chapter we have explored several important policy issues relating to the offset effect. The Michigan finding, that there exists some minimum number of mental health treatment visits necessary to "capture" an offset, creates a dose-response conundrum for policymakers: to capture the savings generated by an offset effect, they must structure benefit packages so as to motivate the mentally ill to seek care, but (at least in the Michigan population) not just a little care—not one, two, or three visits—but more. And, as mental health treatment visits increase, at least between one and six visits, the expenses (both physical and mental) increase.

Exhibit 6.10

Average Number of Outpatient Mental Health Visits per Person
with at Least One Mental Health Visit by Primary Setting
and Region, 1980

| Region Setting | All Settings | Office-Based Setting | | | Organized |
		Psychiatrist	Psychologist	Other	
Northeast	10.5	11.8	18.8	6.6	5.0
North Central	6.0	6.8	7.0	5.1	3.8
South	6.0	8.4	6.2	5.0	3.7
West	10.0	15.9	16.1	4.0	4.6

Source: Adapted from American Psychiatric Association, 1987, page 138.

How many visits should be encouraged? How many should be insured? Clearly, unlimited coverage is not an attractive or viable alternative: the empirical findings suggest that eventually the offset effect (as we define it) is exhausted (or, in the case of Georgia, gets so close to zero that for all intents and purposes it may be considered virtually identical to zero). Moreover, economic theory suggests that private insurers will provide coverage of visits only up to that number where the marginal private benefits equal the marginal private costs. If mental health treatment visits were costless, then a ceiling on the number of insured visits should be set at the point beyond which there are no additional savings in physical health charges. This number—at least for this particular sample of the Georgia Medicaid population—was found to be forty-two visits for those with inpatient treatment for physical health diagnoses; and for Michiganders with no general health inpatient care it was found to be about eighteen visits. But mental health treatments, of course, are not costless, and the maximum number of insured visits should be, and no doubt would be, far lower.

Another confounding issue is how to ensure that the liberalization of benefit packages does not encourage profligacy or attract other not-so-ill persons. Some type of cap on the number of covered visits would seem to be the best possible solution, but it is not clear whether the savings generated by those already receiving some care (i.e., those in our sample) would be offset by new entrants into mental health treatment programs.[20]

Differences between provider types were also identified. Patients of psychologists did not experience an offset effect in any of the different specifications and subsample groups. In contrast, community mental health centers produced a significant offset effect for patients with no inpatient treatment for physical health problems; while psychiatrists produced a significant offset for patients who had experienced some inpatient treatment for physical illness. Greater specificity as to treatment methods and severity of illness would, for example, allow one to distinguish between offset characteristics within a provider type. Moreover, in the case of community mental health centers, we do not even know the type of personnel providing the care. Consequently, the available data do not enable us to answer why we observe these differential effects between the provider types (after controlling for general characteristics and having found that patient diagnoses do not differ significantly between providers).

What factors might account for the very different nature of the results in Michigan compared to Georgia? There are a host of rival hypotheses as to why no offset was found for the entire Michigan sample. Certainly important are: cultural factors giving rise to the illness and its recognition, definition, and attribution (which together affect the decision to seek care); and institutional factors, such as the obstacles to receiving care, and the structure under which the mentally ill received treatment—including its method, setting, duration, intensity, and continuity. These are all factors which we would expect to be important in conditioning the existence and magnitude of an offset effect.

More precisely, our findings suggest that a limited benefit package of mental health treatments, such as existed under the Michigan Medicaid plan in the early 1980s, is not effectual in achieving a medical offset effect in the entire sample group. One reason for this is that, if an offset exists, a threshold of visits appears to be necessary before the offset can be observed; and the small number of mental health treatment visits allowable under Medicaid, as well as other barriers to access which reduce the number of mental health treatment visits, has kept the threshold from being reached in Michigan (for the entire sample group).

When we segmented the sample to those with more than three treatment visits we did indeed find a significant offset effect. As in Georgia, however, this did not produce a "total" offset. Mental health treatment, in and of itself, cannot be justified therefore solely on the basis of reducing physical health charges. This is not meant to imply that the mental health treatment visits provided have been ineffective in reducing mental illness—nor is it meant to imply its corollary, that policy should aim to eliminate such visits. Indeed, the mental health treatment provided may have alleviated many of the symptoms and perhaps some of the causes of mental illness which afflict the Medicaid population.

It is important to note that these observations and conclusions are limited by many of the same methodological issues that have hampered medical economic research in general and offset studies in particular. In addition, it is clear that this analysis can offer only preliminary suggestions as to why an offset is found in Georgia and not in Michigan. Certainly, the duration and continuity of care issues need to be investigated further. A much greater institutional and sociological analysis, beyond the scope of this report, is also needed to identify why we are observing these differences. In addition, an unanswered question is whether the upsurge in the number and type of community-based mental health clinics used by the Medicaid population in Michigan after 1983 (which more closely parallels the predominant Georgia Medicaid treatment modality of the 1980–82 period) would alter the findings with regard to the offset.

The final issue at hand, which we will address in the last chapter, is how these offset findings fit into the larger picture of mental health care, the mental health industry, and more generally public health care policy, as these complex social phenomena are likely to evolve—through the mid-1990s. Understanding the offset, particularly the finding that a "total" offset may not exist, does much to explain the retrenchment taking place in government, the private insurance industry, and private companies seeking to limit costs. Nevertheless, we argue that this retrenchment is very likely to go too far, if it has not already done so.

Appendix 6.1

Inpatient Mental Health Care Treatment—Michigan

(A) Inpatient Care: Restricted to Those With at Least
One Mental Health Inpatient Day (n=49)

AT LEAST ONE INPATIENT DAY IN YEAR(s)	N	MEAN NUMBER OF DAYS/TREATMENTS				AGE
		TOTAL	1980	1981	1982	
1980 ONLY:	10					
1) Inpatient Mental Health Days		27.1	27.1	0	0	25
2) Outpatient Mental		9.3	4.4	2.5	2.4	25
3) Inpatient General Health Care Days		6.5	0.8	2.9	2.8	25
1980 AND 1981 ONLY:	2					
1) Inpatient Mental Health Days		60.5	34.5	26.0	0	29
2) Outpatient Mental		6.0	4.0	2.0	0	29
3) Inpatient General Health Care Days		7.0	1.0	6.0	0	29

Appendix 6.1 (Continued)

| AT LEAST ONE INPATIENT DAY IN YEAR(s) | N | MEAN NUMBER OF DAYS/TREATMENTS | | | | AGE |
		TOTAL	1980	1981	1982	
1980 AND 1982 ONLY:	2					
1) Inpatient Mental Health Days		45.5	19.0	0	26.5	30
2) Outpatient Mental		10.0	2.5	2.5	5.0	30
3) Inpatient General Health Care Days		2.5	0	0	2.5	30
1980, 1981, AND 1982:	2					
1) Inpatient Mental Health Days		179.5	22.5	114.5	42.5	28
2) Outpatient Mental		17.0	3.5	8.0	5.5	28
3) Inpatient General Health Care Days		4.2	1.6	1.5	1.1	28

152

ALL CASES WITH AT
LEAST ONE MENTAL HEALTH
INPATIENT DAYS: 49

1) Inpatient Mental Health Days	35.1	8.6	18.1	8.5	35
2) Outpatient Mental	8.7	4.0	2.7	2.0	35
3) Inpatient General Health Care Days	5.1	1.3	2.4	1.4	35

ALL CASES--WITH AND
WITHOUT MENTAL HEALTH
INPATIENT DAYS: 331

1) Inpatient Mental Health Days	5.3	1.3	2.7	1.3	32
2) Outpatient Mental	6.1	3.5	1.6	1.0	32
3) Inpatient General Health Care Days	7.0	2.1	2.4	2.4	32

Appendix 6.1 (Continued)

(B) Mental Health Care Inpatient Days By Year

Year	Mean	High	Low	S.D.	Per Cent of Sample With Zero Visits That Year(s)
1980	1.3	107	0	8.0	95%
1981	2.7	198	0	14.7	91%
1982	1.3	83	0	7.0	93%
1980-1982	5.3	303	0	21.9	85%

S.D.: Standard Deviation

154

Appendix 6.2

Means and Standard Deviations—Michigan

```
Variables    Mean   Std Dev

LNET3_12     8.095     1.211
MHTV         6.103     6.874
MHTVSQ      84.350   216.806
Q312DAYM    13.526   123.436
Q312DAYG     4.752    16.693
GENDER        .299      .459
AGE         32.184    14.604
RACE          .471      .500
NPRO3_12     3.258     2.162
Q3_12NDX     3.907     1.834
LPREGHSU     5.152     3.526
NPREDX       1.798     1.215
NPRONDX      5.933     1.643

    N of Cases =    331
```

Appendix 6.3

Correlation Matrix—Michigan

	LNET3_12	MHTV	MHTVSQ	Q312DAYM	Q312DAYG	GENDER	AGE	RACE	NPRO3_12	Q3_12NDX	LPREGHSU	NPREDX	NPRONDX
LNET3_12	1.000	.124	.122	.103	.509	-.244	.183	-.127	.711	.817	.443	.486	.853
MHTV	.124	1.000	.921	.107	.001	.030	.128	-.091	.060	.062	.022	.023	.116
MHTVSQ	.122	.921	1.000	.073	.001	.039	.052	-.042	.048	.065	.043	.071	.111
Q312DAYM	.103	.107	.073	1.000	-.003	.096	-.042	-.087	.014	.005	.012	-.003	.055
Q312DAYG	.509	.001	.001	-.003	1.000	-.150	.094	-.069	.831	.587	.191	.192	.312
GENDER	-.244	.030	.039	.096	-.150	1.000	-.253	.005	-.207	-.259	-.189	-.209	-.279
AGE	.183	.128	.052	-.042	.094	-.253	1.000	.058	.116	.142	.107	.099	.142
RACE	-.127	-.091	-.042	-.087	-.069	.005	.058	1.000	-.088	-.024	.045	.027	-.049
NPRO3_12	.711	.060	.048	.014	.831	-.207	.116	-.088	1.000	.801	.298	.328	.590
Q3_12NDX	.817	.062	.065	.005	.587	-.259	.142	-.024	.801	1.000	.397	.497	.806
LPREGHSU	.443	.022	.043	.012	.191	-.189	.107	.045	.298	.397	1.000	.730	.421
NPREDX	.486	.023	.071	-.003	.192	-.209	.099	.027	.328	.497	.730	1.000	.536
NPRONDX	.853	.116	.111	.055	.312	-.279	.142	-.049	.590	.806	.421	.536	1.000

Notes

1. Note, however, that the severity interaction term is affected; it is no longer significant in this equation. All other independent variables were of similar magnitudes and had identical signs and levels of significance, in comparison with their equation #2 counterparts.

2. Ideally, one would like to control not just for provider types but also for provider experience and provider treatment methods. Unfortunately, data did not exist for making such distinctions.

3. Those whose initial quarter 3 mental health diagnosis was "neurosis," "special symptom," "transient, situational disorder," or "personality disorder" were classified MILD. Those whose initial quarter 3 mental health diagnosis was "psychosis," "organic brain syndrome," or "schizophrenia" were categorized SEVERE.

4. Significant differences which are discussed in the text were found to be consistently significant whether visits to particular provider types were restricted to (1) those with one or more visits or (2) those who visited that provider type exclusively.

5. Keep in mind, there are no statistically significant differences in mental health diagnoses as captured in the SEVERE variable, although it may be that their illnesses are relatively more severe within any given diagnosis. Unfortunately, (again) we have no data by which to assess this hypothesis.

6. In addition, it may be that other poorly measured or unmeasured factors (which cannot be established without more detailed data and further analysis) might help to explain the observed differences in provider type efficacy.

7. Our sample was drawn from those individuals who had been continuously enrolled in Medicaid over the entire period, 1980–82. The sample contained 674 cases drawn from the combined outpatient, inpatient, and prescription drug claims files. From this group, a subgroup of 346 cases was selected which had no mental health treatment in quarters 1 and 2, but did have such a visit in quarter 3. Thus, a two-quarter baseline for physical health care cost was established prior to any mental health treatment intervention. The subgroup was further reduced to 331 cases by eliminating cases for which there was incomplete information.

8. This parallels the common, long-standing interpretation of the health status–utilization relationship of white adult males aged 25–50. They have long been known to enter the health care market less often than other age-sex-race cohorts, and use relatively few ambulatory health care services; conversely, they use relatively more inpatient care. Not seeking care as frequently for illnesses, members of this group (it is explained) are more likely to seek to avoid or to postpone health care utilization, if possible. When they finally do obtain health care, therefore, they are more likely to be more severely ill, and hence more likely to require hospitalization, and more likely to be hospitalized.

9. Performing a type of sensitivity analysis, we eliminated the high-user outliers within the Georgia group (defined as those with more mental health treatment visits than the mean plus two standard deviations) and reestimated the t-statistic. The results did not change.

10. We are using the term "continuous treatment" in a very loose manner, analogous to our use of "episode," to mean simply that the individual received some mental health treatment in each of the years under study. We do not have adequate information

to determine if each visit was part of an unbroken course of treatment by a single provider, or whether the treatment was for the same episode of mental illness defined from a clinical (rather than our utilization) perspective.

11. The calculated F value was 11.78, while the critical F value at the 95 percent confidence level was 1.90 (with degrees of freedom 10,722). Thus we rejected the null hypothesis that the coefficients were equal (stable) across the two samples.

12. The small number of cases (thirty) in the third subsample—that comprised of persons with only mental health inpatient care—precluded its being analyzed using multiple regression.

13. A histogram of the standardized residuals reveals that although there is some clustering toward the center of the distribution, the residuals approximate a normal curve. Examination of scatterplots of the residuals with each of the independent variables revealed that initially the residuals of many variables were characterized by decreasing variance; that is, they exhibited heteroskedasticity. This prompted us to transform all of the non-discrete independent variables (with the exception of MHTV) into natural logarithms, which substantially reduced the degree of heteroskedasticity.

Severity of mental illness was not controlled for in the Michigan sample, due to lack of information. In Georgia, recall, we developed a dichotomous severity of mental illness measure based on categorizing the initial mental health diagnosis. For the purpose of maximizing the comparability of our analysis of the two states, we reestimated the Georgia equations omitting this variable. We found little change in the size or statistical significance of the coefficients; that is, excluding the severity variable did not prevent the identification of an offset. The severity variable was included in the reported Georgia results, and appropriately so; its deletion would make the estimates subject to a specification error. This bias, of course, is likely to exist for the Michigan estimates. However, based on the Georgia findings, it does not appear that the lack of this variable would prevent the identification of an offset, though we are less confident of its estimated magnitude.

14. We also fitted regressions with alternative specifications of the mental health treatment variable, including semi-logarithmic linear, reciprocal, and double-log, and found virtually identical results, including no offset effect.

15. When those persons with some mental health inpatient care were excluded from subsample A, and the model fitted for those with more than one, two, and three visits, the results paralleled those described here. The MHTV and MHTVSQ coefficients changed very little (e.g., the counterparts to those presented in equation #3 of exhibit 6.9 were -4.197 and 0.120, respectively), although the levels of significance were slightly less; the t-values were 1.86 and 2.04, respectively.

16. What might account for the higher average treatment costs in Michigan compared to Georgia? One hypothesis is that there are high "start-up" costs associated with mental health treatment, for example, psychological testing, evaluation, and the like. Thus we might expect the initial mental health treatment to cost more than additional follow-up visits. When these fixed (or sunk) costs are spread over only a few visits, they tend to create a high average cost. By contrast, if a patient has many follow-up visits, the average cost tends to decrease. According to this line of reasoning, Michigan has higher average mental health treatment charges than Georgia because Michigan patients had far fewer visits over which to spread these fixed costs (six visits on average in Michigan compared to seventeen in Georgia).

To evaluate this hypothesis, we compared average mental health treatment charges for those with only one mental health treatment visit to those with more than one and found:

	Treatment Visits	Average Charge
Michigan:	Only one	$117.89
	More than one	$92.87
Georgia:	Only one	$126.99
	More than one	$62.48

In both states the average charge for those with only one mental health treatment are approximately the same, and are higher than those with more than one mental health treatment—supporting, but not by any means proving, our start-up costs cum duration—intensity of treatment hypothesis.

17. Similarly, because the small number of cases (thirty) in the third subsample—that comprised of persons with only mental health inpatient care—no analysis was made of this group.

18. In 1960 there were over nineteen thousand residents in mental institutions in Michigan. Following a steady trend of deinstitutionalization, this inpatient population numbered just five thousand in 1975; and by 1985 it numbered 4,300 (Michigan Department of Mental Health, 1986).

19. This is consistent with other, more general findings about geographic variation in mental health treatment. As the Office of Economic Affairs of the American Psychiatric Association has noted, "Utilization rates vary geographically as does length of stay and this geographic variation appears to be consistent over time" (American Psychiatric Association, 1987: 67).

20. In fact, evidence suggests just the opposite. Recall that in the review of the demand for mental health care literature (chapter 3), we saw that entry into treatment has been found to be much more sensitive to liberalization of insurance coverage than has the level of care.

7

IMPLICATIONS OF THE OFFSET EFFECT AND BEYOND: CHARTING THE COURSE OF THE MENTAL HEALTH INDUSTRY

> This is the great error of our day in the treatment of the human body that physicians separate the soul from the body.
>
> —Plato

> Men condemn what they do not understand.
>
> —Cicero

INTRODUCTION

The mental health industry, as we have seen, is at an evolutionary, developmental crossroads. It is a crossroads of structural transformation which most of the rest of the health care industry—propelled by radical change in its financing mechanism—has already begun to pass through.

The mental health component of the industry has been slower in coming to this crossroads because of its unique character and its peculiar mix of:

1. Long-standing government involvement,

2. the growing recognition that mental illness is relatively widespread, affecting a larger portion of society than cross-sectional profiles suggest, because of the relatively large number of relatively minor illness episodes which are subject to spontaneous remission,

3. the marked discrepancy in the *social* relative to *private* benefits and costs of mental illness,

4. the individual-specific character of treatment which defies development of a standard treatment protocol or regimen, and which has continued to nurture item 5,

5. the still extant doubts about the effectiveness of psychotherapy.

These multifarious, crosscutting factors make it difficult to develop a consensus about the private and social costs of mental health illness, the benefits resulting from treatment, or the desired roles of private and public financing of the industry.

Viewed within this larger framework, it is understandable that the offset effect—its definition, estimation, and interpretation—remains a contentious and elusive issue. Many mental health care providers believe emphatically that an offset exists, and that its existence justifies additional mental health services. On the other hand, many health insurance companies believe just as emphatically that the purported offset effect is wishful thinking at best; at worst, that it is a self-serving, unsubstantiated claim by an effete profession whose policy agenda constitutes a significant threat to their financial well-being, and perhaps their continued existence.

Meanwhile, at least to date, mental health services researchers have for the most part only helped to further obfuscate the issues, developing estimates of this complex phenomenon at specific points in time and space, the results of which are often contradictory and cannot (or should not) be generalized. Wherein lies the truth?

The heart of this turbid matter, we believe, lies in recognizing a key fact: that the interests of public policy and those of private policy (be it that of an insurance company, or that of an employer, or whomever) need not be the same. There are many areas in which the divergence of private and public economic interests is recognized; generally such cases arise, as in this instance, when private economic actions entail substantial external costs or benefits— "externalities" in the nomenclature of economics.

In this chapter we trace the recent evolution of the public's—that is, the governments'—attitudes and philosophies toward mental illness and the mental health care industry (focusing on the federal government). We develop a thumbnail sketch of government involvement and its rationale, and analyze the implications for the (other) key actors in the mental health industry—patients, providers, and private insurance companies. This discussion is central to understanding how the offset controversy must be analyzed within the larger political framework of (oftentimes) competing public and private interests, and is essential to interpreting the empirical findings of this and other offset studies. Recognizing these dimensions is imperative if public policymakers and the private mental health care industry are to chart a reasonably coherent and consistent path for meeting the treatment needs of the mentally ill in the 1990s and beyond.

HOW WE GOT HERE: A STYLIZED INTERPRETATION OF RECENT CHANGES IN THE RATIONALE FOR GOVERNMENT INVOLVEMENT IN THE HEALTH SECTOR

The federal and state governments have long been involved in the mental health industry, both directly and indirectly. In its oldest mode—traditionally the asylum, and more recently the state mental hospital and community mental hospital center— government has been directly involved as a provider of mental health care services.

In terms of molding the present configuration and future directions of the industry, the governments' influence has been exerted primarily indirectly, as a result of its impact on the financing of services. The most prominent examples of this financing are: (1) the provision of public insurance for private providers—viz., Medicare and Medicaid, (2) the payment of health insurance premiums for its employees, (3) the mandating of health insurance carriers in some states to provide or to offer minimum levels of mental health service packages, (4) "tax expenditures" for health insurance premiums, primarily at the federal level, but also at the state level,[1] and (5) licensing requirements and regulations.

Health Care as a "Merit Good"

It is clear that American society and the mental health industry have come a long way from the days of the asylum. Mental health is now generally regarded as one of the two distinct, transactionally related components of total or holistic well being, the other, of course, being physical health. Health care has come to be regarded as a merit good—a type of good or service which everyone is entitled to because of its unique character. That is not to say that everyone is entitled to as much of this good or service as they want, or even as much as they may "need" (as defined by the individual consumer or provider), but entitled to some difficult-to-define, minimal amount.

The public's perception that poor health was largely an unavoidable, random event, coupled with its belief that medical services are generally important and beneficial in the treatment of ill health, were major rationales motivating the development of Medicare and Medicaid. Those who are randomly (that is to say, unfairly) saddled with poor health, it was reasoned, should be given an opportunity to benefit by receiving health services; regardless of income or wealth, everyone *merits* some of these services.[2] Indeed, our society's humanitarian values and humane self-image requires it. What has become an increasingly important and contentious public policy issue in the 1980s (and promises to remain so heretofore) is: To how many of these services are people entitled? What is the absolute minimal level of health services which people merit?

Mental health services, in contrast, have historically (since the 1960s) been accorded the appellation of "merit good" generally only implicitly, and primarily by virtue of their being associated with other health services. A number of factors, however, served to encourage the public's growing (and increasingly explicit) recognition of mental health services as a merit good in their own right. Factors contributing to this change included the reduction in the social stigma of mental illness, the deinstitutionalization movement of the 1960s and early 1970s, the increased availability of an armamentarium of psychotropic drugs to make the behavior of all but the most severely mentally ill more "acceptable" to society, the public's growing belief in the efficacy of psychotherapy, and acceptance of the redefinition of many mental illnesses (most noticeably alcoholism) as diseases with biochemical components which readily fit into the medical paradigm.

The Retrogression to Individualism

Over the course of the last decade and a half, there has been remarkable growth in the general public's knowledge about both physical and mental health, as well as in individuals' efforts to maintain and promote their own health status. One of the major themes of this era has been recognition of the important role of elements of lifestyles—factors within the control of the individual—in determining personal health status. A concomitant of this development has been the growing influence of what has been termed a "victim-blaming" philosophy of health, predicated on what Larry Churchill has termed "ethical individualism" (Churchill, 1987).

In the most articulate, eloquent, and compelling of the first expositions of this philosophy, Victor Fuchs wrote, "the greatest potential for improving health lies in what we do and don't do for and to ourselves" (Fuchs, 1974). Effectively challenging the notion that health is a "random event," this new social philosophy of health—underscored by American society's embracing of a political philosophy emphasizing the need to return to (rugged) individualism—significantly eroded the force of the merit good justification for government involvement in the health sector. When the resulting deteriorating consensus about why we as a society (in the form of government) should provide health was overlaid with the fiscal crisis of the state, backpedaling on the level of government involvement in the health sector became (at least in hindsight) a foregone conclusion.

It was now acceptable to espouse that while Medicare and Medicaid had been important policies, and ones which successfully had accomplished their central objectives of improving access to and utilization of health care, they were no longer so important or necessary, and certainly (though lamentably, of course) were no longer affordable. (As if the need for access to and utilization of health care services was a static, one-time event!) It had come to be acceptable to question whether government intervention was essential to ensuring that all persons be provided access to (some) health care. Efforts could be made, and were made, to begin the process—sure to be a long and slow one—of extricating the government from the health sector. Although there was never any political consensus concerning the degree to which the government should ultimately remain involved in the health sector—and concomitantly the degree of desired extrication—it was assumed to be significantly less than at present.

The extrication work, it was asserted, could and should—and, given the politically defined budget extingencies at the start of the 1980s—*must* begin now; longer-term goals and objectives could be worked out as the process unfolded. In the shorter term, and most immediately, it was possible to reduce the level of government support for health programs, and to reduce the government-defined and government-backed level of what constituted the minimal level of health care that people should be assured. In addition, restrictions were placed on who was "truly deserving" of even that assurance.

As health economist Judith Lave noted in a *Journal of Health Economics* editorial in 1984:

The world has changed since 1965 and in the United States we are seeing a re-evaluation of public commitments made at that time. Medicare and Medicaid will continue to subsidize the care for the elderly and the poor . . . . No longer, however, do access to mainstream medicine and freedom of choice appear to be sacrosanct. Moreover, the goals of the programs are no longer clear. In recent years the government has increasingly set a goal of cost containment often with seemingly little regard for the consequences for the health care for the poor and the elderly. Just as the denial that economic incentives were unimportant was foolish in 1965, so is the sole focus on cost containment foolish in 1984. The Congress needs to clarify priorities attached to these goals; otherwise, HCFA may engage in increasingly contradictory policies. . . . (Lave, 1984: 198)

Unfortunately, Dr. Lave's call has not been heeded. Between 1980 and 1986, Congress enacted no less than thirty-three laws that affected the Medicare and Medicaid programs (GAO, April 1987).

THE FACE OF THE FUTURE

We, therefore, have slowly become, and remain today, a society in the process of radically restructuring our health sector, without a vision of where we are going, what the impact of our new policies will be, or what we want. This is dangerous. Reshaping the health sector, by simply capping the financing level of programs or by continually "fine-tuning" policies predicated on an ongoing redefinition of what constitutes an "appropriate" government role in the sector, makes it too subject to buffeting by capricious and myopic politics and their unanticipated consequences.

One of the best examples of this in the mental health sector is the extension of DRGs to all but psychiatric illnesses, and the subsequent boom in the number of private psychiatric beds and hospitals, with private psychiatric facilities expanding in number by 25 percent and beds by 22 percent by 1987 (Keckley

Report, August 31, 1987). (For further details refer back to the discussion in chapter 3.)

Another example is the defunding of community mental health centers, when there was no knowledge about their relative effectiveness, whether or not they could survive "the market test," or what the impact on their clientele or the quality of mental health services might be. In our empirical analysis we found community mental health centers to be particularly effective in generating an offset. It may be, after the budgetary pressures they have experienced in the last seven years (as discussed in chapter 3), that they are no longer. In response to a dramatic reduction in federal funding,

As one therapist put it,

"Our staff meetings began to focus more on clients who could verbalize their problems—and who could pay." Another therapist said that at her center, staff members are instructed to ask their paying or insured clients to come two or three times a week, even though they may not need more than one weekly visit. Therapists who object are told, Go with the system or lose your job. (Hope and Young, 1988: 782)

A third example is the adoption of the strategy of limiting state involvement in the mental health service by relying on publicly funded, private-sector agencies to provide the services, instead of direct state provision of the care. In such arrangements, private agencies competitively bid for the states' service contracts. This approach (not only to mental health but to a growing number of health and social services) has increased significantly in the past decade. Growing reliance on this mechanism has been in large part the result of the assumption that competitive contracting eases program administration, reduces costs, and improves the quality of services. In a case study of mental health care in Massachusetts, however, Schlesinger and two colleagues at Harvard found this presumption not to be borne out by experience. They reported that

few of the expected benefits are achieved. In practice, supposedly competitive bidding systems often degenerate into administratively complicated negotiations between the state and private monopolies. This results in higher costs and lower quality of services. (Schlesinger et al., 1986: 245)

A final example is the deinstitutionalization movement of the late 1960s and early 1970s, with its unintended consequences for the (still) rapidly growing number of homeless who blight our cities, haunt our consciences, and hopefully will pique us to address the issue of basic human needs.[3]

The Medicaid Lesson of the Recent Past and Present

There are also lessons to be learned from the rest of the health care sector which, as already noted, has been more subject to the impact of financial retrenchment. In some instances holding the budget line has, in effect, led to the unplanned and occasionally unconscious transformation of programs—the most obvious and important case being the Medicaid program. With the government paying for an estimated 30 percent of all mental health care, and this being one of the primary programs through which it does so, a brief accounting of the transformation of Medicaid over the past decade is insightful (Horgan, 1985).

Medicaid coverage of the poor peaked in 1975 at 63 percent; since then it has consistently fallen, reaching an estimated 46 percent in 1985 (Curtis, 1986: 278). Over the past decade, while the number of people living below the official poverty line increased dramatically by nearly 70 percent—from 22.9 to 33.7 million—the number of Medicaid recipients has actually fallen from 22 million to slightly more than 21 million. This downward trend is largely attributable to the actions of states responding to budgetary pressures. Between 1975 and 1986, Medicaid income eligibility levels fell on average by 33 percent (Curtis, 1986: 279).

The increasing difficulty in qualifying for Medicaid on the basis of income has reduced Medicaid rolls and thereby effectively lowered program costs. A second way in which the rate of growth of the Medicaid budget has been tempered has been the holding down of reimbursement rates. Relative to private, third-party payers and relative to physician and hospital "costs," Medicaid reimbursement rates have fallen over the past decade. The growing disparity between Medicaid cases-related costs and revenues has encouraged physicians and hospitals alike to cost-shift; that is, to raise their general level of charges in order to shift the amount of costs not covered by one payer to other payers.

But the Medicaid budget still continues to grow in an absolute sense. How can this be explained?—largely by the fact that the basic aim of the program has been altered in a piecemeal, haphazard manner that has largely eluded the general public's awareness, but the outcome and impact of which has been pronounced. As a result of

federal budget cuts, differing state priorities, a growing elderly population, and rapidly increasing acute and long-term health care costs all have exerted their influence on the federal/state program originally designed to increase access to care for the indigent. One trend that has emerged over the past decade is the shift of Medicaid funds away from the poor population to the elderly with chronic care and nursing home needs. This tension for limited funds between two worthy populations was highlighted in a recent report from the American Hospital Association, *Medicaid Options*: "in terms of expenditures, Medicaid largely, and increasingly, has become a secondary insurance program for the elderly, blind, and disabled, rather than a primary insurance program for the poor." (Burwell and Rymer, 1987: 31)

Medicaid now pays for about half of all long-term care for the elderly and disabled (almost all of which is provided in nursing homes (Omenn and Ehreth, 1986: 11), while only about 40 percent of Americans with incomes below the federal poverty level receive assistance from the Medicaid program (Burwell and Rymer, 1987: 30).

Private Insurance and Cost Shifting

At the same time as physicians and hospitals have attempted to cost-shift from one payer or nonpayer to others, however, there has been less opportunity for cost shifting. Even as medical care inflation has abated over the last five years (though it continues to run at 6 to 8 percent per annum), health insurance premiums have continued to climb at double-digit rates, averaging nearly 20 percent in the last few years (American Hospital Association, 1987: 56). In growing numbers, businesses have begun to abandon their traditional quiescent posture and, individually or in combination with a local "business group on health," have sought to effect behavioral change in the health care market, and (more specifically) to contain costs. "Employers, at present, are in control of the market for health plans, with plans of all types responding to employer demands for particular health insurance products" (Dowd et al., 1987: 48).

In their efforts to contain health-care-related costs, employers have adopted a variety of strategies, ranging from (1) utilization review–linked employee benefit redesign; (2) self-insurance; (3) joining an HMO or PPO, which increasingly drive hard bargains to secure price discounts; (4) more closely shopping for and monitoring their health insurance premiums; and (5) developing an employee assistance plan (EAP).

In addition, having become more cognizant of the repercussions of providing uncompensated care, they are more closely examining the level of indigent care provided by their affiliated health-care-providing organizations. This is understandable; the amount of taxes businesses pay to cover medical care for the uninsured through Medicaid is far less than the increase in their insurance premiums due to cost shifting (Wilensky, 1987; Omenn and Ehreth, 1986). The two most common approaches for business are either to continue offering a single health plan but to shop around frequently for the best buy, or to offer employees a variety of plans and rely on the competition thus generated to keep the cost of premiums down.

The cumulative effect of these various, rapidly occurring, and major changes in business practices has been significant. The health care market has increasingly become characterized by price consciousness and price competition. Price competition has reduced the willingness and the ability of insurers to accept higher costs due to cost shifting: it requires them to increase premiums, rendering them less competitive. As the opportunity for cost shifting has eroded, there has been a concomitant growth in hospitals' and physicians' bad debt attributable to uncompensated care. According to the American Hospital Association, of the $7.4 billion in uncompensated care reported in 1985, $1.1 billion was covered through state and local tax revenue transfers, leaving $6.3 billion in bad debt (*Washington Health Costs Letter*, March 27, 1987: 7).

More and more the medically indigent are eschewed altogether, or are being "dumped" at public hospitals predominantly for economic reasons, in spite of the fact that many of them are in unstable condition at the time of transfer" (Schiff et al., 1986: 552). These facilities, with only a small percent of the hospital beds in the country, provide a disproportionate share of the charity care delivered, and incur a disproportionate percentage of the bad debt. The impact of public hospitals' financial position has been predictable; around the country they have been closing at an unprecedented rate, while indicators of access to care and utilization—starting in 1986—have turned downward for the first time in more than two decades (Freeman et al., 1987).

So Goes the Mental Health Sector?

What about—specifically—the mental health care sector? There is no reason to anticipate that its development has been or will be markedly different. Already changes are moving in that direction. The general direction of the health sector as a whole is already fundamentally altering the mental health subsector. Even though the development of DRGs for inpatient mental health care has been postponed (at least until the end of 1988), other transformations in the rapidly changing health industry are already making an impact.

Changes in the financing mechanisms of the health sector have made health care consumers more price-conscious, by forcing them to be at greater financial risk of paying for the care they receive. Greater price consciousness has encouraged insurance companies—standard third-party carriers and HMO-like arrangements, alike—to become more competitive. They have done so by restructuring their service packages, gearing them to particular types of clientele and relying increasingly on individual-rating (sometimes called experience-rating) as opposed to community-rating to set premium levels. This shift does not bode well for the mentally ill.

According to mental health specialists, many of the most severely mentally ill experience a cyclical pattern of heightened acuity followed by remission, followed again by heightened acuity; the time period for a complete cycle to occur may be very long, even years. It is likely, therefore, that one method that insurance companies (including HMOs) are likely to use to "protect" themselves from relatively expensive clientele (or to discourage their being selected by the more severely mentally ill) is the widespread use of clauses excluding "preexisting conditions," or even more restrictive "ever had" clauses.

But in this period of mental health insurance benefit retrenchment, we must try not to move too rashly. A frontal attack has been launched in the last five years and continues to grow in intensity. This is in part a knee-jerk reaction to the dramatic increase in mental health expenditures relative to other health care expenditures. Many of the largest firms in the country reported 15 to 25 percent increases in their mental health care costs in 1986 alone (*Washington Health Costs Letter*, 1987: 74).

Historically mental health costs have been a relatively small component of total employment-related health insurance, averaging between 3 and 7 percent. As such, they neither warranted nor received much attention. But as they have surged in both absolute and relative amounts in the past five years, and with the simultaneous growth in (insurance premium) price consciousness and the practice of redesigning benefit packages, they have attracted attention and prompted reaction. Wholesale retrenchment, however, is not in order, as a review of the composition of total mental health expenditures quickly suggests.

Although only between 3 and 7 percent of private health insurance reimbursement expenditures have been for mental health care, direct treatment costs of mental illness now constitute nearly 20 percent of the total health care bill in the United States; the federal and state governments pick up most of the tab. The overwhelming majority of these costs—about 80 percent—are generated by a tiny proportion of the population: approximately 2.5 persons per 1,000 (0.25 percent) who receive inpatient treatment (Lee, 1987: 9–10). Freestanding psychiatric hospital admissions (documented in chapter 3) have grown meteorically in the 1980s (by more than 30 percent between 1982 and 1984 alone), while admission for children less than eighteen years of age soared (by 450 percent between 1980 and 1984). There is, therefore, cause for concern.

Payers have historically focused their efforts to limit mental health expenses on the curtailing of benefits. But what is needed, and where these initial efforts should focus, is on the mix of mental health insurance coverage—inpatient relative to outpatient. Unfortunately, this has not been the case. Most efforts to curtail mental health benefits to date, like most analysis of costs to date, have not adequately disaggregated mental health benefit packages.

As we saw in chapter 3, insurance coverage of mental health care has long been less than that of general health care. Most of the inequality in benefits has been to the detriment of outpatient as opposed to inpatient care.

The disproportionate skewing of inpatient care results from stringent restraints on outpatient psychiatric benefits. Per visits copayments are generally 50% of the charge, capped at $50-$70.... A 1983 APA study found only 30 plans of 300 large group insurance plans covered outpatient mental health treatment equal to any other medical outpatient coverage. A 1984 Washington Business Group on Health (WBGH) survey of 64 large employers found only 6% that paid more than half of the provider's charge. Outpatient benefits are also often subject to annual maximum outlays or restraints on the number of visits that will be reimbursed.... Some employers have feared that their unlimited inpatient benefit contrasted with high cost sharing for outpatient services has driven patients to psychiatric wards. (Lee, 1987: 9–10)

And, it should be noted, this bias has not been limited to private sector insurance. The initial outpatient mental health treatment benefit established with the passage of Medicare in 1966—$250 per patient per year—did not change until 1988. With treatment costs growing rapidly over the last two decades, this has meant that the level of mental health care covered by Medicare has fallen markedly; conversely, that of inpatients has increased, both absolutely and relatively. In 1985, less than 5 percent of Medicare expenditures for mental illness were made for outpatient services (Mumford and Schlesinger, 1985: 587).

Fortunately this is starting to change. Employers in their efforts to contain health care costs have followed two basic strategies: holding the line on new benefits, and monitoring of inpatient care. Again, a primary reason for skyrocketing mental health costs in the past five years has been the dramatic increase in the number of psychiatric beds being built and filled, coupled with general hospitals transforming their DRG-idled beds into psychiatric beds and marketing effectively to fill them. Although there is no question that hospitals will continue to be a key element in the treatment of some of the mentally ill, a growing number of industry analysts feel that psychiatric beds are being overutilized (Lee, 1987; Kiesler, 1982; Kiesler and Sibulkin, 1983 and 1987; *Washington Health Costs Letter*, 1987). This has resulted in employer backlash to what has been termed "fiscogenic" treatment.

For instance, in 1981 the Blue Cross federal employee plan had an average length of stay of 27.5 days for a 28-day psychiatric inpatient benefit. Similarly, the Toledo Business Coalition on Health survey found a uniform 28-day psychiatric hospital stay for a 28-day inpatient benefit, regardless of diagnosis (Phelan and Rosenbloom, 1986). With the introduction of a 45-day inpatient benefit cap to its previously unlimited inpatient coverage, the Philadelphia American Life Insurance Company experienced a reduction by half, within two years, in the proportion of its clientele with inpatient care in excess of 45 days (Tsai et al., 1987). Econometric analyses too have established the importance of the level and type of reimbursement (per case versus per service) as a major determinant of length of stay (Frank and Lave, 1985; Rupp et al., 1985).

Prepaid Care and False Complacency

Fear of an incipient major rollback in insurance coverage of mental health benefits might initially appear unwarranted and alarmist. After all, most of the rollbacks to date have been by third-party indemnity insurance carriers. The wave of the future is prepaid care, and (it is generally thought) HMOs have better mental health benefit packages and better records of actual service provision of mental health care (i.e., they are commonly perceived as providing more care per enrollee, other things being equal).

Reality is not quite as comfortable as these common perceptions would suggest. In a 1982 national survey of all operational HMOs (group, staff, individual practice association, and preferred provider organizations—which achieved an 86 percent response rate), Levin, Glasser, and Roberts found that

mean hospital utilization rates for all health services and for mental health services were lower when compared to national Blue Cross/Blue Shield data and other selected indemnity health plan rates. HMO ambulatory care utilization rates for physical and mental health services remained higher than third party insurance plan ambulatory utilization rates. Additionally, both hospital utilization for all HMO health services and mental health services were lower in 1982 than in 1978. (Levin et al., 1984: 456–57)

Moreover, HMOs' major cost savings are generated from their approach to inpatient care: namely, their patients' relatively shorter average lengths of stay. Hence, it might be presumed that the restructuring of the U.S. health care system, in the direction of HMOs, might improve the prospects for not "throwing the baby out with the bath water"—that is, not indiscriminately slashing both inpatient and ambulatory mental health benefits because of the felt need to halt the rapid increase of (aggregated) mental health treatment costs. It might be presumed that HMOs, with their (at least theoretical) advantages of continuity of care (including the integration of mental health services within primary health care delivery), and reduced financial barriers to care (in concert with their relatively higher mental health care benefit levels and higher mental health care utilization rates), might portend an unambiguously brighter day for the mentally ill and mental health specialists. This perception seems further underscored when one notes that HMOs are in a position to capture the financial benefits of any offset effect, and therefore would be expected to maintain their relatively liberal coverage.

But psychiatrists are rarely involved in the structuring of HMO mental health benefit packages, and, in those very few studies which control for the different population characteristics of HMOs and third-party-covered populations, have found that in fact HMOs, despite their higher benefit levels, provide fewer services (Williams et al., 1979; Diehr et al., 1979; Diehr et al., 1984; Diehr et al., 1986; Wells et al., 1986). This of course implies that there may be some type of rationing of, or non-clinically based managerial control of, mental health services as practiced in HMOs. On average (as measured by the median), mental health care consumes only 3 percent of HMO budgets (Levin et al., 1984: 455).

Levin and colleagues also documented that "HMO mental health benefits are approaching a lower structure. . . . "—a trend which was also identified by Patterson (Levin et al., 1984: 456; Patterson, 1982).

As we saw in chapter 3, HMOs have been found to "restrict coverage of mental illness . . . and lack provision for treating chronic and indigent mentally ill patients" (Flinn et al., 1987: 255). The growth of HMOs and price competition among insurers are likely to result in the increasing tendency to undertreat mental health patients, to not insure the mentally ill, and to transfer mental health patients—particularly the more severely mentally ill—to public providers/institutions—the so-called "dumping" phenomenon (Frank and Lave, 1985; Diamond et al., 1985; Sullivan et al., 1987).[4]

Advice provided by two physicians in a recent article of *Hospital and Community Psychiatry* is telling. Although intended for inpatient care, Fogel and

Slaby's advice is equally applicable to a world in which outpatient care is prospectively financed:

One option for reducing hospital cost is to limit admission of patients who are likely to incur high treatment costs. Unit leaders must decide which kinds of high-cost patients the unit is obliged to care for.... After determining the categories of high-cost patients whose care must be undertaken for political or ethical reasons, unit leaders can further define their priorities by identifying the high-cost patients likely to have the best outcome. It is reasonable to apply the limited amount of money available for expensive treatment to patients for whom a costly intervention would make the most difference. (Fogel and Slaby, 1985: 761)

As our empirical work in chapters 5 and 6 demonstrates, it makes (private) economic sense to do so: mental health care does not pay for itself—that is, there is no total medical offset effect. Moreover, the increased cost associated with the provision of mental health services is greater (i.e., the medical offset effect is smaller) for the more severely mentally ill.

What then is to become of such persons? In a world of ever-heightening price competition cum individual rating, they are increasingly likely to be "flagged," forced to pay higher premiums, and/or become uninsurable, and/or become insured by or treated by the state. Whichever the outcome, it seems certain that the evolving system will provide less access to care and more instances of inadequate treatment. This is troubling; as Sharfstein and Beigel have noted, "The potential for greater chronicity is high in some of these persons who are untreated or inadequately treated as a result of access problems" (1985: 235).

Although federal law prohibits states from adopting Medicaid eligibility or coverage policies which discriminate on the basis of diagnosis, nothing prevents private insurance companies from doing so; and in fact they are increasingly doing so. Moreover, the 1974 Employment Retirement Income Security Act (ERISA) proscribes any state regulation of self-insured employers. With more than half of all large employers (over 500 employees) already self-insured, the government is left on the sidelines only able to observe the most rapidly occurring major structural change in the health insurance market.

Furthermore, there is no reason to think that the completion of the transformation of Medicaid to a capitated, prepayment system will result in the mentally ill receiving treatment any better than that provided at present by HMOs.[5] On the contrary, in light of the growing gap between Medicaid reimbursement and the costs of care, the economic incentives will exacerbate the already relatively poor record of HMOs in treating the mentally ill, unless special regulations are established and enforced. Furthermore, the lack of choice among alternative providers/organizations (inherent in some states' present approach to Medicaid capitated systems) provides even greater opportunity for diagnosis-based discrimination, without fear of consumer retaliation; the Medicaid enrollees in some states, after all, are a captive clientele of the prepaid provider organization—which (from the perspective of the enrollees) is a monopolist.

Hence, we are likely to experience a significant acceleration in growth of the (already existing) two-tiered system of care in the United States. Mental health care benefits are likely to be singled out and dropped from health insurances' "standard plan" package, to the extent that other forces (e.g., state mandates or improved marketability to groups) allow them or encourage them to do so. As this process unfolds, those individuals in need of mental health services will be increasingly attracted to those diminishing numbers of (ever more expensive) plans still offering such coverage. Without government intervention, this situation could very easily lead to a very grim scenario, in which we ultimately end up with very little (and very expensive) or no insurance coverage of mental health services for those most in need of them.

The Positive Externalities of Mental Health Treatment

The preceding scenario is rather frightening and is one which we are all too likely to glibly dismiss as unlikely. But it is unlikely *only* because, looking at the indispensability of government intervention in this market in its most stark form, we know that "we" (as a society) could not and would not let that happen.

Why? Because we know that (again, as a society) we have goals which embody more than simply economic considerations, and because most of us have an intuitive grasp of the notion that mental health services exhibit what economists refer to as "positive externalities."[6]

A positive externality exists when someone who is "external" to the market—that is, not a direct purchaser of the good or service in question, nor a producer of it—enjoys some of the positive benefits of its consumption but does not have to pay for them. The benefits to society generated by the consumption of this good or service include both private and external benefits; consequently, when positive externalities are present, *social* benefits invariably exceed *private* benefits. Society can be better off if it could somehow encourage more consumption (and production) of this service than will occur in the laissez-faire marketplace. To the extent that an offset effect exists, mental health treatment generates a private benefit for insurance companies based on savings in physical health charges. But other external benefits are also produced.

There are two fundamentally different types of positive externalities which are of interest in assessing the nature and extent of the public role in the mental health care market. Probably the more common (and intuitively understood) view is that described by Randall Bovbjerg, Phillip Held, and Mark Pauly:

The most persuasive normative rationale for public provision of health care is a consumption "externality"; that is, individuals feel altruistic concern about the health or level of medical-care consumption of their fellow citizens, mainly those with fewer resources than themselves. Seeing the public role as altruism resembles the conception of health care as a "merit good" or a "natural right" to which people are entitled. The difference is that merit goods and rights come with an expectation about the level of care, whereas unlike rights, altruistic impulses can come in varying degrees of strength and are appropriately varied in quantity and quality when price or cost varies. (Bovbjerg et al., 1987: 650)

The second type of positive externality relates to more direct and unambiguous benefits which are not as subject to variations over time as are the impulses of altruism. They are, therefore, less subject to significant changes in social concern and commitment or to changes in the political spectrum. It is this second type of positive externality which has not been, but should be, the primary basis on which we as a society predicate our mental health policies. These positive externalities of mental health treatment include reduced morbidity, reduced absenteeism, increased productivity, improved interpersonal relations, and less crime.

The value of some of these external benefits has been the subject of two cost-of-illness studies sponsored by the National Institute for Mental Health (a third is to be completed by 1990). The total costs to society of mental illness have been estimated to be in excess of $50 billion annually. The Research Triangle Institute estimated that the figure for 1980 was $54,236 million (independent of alcohol and other drug abuse costs). Of this total, less than half ($23,558 million, or 43 percent) consisted of treatment and support costs, with the bulk of the remainder a combination of the indirect costs of increased morbidity (reduced productivity and lost employment) valued at $21,664 million, and premature mortality worth $7,196 million (see exhibit 7.1).

Given that positive externalities in mental health care exist, how much more of this service should be provided? Theoretically the answer is simple: from society's perspective, the optimal level is where the marginal social benefits derived from treatment (private benefits plus external benefits) are equal to the marginal social costs of production. Quantifying these levels, however, is exceedingly difficult; rivaling the degree of difficulty in doing so is the difficulty of determining how they are to be financed. Ultimately, this determination boils down to the contentious political issues of relative priorities (trade-offs) and income redistribution (from the non-mentally ill to the mentally ill).

Although most Americans view some combination of government mandating, government financing, and government provision of mental health care as acceptable and desirable, they generally do so primarily because of altruistic motivations (the normative consumption externality cited by Bovbjerg, Held, and Pauly above). But as long as altruism remains the primary concern and motivation, it is probably safe to say that we can expect American society to be unwilling to finance anything closely approaching the socially optimal level of mental health care.

The consensus that mental illness is significantly underrecognized and undertreated in our society (as detailed in chapter 3) suggests that the manifes-

Exhibit 7.1

Costs to Society of Mental Illness
(in Millions of Nominal Dollars)

CORE COSTS	$52,418
Direct	
Treatment	20,961
Support	2,597
Indirect	
Mortality	7,196
Morbidity	21,664
Reduced Productivity	(3,122)
Lost Employment	(18,542)
OTHER RELATED COSTS	$1,818
Direct	
Crime	870
Public	(635)
Private	(235)
Social Welfare Programs	201
Other	659
Indirect	
Incarceration	88
TOTAL	$54,236

*Components are indicated in parentheses.

Source: Research Triangle Institute, 1984, Table III-1, page 34.

tations and implications of mental illness are analogously little understood or appreciated. It is hardly surprising, therefore, that many of the external costs of mental illness (the obverse of the benefits of effective mental health treatment) are rarely attributed to it. The public's continuing ignorance of these costs contributes to the likelihood that American society will remain unwilling to provide the socially optimum amount of mental health care. Explicitly recognizing these costs and demonstrating that mental health care can reduce them (and thereby produce positive externalities) is an important point about which the public must be educated.

For some, fighting for an increased government commitment to mental health care on the basis of "external benefits" may sound like wishful thinking from an academic ivory tower. The American polity, many will argue, is not responsive to such theoretical arguments. This is where mental health care researchers have an important function to fulfill: they can translate the theoretical into the concrete, and monetarily quantify the concept. Medical offset research, in particular, has an important role to play in this more general activity. But, more immediately, it can (already) be demonstrated that these "external benefits" are not merely metaphysical constructs of the "dismal science of economics." There are some agents in American society who are positioned to internalize some of the external benefits of effective mental health treatment; and they are already reaping the very real economic gains of doing so.

Internalizing the External Benefits

As already suggested, we do not have the adequately detailed data which would allow us to identify the socially optimal amount of mental health services (based solely on economic critera, devoid of political considerations and the trade-offs inherent in the present fiscal crisis).

Turning specifically to the offset, the private benefits of treatment accrue to health insurance companies as reductions in physical health charges due to mental health treatment. But, as we indicated in the empirical sections, this private offset is not sufficient to pay for the total treatment costs. Thus, the private health insurance market will not voluntarily provide this service, or will provide less than is socially desirable. From society's viewpoint, this situation reflects some degree of market failure, since substantial positive externalities of mental health treatment are known to exist.

But it is clear that there are elements of the private market—other than private health insurance companies—that are able to "internalize" some of these external benefits; and in fact have sought to do so. The clearest example is the growth throughout the 1980s of employee assistance programs (EAPs). Corporations have grasped the significance of the level of positive externalities which may be gained (in the form of reduced absenteeism and increased productivity) by alleviating mental illness, and have accordingly invested in EAPs.[7]

Why have corporations done so? Why, when—often at the same time—they have opposed the paying for the expansion of insurance coverage for mental health benefits, or even attempted to roll them back? The EAP alternative is more attractive than mental health insurance because it provides a greater degree of predictability and control—while projecting a very positive, caring image of management to both employees and the general public. Predictability and control are most important in trying to maintain health care costs at a more "acceptable" level; the aim, of course, is that the additional outlays required of the corporation to fund the EAP not exceed the amount of savings to be realized in terms of reduced absenteeism, increased productivity, reduced turnover, and, in instances where the EAP is provided in lieu of mental health insurance coverage, reduced total mental-health-service-related costs.

Another dimension of the control-cost issue is the pattern of mental health treatment expenditures. Generally a very small fraction of the insured population accounts for the overwhelming majority of all utilization and reimbursement costs. An EAP better enables a corporation to target "troubled" employees and to provide them with an intensive level of services, while not becoming as vulnerable to dramatically increased costs resulting from the "not so necessary" utilization that might be encouraged by provision of that same intensive level of care to the "more deserving" employees.

Over the past half decade, in contrast to many corporations voluntarily extending the provision and financing of mental health services in the form of EAPs, most health insurance companies have established maximum levels of mental health services coverage, and others have rolled back their coverage. These differences are easily understood by comparing social versus private costs and benefits, and abilities to internalize benefits. It clearly demonstrates that the external benefits of effective mental health care are more than theoretical abstractions.

But while it can be shown that these external benefits are very real and that their value can be monetized, for a variety of reasons there are not private agents who are able, or in some cases willing, to internalize all of the external benefits. Getting closer to the socially optimum level of mental health care remains the responsibility of government. How much additional mental health care is appropriate, what mix of providers, settings, and services, and what level of government should be involved (local, state, or federal) remain unresolved political issues—but ones which mental health services research can help to address, and which should receive high priority on the research agenda.

TOWARD THE DEVELOPMENT OF A MENTAL HEALTH POLICY EVALUATION FRAMEWORK

It is inevitable that controversy should periodically arise in the consideration of the costs and benefits of mental health treatment.

After years of enthusiastically embracing mandated health insurance benefits, state legislators seem to be taking a step back, to see whether the benefits of the laws outweigh their costs and whether public demand for the coverages warrants the states' continued involvement." (Intergovernmental Health Policy Project, *State Health Notes*, September 1987)

But how are lawmakers measuring benefits and costs? And whose benefits and costs are they assessing? The public's? Or only those of private individuals? Which segments of the public? Whose demand are they assessing? The most visible, articulate, and influential taxpayers? Or the generally far less vociferous, politically inarticulate mentally ill? The need for mental health professionals to get involved in the design of policy has never been more urgent; at stake are much of the gains which have been won over the past four decades.

Efforts must now be directed to the development of a framework for mapping out a policy-relevant research agenda, pursuing that research in as rigorous and scientific a manner as possible, and crafting the findings into a sound, consistent, and explicit public policy framework and agenda for mental health care.[8] What is needed is a better footing in which to ground decisions: a framework with which to direct change and by which to assess change. We, the authors, do not purport to possess such a grand master plan; it must be the eclectic creation of mental health providers, as well as experts from the multifarious other disciplines involved in the mental health industry. What we do have to offer are two far more modest contributions: first, a call to mental health specialists to begin the process of developing such a scheme so that they may become more proactive, and less reactive; and second, we offer a suggestion as to how to begin the construction of the new framework.

It has generally come to be realized that America's social "safety net" has some holes in it, that many of the holes are substantial, and that some of them are growing. Consistent with this growing recognition and concern is the need to reaffirm that the concept of health as a merit good is not dead. The concept of physical and mental health services as merit goods, which served as the primary philosophical basis for justifying continued government intervention in the health care market(s) (until it was eviscerated by the individual-responsibility argument), is not moot. While its force has been vitiated, it must still be recognized as the starting point and backbone of the new, to-be-constructed, philosophical framework. It is imperative to recognize that the "ethical individualism"-based, victim-blaming philosophy, while legitimate, is not absolute; other considerations—one of which is the merit good concept—are at least as compelling, and have very different implications as to what should be the role of government in the health sector. As Larry Churchill has simply and succinctly put it,

a just health care system, whatever its final shape, requires a recognition of our sociality and mutual vulnerability to disease and death. Individual self-sufficiency, which was a virtue in the American frontier of the past, has become a vice in our late 20th-century thinking about health care. A more mature ethics will not discard self-reliance, but temper it with social concerns. (Churchill, 1987)

Complementing the merit good concept are a number of economically based rationales, which may collectively be referred to as market failures. The health care market is characterized by a number of market failures, including artificial restrictions on supply (resulting from licensing regulations); the controlling and limiting of positions in medical schools (to restrict the analysis to only psychiatrists, but there is a parallel argument for all other mental health providers as well); the often one-time, urgent nature of need (which contributes to consumers not being well-informed about either procedures or prices); and general consumer ignorance and incompetence to judge what or how much they need.

These differences are widely recognized and have been widely discussed in the literature. But there is another characteristic of the mental health marketplace which constitutes another rationale for encouraging some type of ameliorative governmental action in this arena: mental health care generates significant positive externalities. As discussed earlier in this chapter, these external benefits are of two fundamentally different types. One, which is conceptually and philosophically very similar to the merit good rationale, is the consumption externality of people "feeling good" as a result of their helping others (especially those economically less well off) secure an "adequate" amount of health care (the Bovbjerg, Held, and Pauly notion).

The second type of external benefit of effective mental health treatment is entirely independent of the merit good, and less value-laden in terms of its recognized legitimacy and its quantification. This is the notion that effective care improves not only the individual patient's mental well-being, but also his interpersonal relationships, his family life, his general health and health care utilization, and his workplace performance. Social decision-making needs to make a more adequate accounting of these considerations.

As our research has shown, the private offset benefits of mental health treatment, while significant, are not sufficient to ensure that the private marketplace will produce the socially optimal amount of mental health care. It is penny-wise and dollar-foolish, from society's point of view, to fail to recognize the positive externalities that link effective mental health treatment with the workplace, home life, the homeless, and our jails and mental institutions. Fifty years from now historians will perhaps look back on the 1980s and early 1990s as an era of financial and moral retrenchment—of the disavowal of the social compact. Perhaps a good part of this rethinking is necessary to eliminate previous excesses; yet retrenchment in the care of the mentally ill should not be the myopic characteristic for which this generation is remembered.

NOTES

1. The term "tax expenditure" refers to government revenue losses which result from the provision of selective tax-exempt status to specific uses of taxpayer monies. Con-

stituting foregone tax revenues, they are not expenditures in the customary sense of making a direct grant, but instead are made through a reduction in taxes. Their impact on the government's balance sheet (tax revenues minus expenditures outlay) is identical, although their impact on resource allocation and in income distribution is very different (as will be discussed below). Under 1986 tax rates, the Congressional Joint Tax Committee estimated the 1987 federal subsidy for health benefits at $26.5 billion (Darling and Bass, 1987: 37).

2. Some have maintained that the merit good argument is (also?) a manifestation of positive externalities in consumption (Bovbjerg et al., 1987).

3. An estimated two-thirds of the homeless are mentally ill—one-half of whom are thought to be alcohol and other drug abusers.

4. The difficulties inherent in establishing a causal relationship largely proscribe investigating the practice of outpatient "dumping," except perhaps in a prospective study. Nor is there much evidence about the extent of the practice of inpatient dumping. That which is available suggests that while both diagnosis and benefit structure are the salient determinants, the patient's diagnosis is the more important of the two (Cotton et al., 1980; Frank and Lave, 1984; Frank and Lave, 1985).

5. This transformation is already well under way and will be completed by 1992, according to the Health Care Financing Administration's chief administrator, William Roper.

6. To explain a positive externality requires a brief digression to understand how a market functions. A market is a mechanism for allocating resources. There are some markets whose characteristics are such that they fail to perform their function of allocating resources in a socially desirable manner. That is, the market does not allocate the "appropriate" amount of resources to the production or consumption of that good. While there exist a handful of different types of "market failures" (as economists categorize this phenomenon), we will focus on only one: the positive externality.

7. Employee assistance programs have long existed in the United States. They have taken on numerical significance only in the last quarter-century, especially since the passage of the 1970 federal Comprehensive Alcohol Abuse and Alcoholism Treatment and Rehabilitation Act, which required that all federal agencies and military commands institute alcoholism programs. Over time, EAPs have evolved from alcohol- and drug-abuse-focused programs into efforts with a more comprehensive approach. While alcohol and drug abuse remain an important focus of their activities, EAPs now "take an interest in troubled employees whose work performance was adversely affected by a variety of personal problems, some of which were symptomatic of covert psychiatric illness" (Brill et al., 1985: 728).

8. This is not to imply that there has not already been a great deal of rigorous analysis of mental health services. It is, however, meant to suggest that more works are in order; exercises which consist primarily of comprehensive stock-taking reviews of literature, which seek to synthesize what we do know, at the same time that they identify holes in our understanding, and direct future research efforts.

BIBLIOGRAPHY

Aday, LuAnn. "Economic and Noneconomic Barriers to the Use of Needed Medical Services." *Medical Care* 13 (1975): 447–65.

Aday, LuAnn, and Andersen, R. *Development of Indices of Access to Medical Care.* Ann Arbor: Health Administration Press, 1975.

———."The National Profile of Access to Medical Care: Where Do We Stand?" *American Journal of Public Health* 74 (1984): 1331–39.

Aday, LuAnn, Andersen, R., and Fleming, G. V. *Health Care in the United States: Equitably for Whom.* Beverly Hills: Sage, 1980.

Aday, LuAnn, and Eichhorn, Robert. *The Utilization of Health Services: Indices and Correlates.* Washington, D.C.: National Center for Health Services Research and Development, 1972.

Alcohol, Drug Abuse and Mental Health Administration. *Alcohol, Drug Abuse and Mental Health Services under National Health Insurance: Alternative Levels of Benefits and Estimated Costs.* Office of Program Planning and Evaluation. Washington, D.C.: GPO, 1979.

Altman, Laura S., and Frisman, Linda K. "Preferred Provider Organizations and Mental Health Care." *Hospital and Community Psychiatry* 38(4) (April 1987): 359–62.

American Hospital Association. "High Insurance Rates Prompt Self-Insurance." *Hospitals* (July 5, 1987): 56–57.

American Psychiatric Association, Office of Economic Affairs. *Economic Factbook for Psychiatry.* Washington, D.C.: American Psychiatric Press, 1983. 2d ed. 1987.

Andersen, R. "Health Status Indices and Access to Medical Care." *American Journal of Public Health* 68 (1978): 458–65.

Andersen, R., and Benham, Lee. "Factors Affecting the Relationship between Family Income and Medical Care Consumption." In H. R. Klarman, ed., *Empirical Studies in Health Economics.* Baltimore: Johns Hopkins University Press, 1970.

Andersen, R., and Newman, J. F. "Societal and Individual Determinants of Medical Care Utilization in the U.S." *Milbank Memorial Fund Quarterly* 51 (1973): 95–124.

Andersen, R., Francis, A., Lion, J., et al. "Psychologically Related Illness and Health Services Utilization." *Medical Care* (Supplement) (May 1977): 59–73.

Andersen, R., Kravitz, J., and Anderson, O., eds. *Equity in Health Services.* Cambridge: Ballinger, 1975.

Anderson, James G. "Health Services Utilization: Framework and Review." *Health Services Research* 8 (1973): 184–206.

Anderson, Odin W., and Andersen, R. M. "Patterns of Use of Health Services." In H. E. Freeman, S. Levine, and L. G. Reeder, eds., *Handbook of Medical Sociology.* Englewood Cliffs, N.J.: Prentice-Hall, 1972, pp. 386–406.

Andrews, G., Schonell, M., and Tennant, C. "The Relation between Physical, Psychological and Social Morbidity." *AMJ Epidem* 105 (1977): 324–29.

Babigian, H. M. "The Impact of Community Mental Health Centers on the Utilization of Services." *Archives of General Psychiatry* 34 (1977): 385–94.

Babigian, H. M., and Odoroff, C. L. "The Mortality Experience of a Population with Psychiatric Illness." *American Journal of Psychiatry* 126 (1969): 470–80.

Bachrach, Leona L. *Marital Status and Mental Disorder: An Analytical Review.* DHEW, Public Health Service. ADAMHA, Pub. No. (ADM): 75-217. Washington, D.C.: GPO, 1975.

———. "The Future of the State Mental Hospital." *Hospital and Community Psychiatry* 37(5) (May 1986): 467–74.

Balint, M. *The Doctor, His Patient and the Illness.* New York: International Universities Press, 1957.

Beck, A. T., Ward, C. H., et al. "An Inventory for Measuring Depression." *Archives of General Psychiatry* 4 (1961): 561–71.

Becker, M. H., Haefner, D. P., Kasl, S. V., et al. "Selected Psycho-Social Models and Correlates of Individual Health-Related Behaviors." *Medical Care* (Supplement) (May 1977): 27–46.

Beigel, Allan. "The Remedicalization of Community Mental Health." *Hospital and Community Psychiatry* 35(11) (November 1984): 1114–17.

———. "Planning Psychiatry's Future." *Hospital and Community Psychiatry* 37(6) (June 1986): 551–54.

Bender, Paul. "Controlling Costs of Outpatient Mental Health Care." *Business and Health* (November 1986): 6–38.

Benham, L., and Benham, A. "The Impact of Incremental Medical Services on Health Status, 1963–1970." In Andersen, Kravitz, and Anderson, *Equity*, 1975.

Bennett, S., and Bowers, D. *An Introduction to Multivariate Techniques for Social and Behavioral Sciences.* New York: Halsted Press, 1976.

Bergin, A. E., and Lambert, M. J. "The Evaluation of Therapeutic Outcomes." In S. L. Garfield and A. E. Bergin, eds., *Handbook of Psychotherapy and Behavior Change: An Empirical Analysis.* New York: Wiley, 1978, pp. 139–89.

Bittker, Thomas E. "The Industrialization of American Psychiatry." *American Journal of Psychiatry* 142(2) (1985): 149–54.

Bittker, Thomas E., and George, J. "Psychiatric Service Options within a Health Maintenance Organization." *Journal of Clinical Psychiatry* 41 (1980): 192–98.

Bittker, Thomas E., and Idzorek, S. "The Evolution of Psychiatric Services in a Health Maintenance Organization." *American Journal of Psychiatry* 135 (1978): 339–42.

Bloomfield, P. *Fourier Analysis of Time Series: An Introduction.* New York: Wiley, 1976.

Borus, J. F., Olendzki, M. C., et al. "The Offset Effect of Mental Health Treatment on Ambulatory Medical Care Utilization and Charges." *Archives of General Psychiatry* 42(6) (1985): 573–80.

Boskin, M., and Nold, F. "A Markov Model of Turnover in Aid to Families with Dependent Children." *Journal of Human Resources* 10 (1975).

Bovbjerg, Randall R., Held, Phillip J., and Pauly, Mark V. "Privatization and Bidding in the Health Care Sector." *Journal of Policy Analysis and Management* 6 (1987): 648–65.

Breslau, N., and Haug, M. "Service Delivery Structure and Continuity of Care: A Case Study of a Pediatric Practice in Process of Re-organization." *Journal of Health and Social Behavior* 17 (1976): 339–51.

Brill, Peter, Herzberg, Joseph, and Speller, Jeffrey Lynn. "Employee Assistance Programs: An Overview and Suggested Roles for Psychiatrists." *Hospital and Community Psychiatry* 36(7) (July 1985): 727–31.

Brody, D. S. "Physician Recognition of Behavioral, Psychological and Social Aspects of Medical Care." *Archives of Internal Medicine* 140 (1980): 1286.

Brook, R. H., Ware, J. E., et al. "Does Free Care Improve Adults' Health?" *New England Journal of Medicine* 309 (1983): 1426–34.

Broskowski, Anthony. "The Health-Mental Health Connection." In Broskowski et al., eds., *Linking Health*, 1981, pp. 13–26.

Broskowski, Anthony, and Baker, F. "Professional, Organizational and Social Barriers to Primary Prevention." *American Journal of Orthopsychiatry* 44 (1974): 707–19.

Broskowski, Anthony, et al., eds. *Linking Health and Mental Health.* Beverly Hills: Sage, 1981.

Brown, G. W., and Harris, T. *Social Origins of Depression: A Study of Psychiatric Disorders in Women.* New York: Free Press, 1978.

Budman, Simon H., and Gurman, A. S. "The Practice of Brief Therapy." *Professional Psychology: Research and Practice* 14(3) (1983): 277–92.

Budman, Simon H., Demby, A., and Feldstein, M. L. "Insight into Reduced Use of Medical Services after Psychotherapy." *Professional Psychology: Research & Practice* 15(3) (1984): 353–71.

Budman, Simon H., Demby, A., and Randall, M. "Psychotherapeutic Outcome and Reduction in Medical Utilization: A Cautionary Tale." *Professional Psychology* 13(2) (1982): 200–207.

Budman, Simon H., ed. *Forms of Brief Therapy.* New York: Guilford Press, 1981.

Burns, B. J., Burke, J. D., Jr., and Kessler, L. G., eds. "Promoting Health-Mental Health Coordination." In Broskowski et al., *Linking Health*, 1981: pp. 27–43.

Burwell, Brian O., and Rymer, Marilyn P. "Trends in Medicaid Eligibility." *Health Affairs* 6 (1987): 31–45.

Cannell, C. F., Marquis, K. H., and Laurent, A. "A Summary of Studies of Interviewing Methodology." *Vital and Health Statistics*, Series 2, No. 69. DHEW, National Center for Health Statistics. Pub. No. (HRA) 77-1343. Washington, D.C.: GPO, 1977.

Carey, K., and Kogan, W. S. "Exploration of Factors Influencing Physician Decisions to Refer Patients for Mental Health Service." *Medical Care* 9 (1971): 55–66.

Cassell, W. A., Fraser, H. N., and Spellman, A. "Psychiatric Morbidity and Utilization of Insured Health Services." *Canadian Psychiatric Association Journal* 17 (1972): 417–21.

Cheifitz, D. I., and Salloway, J. C. "Patterns of Mental Health Services Provided by HMOs." *American Psychologist* 39 (1984): 495–502.

Chow, Gregory C. "Tests of Equality between Sets of Coefficients in Two Linear Regressions." *Economica* 28(3) (1960): 591–605.

Churchill, Larry R. *Rationing Health Care in America: Perceptions and Principles of Justice*. Notre Dame, Ind.: University of Notre Dame Press, 1987.

Cleary, P. D., Goldberg, I. D., Kessler, L., et al. "Screening for Mental Disorders among Primary Care Patients: Utilization of the General Health Questionnaire (GHQ)." *Archives of General Psychiatry* 39 (1982): 837–46.

Clyne, M. B. "Psychotherapy by General Practice BP and BS" and "Social and Cultural Influences on Psychotherapy." *Annual Review of Psychology* 25 (1974): 417–52.

Coe, Richard. "Welfare Dependency: Fact or Myth?" *Challenge* (October 1982).

Colle, Ann D., and Grossman, Michael. "Determinants of Pediatric Care Utilization." *Journal of Human Resources* 13 (Supplement) (1978): 115–58.

Commission on Chronic Illness. *Chronic Illness in the United States*. Cambridge: Harvard University Press, 1957.

Cook, Thomas D., and Campbell, Donald T. *Quasi-Experimentation: Design and Analysis Issues for Field Settings*. Boston: Houghton-Mifflin, 1979.

Cook, Thomas D., Dintzer, L., and Mark, M. "The Causal Analysis of Concomitant Time Series." In Leonard Bickman, ed., *Applied Social Psychology Annual*. Beverly Hills: Sage, 1980, pp. 93–135.

Cooper, B., Fry, J., and Kalton, G. "A Longitudinal Study of Psychiatric Morbidity in a General Practice Population." *British Journal of Preventive Social Medicine* 23 (1969): 210–25.

Cotton, P., Bene-Kociemba, A., and Roses, S. "Transfers from a General Hospital Psychiatric Service to a State Hospital." *American Journal of Psychiatry* 137 (1980): 230–33.

Crede, R. H. "The Physician's Emotions and Human Illness" *Psychosomatics* 9 (1968): 1–3

Cummings, N. A. "Prolonged (Ideal) Versus Short-Term (Realistic) Psychotherapy." *Prof. Psychology* 8 (1977): 491.

Curtis, Rick. "The Role of State Governments in Assuring Access to Care." *Inquiry* 23 (1986): 277–85.

Darling, Helen, and Bass, Kristin. "The Uninsured: Federal Policy and the Working Poor." *Business and Health* (January 1987): 36–40.

Davis, Glenn, and Breslau, Naomi. "DRGs and the Practice of Psychiatry." *Medical Care*, 22(7) (1984): 595–96.

Davis, K., and Reynolds, R. "The Impact of Medicare and Medicaid on Access to Medical Care." In R. N. Rosett, ed., *The Role of Insurance in the Health Services Sector.* New York: National Bureau for Economic Research, 1976.

Delozier, J. E. *National Ambulatory Medical Care Survey, 1973 Summary, United States, May 1973–April 1974.* DHEW Publication No. (HRA) 767-1772. Washington, D.C.: GPO, 1975.

Devine, Elizabeth C., and Cook, Thomas D. "A Meta-analytic Analysis of Effects of Psychoeducational Interventions on Length of Postsurgical Hospital Stay." *Nursing Research* 32 (1983): 267–74.

Diamond, R. J., Alexander, A. A., and Marshall, J. R. "A Chronic Psychiatric Patient in an HMO." *Hospital and Community Psychiatry* 36 (1985): 239–41.

Diehr, Paula. "Factors Related to the Use of Ambulatory Mental Health Services in Three Provider Plans." *Social Science and Medicine* 23(8) (1986): 773–80.

Diehr, Paula, et al. "The Relationship between Utilization of Mental Health and Somatic Health Services Among Low Income Enrollees in Two Provider Plans." *Medical Care* 17 (1979): 937–51.

———. "Ambulatory Mental Health Service Utilization in Three Provider Plan." *Medical Care* 22(1) (1984): 1–13.

Dohrenwend, B., et al. "Nonspecific Psychological Distress and Other Dimensions of Psychopathology in the General Population: Measures for Use in the General Population." *Archives of General Psychiatry* 37 (1980): 1129.

Douvan, E., Kulka R., and Veroff, J. *Study of Modern Living: 1976—Report to Respondents.* Ann Arbor: University of Michigan, Institute for Social Research, 1976.

Dowd, Bryan, Feldman, Roger, and Klein, John. "What Do Employers Really Want in a Health Plan?" *Business and Health* (January 1987): 44–48.

Duehrssen, A., and Jorswick, E. "An Empirical and Statistical Inquiry Into the Therapeutic Potential of Psychoanalytical Treatment." *Der Nervenarzt* 36 (1965): 166–69.

Duncan, Otis D. *Introduction to Structural Equation Models.* New York: Academic Press, 1975.

Dutton, D. B. "Patterns of Ambulatory Health Care in Five Different Delivery Systems." *Medical Care* 17 (1979): 221–43.

Eastwood, M. R. *The Relationship between Physical and Mental Illness.* Toronto: University Press, 1975.

Eastwood, M. R., and Trevelyan, M. H. "Relationship between Physical and Psychiatric Disorder." *Psychology of Medicine* 2 (1972): 363–72.

Eisenberg, L. "Interfaces between Medicine and Psychiatry." *Comprehensive Psychiatry* 20 (1979): 1–14.

Ejlertsson, Goran, and Berg, Sven. "Continuity of Care Measures: An Analytic and Empirical Comparison." *Medical Care* 22(3) (1984): 231-39.

Ellis, R. P., and McGuire, T. G. "Cost Sharing and Demand for Ambulatory Mental Health Services: Interpreting the Results of the Rand Health Insurance Study." Boston: Department of Economics, Boston University, 1984.

Ellsworth, R. B., Casey, N. A., Hickey, R. H., Twemlow, S. W., et al. "Some Characteristics of Effective Treatment Programs." *Journal of Consulting and Clinical Psychology* 47(5) (1979): 799–817.

Ellwood, Paul. "The HMO Summary." Excelsior, Minn.: InterStudy, June 1986.

Engle, Robert F. "Specification of the Disturbances for Efficient Estimation." *Econometrica* (1973).

Estes, Carroll L., and Wood, Juanita B. "A Preliminary Assessment of the Impact of Block Grants on Community Mental Health Centers." *Hospital and Community Psychiatry* 35 (1984): 1125–29.

Evans, Robert G. "Supplier-Induced Demand: Some Empirical Evidence and Implications." In Mark Perlman, ed., *The Economics of Health and Medical Care.* New York: Wiley, 1974, pp. 162–73.

Feldstein, Paul J. *Health Care Economics.* 2d ed. New York: John Wiley, 1983.

Fiedler, John L. "A Review of Access and Utilization of Medical Care with Special Emphasis on Rural Primary Care." *Social Science and Medicine* 15c (1981): 129–42.

Fink, R., and Goldensohn, S. S. *Use of Mental Health Services by Medicaid Enrollees in a Prepaid Group Practice.* Report to NIMH pursuant to contract HSM-42-77-70. Rockville: 1977.

Fink, R., Shapiro, S. S., and Goldensohn, S. S. *Psychiatric Treatment and Patterns of Medical Care.* Report to NIMH pursuant to contract MJ 02321. Rockville: 1969a.

Fink, R., Shapiro, S. S., et al. "The 'Filter-Down' Process to Psychotherapy in a Group Practice Medical Care Program." *AJPH* 59(2) (1969b): 245–60.

Flinn, Don E., McMahon, Terry C., and Collines, Michael F. "Health Maintenance Organizations and Their Implications for Psychiatry." *Hospital and Community Psychiatry* 38 (1987): 255–69.

Flynn, T., et al. "Predicting Client Improvement from and Satisfaction with Community Mental Health Clinic Services." *American Journal of Community Psychology* 9(3) (1981): 339–46.

Fogel, Barry S., and Slaby, Andrew E. "Beyond Gamemanship: Strategies for Coping with Prospective Payment." *Hospital and Community Psychiatry* 36, No. 7 (July 1985): 760–63.

Follette, W., and Cummings, N. A. "Psychiatric Services and Medical Utilization in a Prepaid Health Plan Setting." *Medical Care* 5 (1967): 25.

Frank, Jeanine. "Economic Changes and Mental Health." *American Journal of Community Psychology* 9(4) (1981): 395–411.

Frank, Richard G. "Pricing and Location of Physician Services in Mental Health." *Economic Inquiry* 23 (1985): 115–33.

Frank, Richard G., and Kamlet, Mark S. "Direct Costs and Expenditures for Mental Health Care in the United States in 1980." *Hospital and Community Psychiatry* 36 (1985): 165–68.

Frank, Richard G., and Kessler, L. G. "State Medicaid Limitations for Mental Health Services." *Hospital and Community Psychiatry* 35 (1984): 213–15.

Frank, Richard G., and Lave, Judith R. *Effect of Benefit Design on Length of Medicaid Psychiatric Patients.* Pittsburgh: University of Pittsburgh Press, 1984.

———. "The Impact of Medicaid Benefit Design on Length of Hospital Stay and Patient Transfers." *Hospital and Community Psychiatry* 36, No. 7 (July 1985): 749–53.

———. "Per Case Prospective Payment for Psychiatric Inpatients: An Assessment and Alternatives." *Journal of Health Politics, Policy and Law* 11(1) (Spring 1986): 83–96.

Frank, Richard G., and McGuire, T. G. "A Review of Studies of the Impact of Insurance on the Demand and Utilization of Specialty Mental Health Services." *Health Services Research* 21:2, Part II (June 1986): 291–320.

Freeburg, Linnea C., Lave, Judith R., Lave, Lester B., and Leinhardt, Samuel. *Health Status, Medical Care Utilization and Outcome: An Annotated Bibliography of Empirical Studies.* DHEW Pub. No. (PHS) 80-3263. Washington, D.C.: GPO, 1979.

Freedman, D. "Psychiatry." *Journal of American Medical Association* 239(6) (1978): 510–12.

Freeman, Howard E., et al. "Americans Report on Their Access to Care." *Health Affairs* 6(1) (Spring 1987): 6–18.

Freiman, Marc P., Mitchell, J. B., and Rosenbach, M. L. "An Analysis of DRG-Based Reimbursement for Psychiatric Admissions to General Hospitals." *American Journal of Psychiatry* 144(5) (1987): 603–9.

Frisman, L. K., McGuire, T. G., and Rosenbach, M. L. "Costs of Mandates for Outpatient Mental Health Care in Private Health Insurance." *Archives of General Psychiatry* 42 (1985): 558–61.

Fuchs, Victor. *Who Shall Live?* New York: Basic Books, 1974.

———. "The Supply of Surgeons and the Demand for Operations." *Journal of Human Resources* 13 (Supplement) (1978): 35–56.

Gavin, Norma I. "An Application of Statistical Matching with the Survey of Income and Education and the 1976 Health Interview Survey." *Health Services Research* 20(2) (June 1985): 183–98.

General Accounting Office. *Medicare and Medicaid: Effects of Recent Legislation on Program and Beneficiary Costs.* Washington D.C.: GAO/HRD 87-53, April 1987.

———. *Medicaid: Interstate Variations in Benefits and Expenditures.* Washington D.C.: GAO/HRD 87-67BR, May 1987.

Gibson, Rosemary. "Quiet Revolutions in Medicaid." In Jack Meyer, ed., *Market Reforms in Health Care: Current Issues, New Directions, Strategic Decisions.* Washington D.C.: American Enterprise Institute for Public Policy Research, 1983, pp. 75-102.

Glasscote, R. M., Gudeman, J. E., and Mills, D. G. "Creative Mental Health Services for the Elderly." Washington D.C.: Joint Information Service of APA & MHA, 1977.

Glasser, M. A., Duggan, T. J., and Hoffman, W. S. *Obstacles to Pathways to Prepaid Mental Health Care.* NIMH, DHEW, Pub. No. (ADM) 76-383. Washington, D.C.: GPO, 1977.

Goldberg, D. *The Manual of the General Health Questionnaire.* London: (GHQ), NFER, 1978.

Goldberg, I. D., Allen, G., et al. "Utilization of Medical Services After Short Term Psychiatric Therapy in a Prepaid Health Plan Setting." *Medical Care* 19 (1981): 672.

Goldberg, I. D., Krantz, G., and Locke, B. Z. "Effect of Short Term Outpatient Psychiatric Benefit on the Utilization of Health Care." *Medical Care* 8 (1970): 419–28.

Goldberg, D., Rickels, K., Downing, R., et al. "A Comparison of Two Psychiatric Screening Tests." *British Journal of Psychiatry* 129 (1974): 61–70.

Goldensohn, S. S., and Fink, R. "Mental Health Services for Medicaid Enrollees in a Prepaid Group Practice Plan." *American Journal of Psychiatry* 136(2) (February 1979): 160–64.

Goldman, Fred, and Grossman, Michael. "The Demand for Pediatric Care: An Hedonic Approach." *Journal of Political Economy* 85 (1978): 259–80.

Goldman, H. H., Pincus, H. A., Taube, C. A., et al. "Prospective Payment for Psychiatric Hospitalization: Questions and Issues." *Hospital and Community Psychiatry* 35 (1984): 460–64.

Gottman, J. M. *Time Series Analysis.* Cambridge: Cambridge University Press, 1981.

———. "Detecting Cyclicality in Social Interaction." *Psychological Bulletin* 86 (1979): 338–48.

Graves, R., and Hastrup, J. "Effects of Psychological Treatment on Medical Utilization in a Multidisciplinary Health Clinic for Low Income Minority

Children." Presented at the annual meeting of the Southern Psychological Association, New Orleans, 1978. Cited in Hankin et al., "A Longitudinal Study," 1983.

Gray, L. "Consumer Satisfaction with Physician Provided Services: A Panel Study." *Social Science and Medicine* 14 (1980): 65–73.

Greenley, James R., and Mechanic, David. "Social Selection in Seeking Help for Psychological Problems." *Journal of Health and Social Behavior* 17 (1976): 249–62.

Greenley, James R., Mechanic, David, and Cleary, Paul D. "Seeking Help for Psychologic Problems: A Replication and Extension." *Medical Care* 25(12) (December 1987): 1113–28.

Greenspan, S. I., and Sharfstein, S. S. "Efficiency of Psychotherapy: Asking the Right Questions." *Archives of General Psychiatry* 38 (l981): 1213–19.

Grossman, Michael. *The Demand for Health: A Theoretical and Empirical Investigation.* New York: Columbia University Press, NBER, 1972.

Grossman, Michael, and Benham, Lee. "Health, Hours and Wages." In M. Perlman, ed., *The Economics of Health and Medical Care.* New York: Wiley, 1974.

Group for the Advancement of Psychiatry. *Medical Practice and Psychiatry: The Impact of Changing Demands.* New York: Report No. 58, 1964, pp. 327–69.

———. *The Effect of the Method of Payment of Mental Health Practice.* New York: Report No. 95, vol. 9, 1975.

Gujarati, Damodar. "Use of Dummy Variables in Testing for Equality between Sets of Coefficients in Two Linear Regressions: A Note." *American Statistician* (January 1970a): 50–52.

———. "Use of Dummy Variables in Testing for Equality Between Sets of Coefficients in Two Linear Regressions: A Generalization." *American Statistician* (December 1970b): 18-22.

———. *Basic Econometrics.* New York: McGraw-Hill, 1978.

Gurin, G., Veroff, J., and Feld, S. *Americans View Their Mental Health.* New York: Basic Books, 1960.

Guzick, David S. "The Demand for General Practitioner and Internist Services." *Health Services Research* (1978): 351.

Hadley, Jack. *More Medical Care, Better Health?* Washington D.C.: Urban Institute Press, 1982.

Hall, J. A., Roter, D. L., and Rand, C. S. "Communication of Affect between Patient and Physician." *Journal of Health and Social Behavior* 22 (1981): 18-30.

Hankin, J. R. "Psychological Distress and the Use of Medical Services." Unpublished Ph.D. dissertation. University of Wisconsin-Madison. 1974.

Hankin, J. R., and Oktay, J. S. *Mental Disorder and Primary Medical Care: An Analytic Review of the Literature.* NIMH, Series D, No. 5, DHEW Pub. No. (ADM) 78-661. Washington, D.C.: GPO, 1979.

Hankin, J. R., and Shapiro, S. "The Demand for Medical Service by Persons under Psychiatric Care." In Robins, L., Clayton P., and Wing, J., eds., *Social Consequences of Psychiatric Illness*. New York: Brunner/Mezel, 1980.

Hankin, J. R., Kessler, L. G., Goldberg, I. D., Steinwachs, D. M., and Starfield, B. H. "A Longitudinal Study of Offset in the Use of Nonpsychiatric Services Following Specialized Mental Health Care." *Medical Care* 21(11) (November 1983): 1099–1110.

Hankin, J. R., Steinwachs, D. M., Regier, D. A., et al. "Use of General Medical Care Services by Persons with Mental Disorders." *Archives of General Psychiatry* 39 (1982): 225–31.

Hansen, W. Lee. "The Supply of Mental Health Manpower." In McGuire and Weisbrod, eds., *Mental Health Service System Reports*, 1981, pp. 85–88.

Hanushek, Eric A., and Jackson, John C. *Statistical Methods for Social Scientists*. New York: Academic Press, 1977.

Harrison, Bennett. "Welfare Payments and the Reproduction of Low-Wage Workers and Secondary Jobs." *Review of Radical Political Economy* 11(2) (Summer 1979): 1–16.

Hausman J., and Wise, D. D. "Social Experimentation, Truncated Distributions and Efficient Estimators." *Econometrica* 45(4) (1977): 918–38.

Hershey, John C., Luft, Harold S., and Giannaris, Joan M. "Making Sense Out of Utilization Data." *Medical Care* 13 (1975): 838–54.

Hilkevitch, A. "Psychiatric Disturbances in Outpatients of a General Medical Outpatient Clinic." *International Journal of Neuropsychiatry* 1 (1965): 371–75.

Hill, B. J. "Sensory Information, Behavioral Instructions and Coping with Sensory Alteration Surgery." Ph.D. dissertation, Wayne State University, 1979, Dissertation Abstracts 40 (1979): 1631B.

Hine, F. R., Werman, D. S., and Simpson, D. M. "Effectiveness of Psychotherapy: Problems of Research on Complex Phenomena." *American Journal of Psychiatry* 139 (1982): 204–8.

Hoeper, E. W., Nycz, G. R., et al. "Estimated Prevalence of RDC of Emotional Disorder in Primary Medical Care." *International Journal of Mental Health*, 8 (1980a): 6–15.

Hoeper, E. W., Nycz, G. R., Regier, D. A., Goldberg, I. D., et al. "Diagnosis of Mental Disorder in Adults and Increased Use of Health Services in Four Outpatient Settings." *American Journal of Psychiatry* 137(2) (1980b): 207–10.

Holder, Harold D., and Blose, James O. "Changes in Health Care Costs and Utilization Associated with Mental Health Treatment." *Hospital and Community Psychiatry* (October 1987).

Hope, Marjorie, and Young, James. "Who Cares for the Mentally Ill?" *The Nation* (December 26, 1987–January 2, 1988): 782–84.

Horgan, C. M. "Specialty and General Ambulatory Mental Health Services: Comparisons of Utilization and Expenditures." *Archives of General Psychiatry* 42 (1985): 565–72.

————. "The Demand for Ambulatory Mental Health Services from Specialty Providers." *Health Services Research* 21:2 (June 1986, Part II): 291–320.

Horn, S. D., Yesalis, C. E., and Bartels, R. H. "Selection of Regression Models for Health Care Data." *Medical Care* 16(7) (1978): 574–83.

Horney, K. *The Neurotic Personality of Our Time.* New York: Norton, 1937.

Houpt, Jeffrey L., Orleans, C. Tracy, George, Linda K., and Brodie, Keith H.. *The Importance of Mental Health Services to General Health Care.* Cambridge: Ballinger, 1979.

Houpt, Jeffrey L., Orleans, C. Tracy, George, Linda K., et al. "The Role of Pyschiatric and Behavioral Factors in the Practice of Medicine." *American Journal of Psychiatry* 137 (1980): 37–47.

Howell, Embry, Corder, Larry, and Dobson, Allen. "Out-of-Pocket Health Expenses for Medicaid and Other Poor and Near-Poor Persons in 1980." Series B, Descriptive Report No. 4, USDHH&S, HCFA, PHS, NCHS. Washington D.C.: GPO, August 1985.

Huberty, Carl J. "Issues in the Use and Interpretation of Discriminant Analysis." *Psychological Bulletin* 95(1) (1984): 156–71.

Hughes, C. C., Tremblay, M., et al. *People of Cove and Woodlot.* New York: Basic Books, 1963.

Hustead, E. C., and Sharfstein, S. "Utilization and Cost of Mental Illness Coverage in the Federal Employees Health Benefits Program, 1973." *American Journal of Psychiatry* 135(3) (1978): 315–20.

Hyams, L., Green, M. R., et al. "Varied Needs of Primary Physicians for Psychiatric Resources. I. Behavioral Indices." *Psychosomatics* 12 (1971): 36–45.

Intergovernmental Health Policy Project. *State Health Notes.* September 1987. George Washington University, Washington, D.C.

————. "Mandated Insurance Benefits." *State Health Reports: Mental Health, Alcoholism, and Drug Abuse.* No. 7, March 1984.

————. "State Mental Health Agencies: An Expenditure Study." *State Health Reports: Mental Health, Alcoholism, and Drug Abuse.* No. 8, Washington: George Washington University, June/July 1984.

Jacobson, A. M., Regier, D. A., and Burns, B. J. "Factors Relating to the Use of Mental Health Services in a Neighborhood." *PH Reports* 93 (1978): 232–39.

Jameson, J., Shuman, L., and Young, W. "The Effects of Outpatient Psychiatric Utilization on the Costs of Providing Third Party Coverage." *Medical Care* 16 (1978): 383.

Jemmott, J. B. III, and Locke, S. E. "Psychosocial Factors, Immunologic Mediation and Human Susceptibility to Infectious Diseases: How Much do We Know?" *Psychological Bulletin* 95(1) (January 1985): 78–108.

Jencks, Stephen F., Goldman, Howard H., and McGuire, Thomas G. "Challenges in Bringing Exempt Psychiatric Services under a Prospective Payment Systems." *Hospital and Community Psychiatry* 36, No. 7 (July 1985): 764–69.

Jenkins, Rachel. "Sex Differences in Minor Psychiatric Morbidity." *Social Science and Medicine* 20 (1985): 887–99.

Jones, K., and Vischi, T. "The Impact of Alcohol, Drug Abuse and Mental Health Treatment on Medical Care Utilization." *Medical Care* 17 (Supplement) (1979).

Jones, Kenneth, ed. "Report of a Conference on the Impact of Alcohol, Drug Abuse, and Mental Health Treatment on Medical Care Utilization." Final Draft, Alcohol, Drug Abuse, and Mental Health Administration (ADAMHA). Washington, D.C.: GPO, October 1980.

Judge, George G., et al. *The Theory and Practice of Econometrics.* New York: Wiley, 1985.

Karon, B. P., and VandenBos, G. P. "The Consequences of Psychotherapy for Schizophrenic Patients." *Psychotherapy: Theory, Research and Practice* 9 (1972): 111–19.

Keckley Report: Supplement to Health Care Competition Weekly. "Employers ... the New Big Stick in Health Care." Nashville, Tenn.: July 27, 1987.

————.: "Mental Health Services: One in Five of Us Would Benefit from Them." August 31, 1987.

Kellner, R., Simpson, G. M., and Winslow, W. "The Relationship of Depressive Neurosis to Anxiety and Somatic Symptoms." *Psychosomatics* 13 (1972): 358–62.

Kelvorick, A. K. "Regulation and Cost Containment in the Delivery of Mental Health Services." McGuire and Weisbrod, eds., *Mental Health Service System Reports,* 1981, pp. 62–71.

Kessel, N. "Who Ought to See a Psychiatrist?" *The Lancet* 1 (May 1963) pp. 1092–95.

Kessler, Larry G. *Episodes Of Psychiatric Care and Medical Utilization in a Prepaid Group Practice.* Unpublished Ph.D. dissertation, Johns Hopkins University. 1978.

Kessler, Larry G., Amick, B. C. III, and Thompson, J. "Factors Influencing the Diagnosis of Mental Disorder among Primary Care Patients." *Medical Care* 23(1) (1985): 50–62.

Kessler, Larry G., Cleary, Paul D., and Burke, Jack D. "Psychiatric Disorders in Primary Care." *Archives of General Psychiatry* 42 (1985): 583–87.

Kessler, Larry G., Steinwachs, Donald M., and Hankin, Janet R. "Episodes of Psychiatric Care and Medical Utilization." *Medical Care* 20 (1982): 1209–21.

Kiesler, C. A. "Public and Professional Myths about Mental Hospitalization: An Empirical Reassessment of Policy-Related Beliefs." *American Psychologist* 37 (1982): 1323–30.

Kiesler, C. A., and Sibulkin, A. E. "Proportion of Inpatient Days for Mental Disorders: 1969-1978." *Hospital and Community Psychiatry* 34 (1983): 606–11.

————. *Mental Hospitals: Myths and Facts about a National Crisis*. Newbury Park, Calif.: Sage, 1987.

Klecka, W. R. *Discriminant Analysis, #19: Quantitative Approaches in the Social Sciences*. Beverly Hills: Sage, 1980.

Klerman, G. L. "Trends in Utilization of Mental Health Services: Perspectives for Health Services Research." *Medical Care* 23(5) (1985): 584–97.

Kmenta, J. *Elements of Econometrics*. New York: Macmillan, 1971.

Kogan, W. S., Thompson, D. J., Brown, J. R., et al. "Impact of Integration of Mental Health Services and Comprehensive Medical Care." *Medical Care* 13 (1975): 934–42.

Koranyi, E. H. "Fatalities in 2,090 Psychiatric Outpatients." *Archives of General Psychiatry* 34 (1977): 1137–42.

Koutsoyiannis, A. *Theory Of Econometrics*, 2d ed. Totowa, N.J.: Barnes and Noble Books, 1977.

Krizay, J. "Measuring Psychiatric Utilization: The Rubber Yardstick." *American Journal of Psychiatry* 137 (1980): 1589–92.

Lachenbruch, P. A. *Discriminant Analysis*. New York: Halsted Press, 1976.

Langner, T. S. "A Twenty-Two Item Screening Score of Psychiatric Symptoms Indicating Impairment." *Journal of Health and Social Behavior* 3 (1962): 269–76.

Lantz, Alma J., Carlberg, Conrad G., and Wilson, Nancy Z. "Mental Health Treatment Outcome by Sex, Diagnosis, and Treatment Agency." *Professional Psychology: Research and Practice* 14 (1983): 293–309.

Lave, Judith R. "Competitive Bidding and Public Insurance Programs." *Journal of Health Economics* 3 (1984): 194–98.

Leaf, P. J., Bruce, M. L., Tischler, G. L., Freeman, D. H., Weissman, M. M., and Myers, J. K. "Factors Affecting the Utilization of Specialty and General Medical Mental Health Services." *Medical Care* 26(1) (January 1988): 9–26.

Lebow, Jack L. "Consumer Assessment of the Quality of Medical Care." *Medical Care* 12 (1974): 328–34.

Lee, Frederick C. "Purchasers Address Escalating Psychiatric and Substance Abuse Utilization." *Employee Benefits Journal* (March 1987): 9–13.

"Legislative Update: Consolidated Omnibus Budget Reconciliation Act of 1985 (Public Law 99-272)." *Health Care Financing Review* 8(3) (Spring 1987): 95–119.

Leighton D. C., Harding J. S., et al. *The Character of Danger*. New York: Basic Books, 1963.

Levin, Bruce Lubotsky, Glasser, Jay H., and Roberts, Robert E. "Changing Patterns in Mental Health Service Coverage within Health Maintenance Organizations." *American Journal of Public Health* 74(5) (May 1984): 453–58.

Levitan, S. J., and Kornfeld, D. S. "Clinical and Cost Benefits of Liaison Psychiatry." *American Journal of Psychiatry* 138 (1981): 790–93.

Link, Bruce G., Cullen, Francis T., Frank, James, and Wozniak, John F. "The Social Rejection of Former Mental Patients: Understanding Why Labels Matter." *American Journal of Sociology* 92(6) (May 1987): 1461–1500.

Linn, M. W., Sandfer, R., Locke, B. Z., and Gardner, E. "Psychiatric Disorders Among the Patients of General Practitioners and Internists." *Public Health Reports* 84 (1969): 167–73.

Locke, B. Z., and Gardner, E. "Psychiatric Disorders among the Practices of General Practitioners and Internists." *Public Health Reports* 84 (1969): 167–73.

Locke, B. Z., Krantz, G., and Kramer, M. "Psychiatric Need and Demand in a Prepaid Group Practice Program." *AJPH* 56 (1966): 895–90.

Luft, Harold S. "Factors Affecting the Use of Physician Services in a Rural Community." *American Journal of Public Health* 66 (1976): 865–72.

MacMillan, A. M. "The Health Opinion Survey: Technique for Estimating Prevalence of Psychoneurotic and Related Types of Disorders in Communities." *Psychological Reports* 3 (1957): 325–29.

Maddala, G. S. *Econometrics*. New York: McGraw-Hill, 1977.

Malan, D. H., et al. "Psychodynamic Change in Untreated Neurotic Patients. II. Apparently Genuine Improvements." *Archives of General Psychiatry* 32 (1975): 110–26.

Manderscheid, Ronald W., Witkin, M. J., Rosenstein, M. J., and Bass, R. D. "The National Reporting Program for Mental Health Statistics: History and Findings." *Public Health Reports* 101(5) (September–October 1986): 532–39.

Manning, Willard G., Jr., and Phelps, Charles E. "The Demand for Dental Care." *The Bell Journal of Economics* 10 (1979): 503–25.

Manning, Willard G., Jr., Wells, K. B., Duan, N., Newhouse, J. P., and Ware, J. E., Jr. "Cost Sharing and the Use of Ambulatory Mental Health Services." *American Psychologist* 39 (1984): 1077–89.

Mark, Melvin M. "Inferring Cause from Passive Observation." In Cook and Campbell, *Quasi-Experimentation*, 1979, pp. 295–340.

Marks, J. N., Goldberg, D. P., and Hillier, V. F. "Determinants of the Ability of General Practitioners to Detect Psychiatric Illness." *Psychological Medicine* 9 (1979): 337–53.

Martinsons, Jane Newald. "Are HMOs Slamming the Door on Psych Treatment?" *Hospitals* (March 5, 1988): 50–56.

Mayer, T. F., and Arney, W. R. "Spectral Analysis and the Study of Social Change." In H. L. Costner, ed., *Sociological Methodology 1973–1974*. San Francisco: Jossey-Bass, 1974.

McCain, L. J., and McCleary, Richard. "The Statistical Analysis of the Simple Interrupted Time-Series Quasi-Experiment." In Cook and Campbell, *Quasi-Experimentation*, 1979, pp. 233–94.

McCleary, Richard, and Hay, Richard A., Jr. *Applied Time Series Analysis for the Social Sciences*. Beverly Hills: Sage, 1980.

McDowall, D., McCleary, R., Meidinger, E. E., and Hay, Richard A., Jr. *Interrupted Time Series Analysis, #21: Quantitative Approaches in the Social Sciences.* Beverly Hills: Sage, 1980.

McGuire, Thomas G. "Financing and Demand for Mental Health Services." *Journal of Human Resources* XVI(4) (1981): 501–21.

McGuire, Thomas G. *Financing Psychotherapy.* Cambridge: Ballinger Publishing Co., 1981.

McGuire, Thomas G., and Montgomery, J. T. "Mandated Mental Health Benefits in Private Health Insurance." *Journal of Health Politics, Policy aaand Law.* 7(2) (1982): 380–406.

McGuire, Thomas G., and Weisbrod, B. A., eds. *Mental Health Service System Reports: Economics and Mental Health.* U.S. Department of Health and Human Services. Rockville: NIMH, 1981.

McGuire, Thomas G., Dickey, Barbara, Shively, Gerald E., and Strumwasser, Ira. "Differences in Resource Use and Cost among Facilities Treating Alcohol, Drug Abuse, and Mental Disorders: Implications for Design of a Prospective Payment System." *American Journal of Psychiatry* 144 (5) (May 1987): 616–20.

McHugh, J. P., Kahn, M. W., and Heiman, E. "Relationships between Mental Health Treatment and Medical Care Utilization among Low-Income Mexican-American Patients: Some Preliminary Findings." *Medical Care* 15 (1977): 439–44.

McKinlay, John B. "Some Approaches and Problems in the Study of the Use of Services—An Overview." *Journal of Health and Social Behavior* 13 (1972): 115–42.

Mechanic, David. "Social Psychologic Factors Affecting the Presentation of Bodily Complaints." *New England Journal of Medicine* 286 (1972): 1132–39.

———. "Sex, Illness, Illness Behavior and the Use of Health Services." *Journal of Human Stress* 2 (1976): 29–40.

———. *Medical Sociology.* 2d ed. New York: Free Press, 1978a.

———. "Considerations in the Design of Market Health Benefits under National Health Insurance." *AJPH* 68(5) (1978b): 482–88.

———. "Mental Health and Social Policy: Initiatives for the 1980s." *Health Affairs* 4(1) (1985): 75–88.

Mechanic, David, Cleary, P. D., and Greenley, J. R. "Distress Syndromes, Illness Behavior, Access to Care and Medical Utilization in a Defined Population." *Medical Care* 20(4) (1982): 361–72.

Mechanic, David, ed. *Improving Mental Health Services: What the Social Sciences Can Tell Us.* San Francisco: Jossey-Bass, 1987.

Menzel, Paul T. *Medical Costs, Moral Choices: A Philosophy of Health Care Economics in America.* New Haven: Yale University Press, 1983.

Mitchell, Janet B., Dickey, B., Liptzin, B., and Sederer, L. I. "Bringing Psychiatric Patients into the Medicare Prospective Payment System: Alternatives to DRGs." *American Journal of Psychiatry* 144(5) (May 1987): 610–15.

Monheit, Alan C., Hagan, M. M., Berk, M. L., and Farley, P. J. "The Employed Uninsured and the Role of Public Policy." *Inquiry* 22 (Winter 1985): 348–64.

Monsma, G. "Marginal Revenue and the Demand for Physician Services." In Herbert Klarman, ed., *Empirical Studies in Health Economics*. Baltimore: Johns Hopkins University Press, 1970, pp. 145–60.

Morris, C. N. "A Finite Selection Model for Experimental Design of the Health Insurance Study (Experimental Design in Econometrics)." *Journal Of Econometrics* 11(1) (1979): 43–62.

Moskowitz, J. A. "The Pediatrician Calls for Psychiatric Referral." *Clinical Pediatrics* 7 (1968): 733–38.

Muller, C. "Timeliness and Equaity in Access." *American Journal of Public Health* 68 (1978): 539–45.

Mumford, Emily, and Schlesinger, Herbert J. "Economic Discrimination against Elderly Psychiatric Patients under Medicare." *Hospital and Community Psychiatry* 36(6) (June 1985): 587–89.

Mumford, Emily, Schlesinger, Herbert J., and Glass, Gene V. "Reducing Medical Costs through Mental Health Treatment: Research Problems and Recommendations." In Anthony Broskowski et al., ed., *Linking Health*, 1981, pp. 257–73.

———. "The Effects of Psychological Intervention on Recovery from Surgery and Heart Attacks: An Analysis of the Literature." *American Journal of Public Health* 72 (1982): 141–51.

Mumford, Emily, Schlesinger, Herbert J., Glass, Gene V., Patrick, C., and Cuerdon, T. "A New Look at Evidence about Reduced Cost Medical Utilization Following Mental Health Treatment." *American Journal of Psychiatry* 141:10 (1984): 1145–58.

Murphy, J. M. "Continuities in Community Based Psychiatric Epidemiology." *Archives of General Psychiatry* 37 (1980): 1215.

Murphy, J. M., Sobol, A. M., et al. "Stability of Prevalence." *Archives of General Psychiatry* 41 (1984): 990–97.

Myers, J. K., Weissman, M. M., Tischler, G. L., et al. "Six Month Prevalence of Psychiatric Disorders in Three Communities." *Archives of General Psychiatry* 41 (1984): 959–67.

National Center for Health Statistics. *Health: United States, 1975*. DHEW Pub. No. (HRA) 76-1232. Washington, D.C.: GPO, 1976.

Newhouse, J. P. "A Design for a Health Insurance Experiment." *Inquiry* 11 (1974): 5–27.

———. "The Demand for Medical Care Services: A Retrospect and Prospect." In van den Gaag and Perlman, eds., *Health*, pp. 85–102.

Newhouse, J. P., and Friedlander, L. J. "The Relationship Medical Research and Measures of Health: Some Additional Evidence." *Journal of Human Resources* 15 (1980): 200–218.

Newhouse, J. P., and Marquis, M. Susan. "The Norms Hypothesis and the Demand for Medical Care." *Journal of Human Resources* 13 (Supplement) (1978): 159–82.

Newhouse, J. P., and Phelps, C. E. "Price and Income Elasticities and the Demand for Medical Care Services." In Mark Perlman, ed., *The Economics of Health and Medical Care*. New York: Wiley, 1974.

———. "New Estimates of Price and Income Elasticities." In R. N. Rosett, ed., *The Role of Health Insurance in the Health Services Sector*. New York: National Bureau of Economic Research, 1976.

Newman, J. P. "Sex Differences in Symptoms of Depression: Clinical Disorder or Normal Distress?" *Journal of Health and Social Behavior* 25 (1984): 136–59.

O'Brien, Margaret, and Savich, John. "Initial Findings from the Medicaid Tape-to-Tape Project: Tennessee and Georgia, 1980." Bethesda, Md.: SysteMetrics, Inc., no date.

O'Donovan, T. M. *Short Term Forecasting: An Introduction to the Box-Jenkins Approach*. New York: Wiley, 1983.

Office of Technology Assessment. "The Efficacy and Cost-Effectiveness of Psychotherapy." Background paper No. 3 of *The Implications of Cost-Effectiveness Analysis of Medical Technology*. Washington D.C.: 1980.

Okin, Robert L. "How Community Mental Health Centers Are Coping." *Hospital and Community Psychiatry* 35 (1984): 1118–24.

Olbrisch, Mary Ellen. "Psychological Intervention and Reduced Medical Care Utilization: A Modest Interpretation." *American Psychologist* 35 (August 1980): 760–61.

Omenn, Gilbert S., and Ehreth, Jennifer S. "A New Look for Medicaid." *Business and Health* (December 1986): 7–11.

Orleans, C. Tracy, George, Linda K., Houpt, Jeffrey L., and Brodie, Keith H. "How Primary Care Physicians Treat Psychiatric Disorders: A National Survey of Family Practitioners." *American Journal of Psychiatry* 142 (1985): 52–57.

Pardes, H., and Pincus, H. A. "Report of the Graduate Medical Education National Advisory Committee on Health Manpower Development: Implications for Psychiatry." *Archives of General Psychiatry* 40 (1983): 97–102.

Parloff, M., Wolfe, B., Hadley, S., and Waskow, I. "Assessment of Psychosocial Treatment of Mental Disorders." *NIMH* Working Group, Advisory Committee on Mental Health, National Academy of Sciences, 1978.

Parron, D. L., and Solomon, F., eds. *Mental Health Services in Primary Care Settings*. DHHS Pub. No. (ADM) 80-995, April 2–3, 1979. Washington D.C.: GPO, 1980.

Parry, H. J., Batter, M. B., Mellinger, G. D., et al. "National Patterns of Psychotherapeutic Drug Use." *Archives of General Psychiatry* 29 (1973): 769–83.

Pasamanick, B., Roberts, D. S., et al. "A Survey of Mental Disease in an Urban Population." *AJPH* 47 (1956): 923–29.

Patterson, D. Y., "The Future of Health Maintenance Organizations." *Hospital and Community Psychiatry* 33 (1982): 746–49.

Patterson, D. Y., and Bise, B. Report pursuant to contract #282-77-0219-MS. Unpublished report to *NIMH*, 1978.

Pedhazur, Elazar J. *Multiple Regression in Behavioral Research: Explanation and Prediction.* 2d ed. New York: Holt, Rinehart and Winston, 1982.

Phelan, John L., and Rosenbloom, Alfred. "What Do Employers Think About Mental Health Benefits?" *Business and Health* (November 1986): 37.

Phelps, C. E. "Effects of Insurance on Demand for Medical Care." In R. Andersen et al., eds., *Equity in Health Services.* Cambridge: Ballinger, 1975.

Pierce, D. A., and Haugh, L. D. "Causality in Temporal Systems: Characterizations and a Survey." *Journal of Econometrics* 5 (1977): 265–93.

Piper, William, Debbane, E. G., Bienvenu, J. P., and Garant, J. "A Comparative Study of Four Forms of Psychotherapy." *Journal of Consulting and Clinical Psychology* 52(2) (1984): 268–79.

Pond, D. A. "Doctors' Mental Health." *The New Zealand Medical Journal* 69 (1969): 131–35.

President's Commission on Mental Health. *Final Report to the President.* Washington D.C.: GPO, 1978.

Quesada, G. M., Spears, W., and Ramos, P. "Interracial Depressive Epidemiology in the Southwest." *Journal of Health and Social Behavior* 19 (1978): 77–85.

Raft, D. "How to Refer a Reluctant Patient to a Psychiatrist." *American Family Physician* 7 (1973): 109–14.

Reed, L. "Utilization of Care for Mental Disorder under the Blue Cross and Blue Shield Plan for Federal Employees, 1972." *American Journal of Psychiatry*, 13 (1974): 964–75.

———. *Coverage and Utilization of Care for Mental Conditons under Health Insurance–Various Studies* 1973–1984. Washington D.C.: Am Psychiatric Assoc., 1975.

Reed, L., Myers, E., Scheidemandel, Patricia L. Health Insurance and Psychiatric Care: Utilization and Cost. Washington D.C.: Am Psychiatric Assoc., 1972.

Regier, D. A., and Goldberg, I. D. "National Health Insurance and Mental Health Services Equilibrium." Paper presented at the American Psychiatric Association Meeting, 1976, cited in Burns et al., "Promoting Health," 1981.

Regier, D. A., Goldberg, I. D., Burns, B. J., et al. "Epidemiological and Health Services Research Findings." Paper presented at ADAMHA conference on HMOs, Chicago, 1977. Cited in Regier, 1977.

Regier, D. A., Goldberg, I. D., and Taube, C. A. "The De Facto U.S. Mental Health Services System." *Archives of General Psychiatry* 35 (1978): 685–93.

Regier, D. A., Goldberg, I. D., et al. "Overview." *Archives of General Psychiatry* 35 (1978).

Regier, D. A., Myers, J. K., and Kramer, M. "The NIMH Epidemiological Catchment Area (ECA) Program." *Archives of General Psychiatry* 41 (l984): 934.

Regier, D. A., Goldberg, I. D., and Burns, B. J., eds. *Use of Health and Mental Health Outpatient Services in Four Organized Health Care Settings.* DHHS DM80-859, 1980.

Reiser, M. F., ed. *American Handbook of Psychiatry.* Vol. IV, New York: Basic Books, 1975.

Research Triangle Institute. "Costs to Society of Alcohol, Drug Abuse and Mental Illness: 1977." ADAMHA, contract No. 382-79-001. Washington D.C.: GPO, 1980.

Rice, D. P., and Wilson, D. "The American Medical Economy: Problems and Perspectives." *Journal of Health Politics, Policy and Law* 1 (1976): 151–72.

Rischler, G. L., Heinsz, H. E., Myers, J. K., et. al. "The Utilization of Mental Health Services." *Archives of General Psychiatry* 32 (1975): 411–18.

Robbins, L. N. "Psychiatric Epidemiology." *Archives of General Psychiatry* 35 (1978): 697–702.

Robbins, L. N., Helzer, J. E., Croughan, J., Ratcliff, K. F. "NIMH Diagnostic Interview Schedule: Its History, Characteristics and Validity." *Archives of General Psychiatry* 38 (1981): 381–89.

Romano, J. M., and Turner, J. A. "Chronic Pain and Depression: Does the Evidence Support a Relationship?" *Psychological Bulletin* 97(1) (1985): 18–34.

Rosen, B. M., Locke, B. Z., Goldberg, I. D., et al. "Identifying Emotional Disturbance in Persons Seen in Industrial Dispensaries." *Mental Hygiene* 54 (1970): 271–78.

Rosen, B. M., Locke, B. Z., and Goldberg, I. D. "Identification of Emotional Disturbance in Patients Seen in General Medical Clinics." *Hospital Community Psychiatry* 23 (1972): 364–70.

Rosen, J. C., and Wiens, A. N. "Changes in Medical Problems and Use of Medical Services Following Psychiatric Intervention." *American Journal of Psychology* 34 (1979): 420.

———. "On Psychological Intervention and Medical Services Utilization." *American Psychologist* 35 (August 1980): 761–62.

Ross, Catherine E., and Duff, D. S. "A Nonrecursive Causal Model of the Health Care Delivery System." *Sociological Quarterly* 23 (Summer 1982a): 403-20.

———. "Returning to the Doctor: The Effect of Client Characteristics, Types of Practice and Experiences with Care." *Journal of Health and Social Behavior* 23(2) (June 1982b): 119–31.

————. "Physician Characteristics and Client Satisfaction in Two Types of Medical Practice." *Journal of Health and Social Behavior* 23(4) (December 1982c): 317–29.

Ross, Catherine, Mirowsky, John, and Cockerham, William. "Social Class, Mexican Culture and Fatalism: Their Effects in Psychological Distress." *American Journal of Community Psychology* 11(4) (1983): 383–99.

Rundall, T. G. "A Suggestion for Improving the Behavioral Model of Physician Utilization." *Journal of Health and Social Behavior* 22 (1981): 103–4.

Rupp, Agnes, Steinwachs, David M., and Salkever, David. "Hospital Payment Effects on Acute Inpatient Care for Mental Disorders." *Archives of General Psychiatry* 42 (1985): 552–55.

Rush, A. J., Beck, A. T., Kovacs, M., and Hollon, S. "Comparative Efficacy of Cognitive Therapy and Pharmacotherapy in the Treatment of Depressed Outpatients." *Cognitive Therapy and Research* 1 (1977): 17–37.

Russo, Nancy Felipe, and Sobel, Suzanne Barbara. "Sex Differences in the Utilization of Mental Health Facilities." *Professional Psychology* 12 (1981): 7–19.

Santiago, Jose M. "Reforming a System of Care: The Arizona Experiment." *Hospital and Community Psychiatry* 38(3) (March 1987): 270–73.

Schiff, Robert L., Ansell, David A., Schlosser, James El, Idris, Ahamed H., Morrison, Ann, and Whitman, Steven. "Transfers to a Public Hospital." *The New England Journal of Medicine* 314 (1986): 552–57.

Schlesinger, Herbert J., Mumford, Emily, and Glass, Gene V. "Mental Health Services and Medical Utilization." In VandenBos, ed., *Psychotherapy*, 1980.

Schlesinger, Herbert J., Mumford, Emily, Glass, Gene V., Patrick, C. and Sharfstein, S. "Mental Health Treatment and Medical Care Utilization in a Fee-for-Service System: Outpatient Mental Health Treatment Following the Onset of a Chronic Disease." *American Journal of Public Health* 73(4) (1983): 422–29.

Schlesinger, Mark, Dorwart, R. A., and Pulice, R. T. "Competitive Bidding and States' Purchase of Services: The Case of Mental Health Care in Massachusetts." *Journal of Policy Analysis and Management* 5(2) (1986): 245–63.

Schurman, R. A., Kramer, P. D., and Mitchell, J. B. "The Hidden Mental Health Network." *Archives of General Psychiatry* 42 (1985): 89-94.

Schwab, J. J. "Comprehensive Medicine and the Concurrence of Physical and Mental Illness." *Psychosomatics* 11 (1970): 591–95.

Schwab, J. J., Bell, R. A., Warheit, G. J., and Schwab, R. B. *Social Order and Mental Health*. New York: Brunner/Mazel Inc., 1979.

Scull, Andrew. "Deinstitutionalization and Public Policy." *Social Science and Medicine* 20(5) (1985): 545–52.

Shapiro, S. M., Skinner, E. A., Kessler, L. G., et al. "Utilization of Health and Mental Health Services." *Archives of General Psychiatry* 41 (1984): 971–78.

Sharfstein, Steven S. "Third Party Payers: To Pay or Not to Pay." *American Journal of Psychiatry* 135 (1978): 1185–88.

Sharfstein, Steven S., and Clark, H. "Why Psychiatry Is a Low Paid Medical Specialty." *American Journal of Psychiatry*, 137(7) (1980): 832–33.

Sharfstein, Steven S., and Taube, C. A. "Reductions in Insurance for Mental Disorders: Adverse Selection, Moral Hazard, and Consumer Demand." *American Journal of Psychiatry* 139 (1982): 1425–30.

Sharfstein, S., Taube, C., and Goldberg, I. D. "Private Psychiatry and Accountability." *American Journal of Psychiatry* 132(1) (1975): 43–47.

Sharfstein, Steven S., Muszynski, S., and Myers, E. *Health Insurance and Psychiatric Care: Update and Appraisal.* Washington, DC: American Psychiatric Press, 1984.

Sharfstein, Steven S., and Beigel, Allan, eds. *The New Economics and Psychiatric Care.* Washington, D.C.: American Psychiatric Press, 1985.

———. "Epilogue: Less Is More? Today's Economics and Its Challenge to Psychiatry." In Sharfstein and Beigel, eds., *The New Economics*, 1985.

Sharp, K., Ross, C. E., and Cockerham, W. C. "Symptoms, Beliefs and Use of Physician Services among the Disadvantaged." *Journal of Health and Social Behavior* 24(3) (1983): 255–63.

Shepherd, M. "Mental Health as an Integrant of Primary Care." In Parron and Solomon, eds., *Mental Health Services in Primary Care Settings.* DHHS Pub. No. (ADM) 80995. Washington, D.C.: GPO, 1980.

Shepherd, S. M., Cooper, B., Brown, A. C., et al. *Psychiatric Illness in General Practice.* London: Oxford University Press, 1966.

Shortell, Stephen, et al. "The Relationship among Dimensions of Health Services in Two Provider Systems: A Causal Model Approach." *Journal of Health and Social Behavior* 18 (1977): 139–59.

Shuval, J. *The Social Functions of Medical Practice.* San Francisco: Jossey-Bass, 1970.

Simon, G. "NIMH Funds Study of Mental Health Utilization and Costs." *APA Monitor* (July 1976): 7, 26, 55.

Sims, A. "Mortality in Neurosis." *The Lancet* 2 (1973): 1072–75.

Sloane, R. B., Staples, F. R., Cristal, A. H., Yorkston, N. J., and Whipple, K. *Psychotherapy versus Behavior Therapy.* Cambridge: Harvard University Press, 1975.

Sloane, R. B., et al. *Short-Term Analytically Oriented Psychotherapy vs. Behavior Therapy.* Cambridge: Harvard University Press, 1975.

Smith, Christopher J. "Geographic Patterns of Funding for Community Mental Health Centers." *Hospital and Community Psychiatry* 35(11) (November 1985): 1133–40.

Smith, M. L., and Glass, G. V. "Meta-Analysis of Psychotherapy Outcome Studies." *American Psychologist* 32 (1977): 752–60.

Smith, M. L., Glass, G. V., and Miller, T. I. *The Benefits of Psychotherapy.* Baltimore: Johns Hopkins University Press, 1980.

Solon, J. A., Feeney, J. J., Jones, S. H., et al. "Delineating Episodes of Medical Care." *AJPH* 57 (1967): 401–14.

Spitz, Bruce. "Medicaid Case Management Programs: A National Survey." *Health Affairs* 6 (Spring 1967): 1.

Spitzer, R. L., and Endicott, J. *Schedule for Affective Disorders and Schizophrenia*. 3d ed. New York: New York State Psychiatric Institute, 1977.

SPSS Inc., and Norusis, Marija J. *SPSS/PC+ for the IBM PC/XT/AT*. Chicago: SPSS Inc., 1986.

Srole, L. *Mental Health in the Metropolis: The Midtown Manhattan Study*. New York: McGraw-Hill, 1962.

———. "Measurement and Classification in Socio-Psychiatric Epidemiology: Midtown Manhattan Study (1954) and (1974)." *JHSB* 16 (1975): 347–64.

Stanford, B. J. "Counseling: A Prime Area for Family Doctors." *American Family Physician* 5 (1972): 183–85.

Starr, Paul. *The Structural Transformation of American Medicine*. New York: Basic Books, 1982.

Stein, S. "Effects of Utilization on Mental and Physical Health." *American Journal of Public Health* 75 (1985): 502–6.

Stoddart, Greg L., and Barer, Morris L. "Analysis of Demand and Utilization through Episodes of Medical Service." In van den Gaag and Perlman, eds., *Health*, 1981, pp. 149–72.

Strumbo, D., Good, M. D., and Good, B. J. "Diagnostic Profile of a Family Practice Clinic: Patients with Psychosocial Diagnoses." *Journal of Family Practice* 14 (1982): 281–85.

Strupp, H. H., and Hadley, S. "A Tripartite Model of Mental Health and Therapeutic Outcomes with Special Reference to Negative Effects in Psychotherapy." *American Psychologist* 32 (1977): 187–97.

Sullivan, Sean, Flynn, Theresa J., and Lewin, Marion Ein. "The Quest to Manage Mental Health Costs." *Business and Health* (February 1987): 24–28.

SysteMetrics. *Administrative Manual for the Tape-to-Tape Files*. Bethesda, Md.: SysteMetrics, Inc., 1985a.

———. "Assessing and Using the Tape-to-Tape Database." October 31, 1985b.

Talbott, John A. "The Fate of the Public Psychiatric System." *Hospital and Community Psychiatry* 36(1) (January 1985a): 46–50.

———. "National Priorities: Halfway There." *Hospital and Community Psychiatry* 36 (1985b): 5.

Talbott, John A., and Sharfstein, Steven S. "A Proposal for Future Funding of Chronic and Episodic Mental Illness." *Hospital and Community Psychiatry* 37(11) (November 1986): 1126–30.

Taube, Carl A. "Introduction: The Demand for Ambulatory Mental Health Care." *Health Services Research* 21:2 (June 1986), Part II: v-vii.

Taube, Carl A., Kessler, Larry G., and Burns, Barbara J. "Estimating the Probability and Level of Ambulatory Mental Health Services Use." *Health Services Research* 21:2 (June 1986), Part II: 321–40.

Taube, Carl A., Lee, E. S., and Forthofer, R. N. "Diagnosis-Related Groups for Mental Disorders, Alcoholism, and Drug Abuse: Evaluation and Alternatives." *Hospital and Community Psychiatry* 35 (1984): 452.

Taube, Carl A., and Rupp, Agnes. "The Effect of Medicaid on Access to Ambulatory Mental Health Care for the Poor and Near-Poor under 65." *Medical Care* 24(8) (August 1986): 677–86.

Tessler, R., Mechanic, D., and Dimond, M. "The Effect of Psychological Distress on Physician Utilization." *JHSB* 17 (1976): 353–64.

Thompson, James W., and Bass, Rosalyn D. "Changing Staffing Patterns in Community Mental Health Centers." *Hospital and Community Psychiatry* 35(11) (November 1984): 1107–13.

Thompson, T. L., Stoudemire, A., and Mitchell, W. D., et al. "Underrecognition of Patient's Psychological Distress in a University Hospital Medical Clinic." *American Journal of Psychiatry* 140 (1983): 158.

Tischler, G. L., Heinsz, J. E., et al. "Utilization of Mental Health Services: I, Patienthood and the Prevalence." *Archives of General Psychiatry* 32 (1975): 411–18.

Towery, O. B., Sharfstein, S. S., and Goldberg, I. D. "The Mental and Nervous Disorder Utilization and Cost Survey: An Analysis of Insurance for Mental Disorders." *American Journal of Psychiatry* 137(9) (1980): 1065–70.

Tsai, Shan P., Reedy, Susan Miller, and Bernacki, Edward J. "The Effects of Redesigning Mental Health Benefits." *Business and Health* (April 1987): 26–28.

Tsuang, M. J., and Woolson, R. F. "Mortality in Patients with Schizophrenia, Mania, Depression and Surgical Conditions." *British Journal of Psychiatry* 130 (1977): 162–66.

U.S. Department of Labor, Bureau of Labor Statistics. *CPI Detailed Reports.* Washington, D.C.: GPO, 1980–83 (various issues).

Uris, J. "Effects of Mental Health Utilization and Diagnosis on General Medical Care Utilization in a Prepaid Setting." Report by a Western Interstate Commission for Higher Education Intern, Boulder, Colo., 1974. Cited in Hankin et al., "A Longitudinal Study," 1983.

Vaillant, G. E. "Natural History of Male Psychologic Health: Effects of Mental Health on Physical Health." *NEJM* 301 (1979): 1249–54.

Vaillant, G. E., et al. "Natural History of Male Psychological Health, X: Work as a Predictor of Positive Mental Health." *American Journal of Psychiatry* 138 (1981): 1433–40.

VandenBos, Gary. "Introduction." In G. VandenBos, ed., *Psychotherapy*, 1980, pp. 9–22.

VandenBos, Gary, and Pino, C. "Research on the Outcome of Pyschotherapy." In G. VandenBos, ed., *Psychotherapy: Practice, Research, Policy.* Beverly Hills: Sage, 1980, pp. 23–70.

VandenBos, Gary, ed. *Psychotherapy: Practice, Research, Policy.* Beverly Hills: Sage, 1980.

Van den Gaag, Jacques, and Perlman, Mark, eds. *Health, Economics and Health Economics*. Contributions to Economic Analysis, #137. Amsterdam: North Holland Publishing Co., 1981.

Vischi, T. R., Jones, K. R., Shank, E. L., and Lima, L. H. *The Adamha National Data Book*. Office of Program Planning and Coordination. ADAMHA, DHEW Pub. No. (ADM) 80-938. Washington D.C.: GPO, 1980.

Wagner, Lynn. "Government Moving to Outpatient Fixed-fee System." *Modern Healthcare* (January 29, 1988): 30–31.

Wallack, S. S. "Financing Care for the Chronically Mentally Ill: The Implications of the Various Approaches." McGuire and Weisbrod, eds., *Mental Health Service System Reports*, 1981, pp. 72–84.

Wallen, Jacqueline, Roddy, Pamela, and Meyers, Samuel M. "Male-female Differences in Mental Health Visits under Cost-sharing." *Health Services Research* 21 (1986): 341–50.

Ware, John E., Jr., Davies-Avery, A., and Brook, R. H. *Conceptualization and Measurement of Health for Adults in the Health Insurance Study: Volume VI, Analysis of Relationships among Health Status Measures*. The Rand Corporation, R-1987/6-HEW, November 1980.

Ware, John E., Jr., Johnston, S. A., Davies-Avery, A., and Brook, R. H. *Conceptualization and Measurement of Health for Adults in the Health Insurance Study: Volume III, Mental Health*. The Rand Corporation, R-1987/3-HEW, December 1979.

Ware, John E., Jr., Manning, Willard G., Duan, Naihua, Wells, Kenneth B., and Newhouse, Joseph P. "Health Status and the Use of Outpatient Mental Health Services." *American Psychologist* 39 (1984): 1090–1100.

Washington Health Costs Letter. "National Subsidy Considered for Hospital Indigent Care" (March 27, 1987): 7.

Watts, Carolyn A., Scheffler, Richard M., and Jewell, Nicholas P. "Demand for Outpatient Mental Health Services in a Heavily Insured Population: The Case of Blue Cross and Blue Shield Association's Federal Employees Health Benefits Program." *Health Services Research* 21(2) (June 1986), Part II: 267–89.

Weissman, Myrna M., and Klerman, G. L. "Sex Differences and the Epidemiology of Depression." *Archives of General Psychiatry* 34 (1977): 98–111.

———. "Epidemiology of Mental Disorders." *Archives of General Psychiatry* 35 (1978): 705–12.

Weissman, Myrna M., and Myers, J. K. "Affective Disorders in a U.S. Urban Community." *Archives of General Psychiatry* 35 (1978): 1304–11.

Weissman, Myrna M., and Paykel, E. S. *The Depressed Woman: A Study of Social Relationships*. Chicago: University of Chicago Press, 1974.

Weissman Myrna M., Myers, J. K., and Harding, P. S. "Psychiatric Disorders in a U.S. Urban Community: 1975–1976." *American Journal of Psychiatry* 135 (1978): 459–62.

Wells, Kenneth B., Manning, Willard G., Jr., and Benjamin, Bernadette. "A Comparison of the Effects of Sociodemographic Factors and Health Status on Use of Outpatient Mental Health Services in HMO and Fee-for-Service Plans." *Medical Care* 24(10) (October 1986): 949–60.

———."Comparison of Use of Outpatient Mental Health Services in an HMO and Fee-for-Service Plans." *Medical Care* 25(9) (September 1987a): 894–903.

Wells, Kenneth B., Manning, Willard G., Jr., Duan, Naihua, Newhouse, Joseph P., and Ware, John E. "Cost-Sharing and the Use of Ambulatory Mental Health Services." *American Psychologist* 39 (1984): 1077–89.

———. "Cost-Sharing and the Use of General Medical Physicians for Outpatient Mental Health Care." *Health Services Research* 22(1) (April 1987b): 1–17.

Wells, Kenneth B., Manning, Willard G., Jr., Duan, Naihua, et al. "Use of Outpatient Mental Health Services by a General Population with Health Insurance Coverage." *Hospital and Community Psychiatry* 37(11) (November 1986): 1119–25.

Wells, Kenneth B., Manning, Willard G., Jr., et al. *Cost Sharing and the Demand for Ambulatory Mental Health Services*. R-2960-HHS. Santa Monica: The Rand Corporation, 1982.

Wilensky, Gail R. "Viable Strategies for Dealing with the Uninsured." *Health Affairs* 6 (1987): 33–46.

Williams, S. J., Diehr, P., Drucker, W. L., and Richardson, W. "Mental Health Services: Utilization by Low Income Enrollees in a Prepaid Group Practice Plan and in an Independent Provider Plan." *Medical Care* 17 (1979): 139–49.

Wilson, P. A., Griffith, J. R., and Tedeschi, P. J. "Does Race Affect Hospital Use?" *American Journal of Public Health* 75 (1985): 263–69.

World Health Organization. *Working Group on Psychiatry in General Practice Report*, 1973.

Yaffe, R., Shapiro, S., et al. "Medical Economics Survey-Methods Study: Cost Effectiveness of Alternative Survey Strategies." *Medical Care* 16 (1978): 641–59.

Yates, B. T. *Improving Effectiveness and Reducing Costs in Mental Health*. Springfield, Ill.: Charles C. Thomas Publishers, 1980.

INDEX

ABOUT THE AUTHORS

John L. Fiedler is an Associate with Macro Systems, Inc., a health and social service consulting firm headquartered in Silver Spring, Maryland. He received his B.A. in economics from the University of Wisconsin-Madison in 1975, his M.A. from Vanderbilt University in 1981, and his Ph.D. from Vanderbilt in 1986. At Vanderbilt, he specialized in health economics and economic development.

Dr. Fiedler has been a consultant for nearly four years. As a consultant he has worked on a variety of domestic and international projects for a number of different agencies, including the National Institute of Mental Health, the Centers for Disease Control, the Veterans' Administration, the National Heart, Lung, and Blood Institute, the Small Business Administration, and the Agency for International Development. Prior to entering consulting, Dr. Fiedler taught economics for four years at the University of Wisconsin-Eau Claire and two other University of Wisconsin campuses. He also served as a planning analyst and program evaluation specialist with the Wisconsin Department of Health and Social Services for two years.

Dr. Fiedler's main areas of interest are health economics, health and social service program evaluation, behavioral modeling, and Third World development. His publications include "A Review of Access and Utilization of Primary Health Care," "Latin American Health Policy and Additive Reform: The Case of Guatemala," "A Disaggregated Investigation of Learning Functions in Introductory Economics," "Recurrent Costs and Public Health Policy: The Other War in El Salvador," and "El Salvador's Ministry of Health, 1975–1986: A Provisional Performance Assessment."

Jonathan B. Wight is an Associate Professor of Economics in the E. Claiborne Robins School of Business at the University of Richmond, where he has been since 1982. He received his B.A. in economics and public policy studies from Duke University in 1976, his M.A. from Vanderbilt University in 1980, and his Ph.D. from Vanderbilt in 1982, where he specialized in economic development.

Dr. Wight has lived and worked extensively overseas and is fluent in Portuguese. His main research interest centers on economic public policy issues. His empirical research includes analysis and estimation of the costs and benefits of alternative energy, and estimation of the cost of capital and costs of government financial incentives. He has also carried out various industry studies, and authored public policy articles on bank loan quality, tax reform, and international trade.

In addition to his teaching, Dr. Wight has served as a consultant to the World Bank and has presented, discussed, and chaired panel sessions at numerous professional meetings.